AFFIRMED

Also by Lou Sahadi

Johnny Unitas: America's Quarterback

One Sunday in December: The 1958 NFL Championship Game and How It Changed Professional Football

Broncos! The Team That Makes Miracles Happen

Los Angeles Dodgers: Champions of Baseball

Miracle in Miami

The Redskins

The Raiders

The 49ers: Super Champs of Pro Football

Super Sundays I–XII

Super Sundays I–XIV

Super Sundays I–XV

Super Sundays I–XVI

Super Steelers: The Making of a Dynasty

The Pirates

The Clemson Tigers: From 1896 to Glory

Steelers! Team of the Decade

Year of the Yankees

Pro Football's Gamebreakers

The Long Pass

Autobiographies

Len Dawson: Pressure Quarterback

Don Shula: The Winning Edge

Hank Stram: They're Playing My Game

Willie Mays: Say Hey!

Jim Donnan: Winning My Way

AFFIRMED

—— *The Last Triple Crown Winner* ——

*"Affirmed is a better horse than Secretariat because Secretariat
didn't have a horse like Alydar to challenge him."*
—Laz Barrera

Lou Sahadi

Foreword by Steve Cauthen

Thomas Dunne Books
St. Martin's Griffin
New York

THOMAS DUNNE BOOKS.
An Imprint of St. Martin's Press.

AFFIRMED. Copyright © 2011 by Lou Sahadi. Foreword copyright © 2011
by Steve Cauthen. All rights reserved. Printed in the United States
of America. For information, address St. Martin's Press,
175 Fifth Avenue, New York, N.Y. 10010.

www.thomasdunnebooks.com
www.stmartins.com

Design by Rich Arnold

The Library of Congress has cataloged the hardcover edition as follows:

Sahadi, Lou.
    Affirmed : the last triple crown winner / Lou Sahadi.—1st ed.
        p. cm.
    Includes bibliographical references and index.
    ISBN 978-0-312-62808-6 (hardback)
    1. Affirmed (Race horse)   I. Title.
    SF355.A44S34 2011
    798.40092'9—dc22

                                        2010041291

        ISBN 978-1-250-00733-9 (trade paperback)

        First St. Martin's Griffin Edition: May 2012

        D   10   9   8   7   6   5   4   3   2

In memory of Louis Wolfson, a man for the ages, and to his family:
Patrice, Marcia, Steve, Gary, and Marty.

For:

Susan, who got me to finish the line . . .

CONTENTS

FOREWORD

I still look back vividly at the exciting year of 1978, which generated the greatest two-horse duel in the history of racing. Unequivocally, I can say that Affirmed and Alydar produced the greatest Triple Crown races ever witnessed. As a young jockey who had just turned eighteen, I perhaps had an innocence of the magnitude of what winning the Triple Crown meant. I was just happy being part of it.

Some jockeys ride all their lives and never get the chance to ride a horse in that sort of situation. It takes years of preparing yourself so that you're ready for the opportunity when it comes. Basically, all those hours of working hard, riding bad horses at times at little tracks, and getting up at 5:00 a.m. and studying race films are worth it. When I got the opportunity, I capitalized on it and put all that knowledge and hard work to use. Because of all that, it brought a tremendous feeling of satisfaction. I was proud of myself and my horse for having the courage to get through that situation.

I had no belief that it would happen, either. In the winter of 1977, my trainer, Laz Barrera, and he was one of the best, decided to give Affirmed a long rest. He decided that he would begin training Affirmed for the Kentucky Derby the following year in California. But the road to the Derby wouldn't be easy. If your horse isn't primed and in position for the initial win in the Derby, then there is no Triple Crown to pursue.

Barrera didn't expect what would happen in California, and I became a bit skeptical about the circumstances. The winter that year was inundated with rain, so much that it was a record amount. Laz couldn't get Affirmed to gallop on the track because of the constant rain and the mud it created. He didn't want to take any chance of Affirmed's enduring a freakish accident. Instead, Affirmed was limited to walks and jogs in the barn area. "I've never had to train a horse like this in my life," he told me.

Before Affirmed finally got to the post, Alydar was already burning up the tracks in Florida. He was winning easily and impressively while Affirmed was sort of leisurely winning his races. Affirmed was just playing. He was flopping his ears back and forth in the stretch looking for someone to beat. It may not have looked good from the stands, but Laz was bringing Affirmed up to every race a little stronger than he was before.

Amazingly, Laz got Affirmed into great shape. When we arrived at Churchill Downs, all he did was work Affirmed easily. He had him where he wanted him, and his confidence in Affirmed never waned. Affirmed was that good a horse and he was ready for the Derby. I was excited about riding my first Derby. There were no surprises and everything went as planned.

Believe It, a fine horse, moved alongside me and gave Affirmed something to look at, something to fight for. That's the way Affirmed runs best.

I hit my horse a few times as he drew away from Believe It. Then I started hand-riding him again, just trying to keep his mind on his business so he could take off again if Alydar came alongside him. I kept looking for Alydar. By the time I saw him, I knew I had him beat. After the race, one of the writers asked, "Do you think Affirmed could have run a better race?" I looked at him with surprise and replied, "What do you want? He just won the Kentucky Derby."

The field for the Preakness was much smaller, and Laz figured on having Affirmed in or near the lead. He left it up to me to dictate the pace. I did, while waiting for Alydar. Affirmed was going along easy and I knew the pace was slow enough. I could have laid second for as long as I wanted. But going into the first turn, Track Reward bore out a little and I decided to go ahead and get out of his way. Down the stretch, Alydar made his move. But Affirmed had just a little bit more to give and we beat Alydar by a neck.

The Belmont was something else again. You're going into unknown territory because of the extra quarter of a mile, and I was probably least sure of that race. Yet, I also realized that I had a courageous horse under me, and that is really what it comes down to. It turned out to be the greatest race of all time. By the time I got to the stretch, I knew it would be a knock-down, drag-out battle with Alydar right to the end. Affirmed and I had to dig as deep as we could because it was then all or nothing. It was such a tight race and I wasn't sure about winning until I got past the finish line by a head.

I was proud of winning the Triple Crown and proud of the way we did it. In Alydar, we had a great champion to beat each time. In our Triple Crown, unlike with Secretariat or Seattle Slew, where they were the dominant horses, we had a great rival in Alydar, the only horse to finish second in all three Triple Crown races. It was great for racing and it was an excellent moment in my life.

We had a great team. Barrera was a Hall of Fame trainer and the Wolfsons, Louis and Patrice, were great owners. They gave me a lot of confidence. Laz always had a game plan for every race and always ended his explanation of it to me by saying, "You're in charge."

Today, along with my wife, Amy, we have been blessed with another Triple Crown in three beautiful daughters: Katelynn, Karlie, and Kelsey. As for 1978, there'll never be another year like it in racing.

—*Steve Cauthen*
2010

PREFACE

The story of Affirmed and Alydar was larger-than-life and held the sports world spellbound in 1978. A millionaire horse owner, the son of a junk dealer; an immigrant trainer; and a teenage jockey who was short on experience combined to win thoroughbred racing's treasured Triple Crown in 1978 against seemingly improbable odds. The Herculean feat has not been duplicated in the last thirty-one years, and Affirmed, a small horse by breeding standards, had earned turf immortality with three intense head-to-head duels against Alydar in the closest Triple Crown races in history.

The owner, Louis Wolfson, and his wife, Patrice, nurtured Affirmed and eighteen-year-old jockey Steve Cauthen against the long odds that ultimately led both to stardom. Affirmed's margin of victory against Alydar was a minuscule combined 1½ lengths in the Kentucky Derby, the Preakness, and the Belmont, a total of four miles of pulsating racing. It became a legendary rivalry that has galloped through time without any yanking of the reins. They defined the sport, and the nation's sports fans have never witnessed anything quite like it again. The saga of Affirmed and Alydar has never been diminished and grows every year.

They own history all to themselves.

Only one would become champion, but the two are forever linked in racing lore. In the first eighteen races that Affirmed ran, only one horse could beat him—Alydar. They raced a total of ten times, with Affirmed winning seven of them. One of Affirmed's losses was by disqualification in the prestigious Travers Stakes, the last time they faced each other.

There was also the added romance of a teenage jockey holding the reins of Affirmed to become the youngest rider to capture the Triple Crown, amazingly so when considering that at this level of competition excellence occurs only after years of experience. Yet, the innocent-looking, baby-faced Cauthen performed magic, and the virtuoso performance was lifted beyond, in an exhibition of power, speed, and strength, to become a picture of grace. Affirmed and his adolescent jockey withstood Alydar's gallant efforts and ascended into racing glory.

"It was the greatest rivalry and the greatest event of all times," expressed Cauthen. "What made the rivalry great was that it came during the biggest series of races in America, the most prestigious events you can win when everyone was watching."

The decade of the seventies was the golden age of thoroughbred racing. No other decade gave the sport as many surpassing horses. Only the 1940s, with Count Fleet and Citation leading the charts, comes remotely close. The seventies was a glorious stage on which Secretariat, Seattle Slew, Forego, Spectacular Bid, Affirmed, and Alydar strutted their incomparable stuff.

It was also a decade in which the racing crowd cheered such Hall of Fame jockeys as Eddie Arcaro, Willie Shoemaker, Bill Hartack, Angel Cordero, Eddie Delahoussaye, Laffit Pincay, and Chris McCarron. The seventies was rife with such extraordinary trainers as Laz Barrera, LeRoy Jolley, Charlie Whittingham, D. Wayne Lukas, and John Veitch, honing their skills. But it was the dramatic duels between Affirmed and Alydar that captured America's attention and are to this day remembered as racing's greatest rivalry. It was Ali-Frazier, Palmer-Nicklaus, and McEnroe-Connors, right there with them. The three greatest moments in horse racing's archives, embellished above all others, are the 1978 Kentucky Derby, Preakness, and Belmont, with Alydar being the only horse in history to finish second in all three legs of the Triple Crown.

Never in the sport's long history have two horses fought each other so frequently in a rivalry that produced such close margins. It posed several questions:

- Did Barrera, Affirmed's shrewd fifty-three-year-old trainer, outmaneuver his much younger and less experienced counterpart, the thirty-two-year-old John Veitch?
- Should thirty-one-year-old jockey Jorge Velasquez, an excellent finisher noted for his patience, have been replaced by a more gung ho rider who would have used more stick and less carrot to bring Alydar home first?
- Did Admiral and Mrs. Gene Markey, both in their eighties, have too much elegance and confidence to order changes for Alydar as the inherited wealth of the once mighty Calumet

Farm battled the self-made Harbor View Farm of respected Louis and Patrice Jacobs Wolfson?

Each of the Triple Crown events was simply a two-horse race between Affirmed and Alydar, in essence a classic match race. Yet, the strategy used for Alydar was perplexing. It didn't reflect that match-race reality, namely by attacking Affirmed as soon as the starting gate opened. In the early stages of the Triple Crown epics, Alydar never established contact with Affirmed.

The Belmont, in particular, appeared to present a perfect setting for such match-race tactics. Alydar would find the sweeping turns at Belmont Park more suitable to his long-striding style than the tracks at Churchill Downs or Pimlico. Alydar's superior strength and stamina would have enabled him to attack the more versatile Affirmed earlier, keep the pressure on him longer, and eventually wear him down.

However, Affirmed, carrying the pink and black silks of Harbor View, did what he had done in six previous meetings with Alydar, he fought him off. While the racing world teetered on the brink of a nervous breakdown, the two horses stormed down the stretch in a furious side-by-side struggle that resulted in the fastest Belmont ever recorded and a photo-finish victory for Affirmed by a nose.

Barrera charted the race perfectly.

"My horse is gonna go slow the first part," he revealed before the race. "The last part of the race will be fast."

Veitch had other ideas.

"We're not going to let Affirmed do any easy galloping the first half-mile," he countered. "If they try to run the first half-mile as slow as forty-nine seconds, they'll have to be going head-to-head with Alydar."

But on a fast track, Affirmed loafed through the first half-mile in fifty seconds, and surprisingly a bit of daylight was still between the two horses. When they finally started slugging it out in the stretch, Cauthen once more played the counterpunching role and secured the victory. It left the crowd of 65,417 breathless.

Affirmed's breathtaking duels with Alydar in the Triple Crown races of 1978 imprinted his image indelibly in the public's consciousness. In each race, Affirmed established a lead and then held off Alydar at the end by ever-decreasing margins that resulted in the last race's photo finish. It was the way he did it that made Affirmed so beloved. No horse in living memory has more visibly and unforgettably displayed the will to win that so enables the thoroughbred than Affirmed did in his Preakness and Belmont victories.

Alydar never gave up, never quit trying, but Affirmed would simply not let him pass, no matter how fast, no matter how far.

Nothing between Affirmed and Alydar has ever been easy. Their rivalry was so intense that it transcended what is racing's best stage, the Triple Crown. Years later, people not only recalled that Affirmed earned the toughest Triple Crown ever contested, but that Alydar was the first horse to run second in all three races.

"This is something the world will never forget," proclaimed Patrice Wolfson.

She's so right. . . .

It were not best that we should all think alike;
it is difference of opinion that makes
horse races.

—*Mark Twain*

AFFIRMED

ONE

——— *How It All Began* ———

In the opulent kingdom of horse racing, nothing attracts public interest more than an exciting rivalry. It would be difficult for racing pundits to think of the 1977 and 1978 seasons without imagining what those years would have contained without the Affirmed-Alydar duels. For two pulsating campaigns they defined racing, as their spirited rivalry became a part of racing legend. It would make everyone forget whatever happened on a racetrack before and with the ride of Paul Revere would go right into the history books: Alydar from the laudatory Calumet Stable and Affirmed from Harbor View with a trainer, Laz Barrera, who appeared to talk to horses in metaphors of Spanish and broken English; Steve Cauthen, an unexcitable seventeen-year-old jockey who looked as if he should be sweeping chimneys in nineteenth-century London; an owner, Louis Wolfson, who needed to restore his reputation after a conviction, with a horse every inch a thoroughbred for the lithographs. The characters all worthy of a Norman Rockwell portrait.

On a cool February morning in 1976, Wolfson, who had shared his feelings with family members concerning Affirmed, was at Harbor View Farm to observe Affirmed as he had done many times before. Affirmed was a yearling now, an age when horsemen can make a more definitive judgment of an animal and his possibilities of becoming a champion. Wolfson spoke for a few moments with his farm manager, George Gauthier, while watching Affirmed frolic around the paddock.

Wolfson's smile was telling. Apparently pleased with what he had heard, Wolfson then shook hands good-bye with Gauthier and waved to a couple of handlers who were close by. By this time next year, Affirmed would be a two-year-old, saddled at a racetrack and run for the first time.

Melvin James, in Wolfson's employ in 1976, was Affirmed's first trainer as a yearling and also fashioned a liking to Affirmed, even though he gave the appearance of being a lazy horse. James eventually broke Affirmed by teaching him how to handle a bridle along with a bit and a saddle before he ever got on a track.

"I never had any trouble with him," disclosed James. "He was a smart horse and took to instructions easy enough. I had the feeling that he was going to be someone special."

Affirmed was an impressive-looking yearling. His legs tested strong and not the least bit bowed. His alertness was evident in response to talk directed at him. It was almost humanlike when he listened and perked his ears straight up.

"He would pull his head back and nod a couple of times as if he wanted to talk," said James.

With a triangular-shaped, foot-long white stripe from his forehead to the top of his muzzle, Affirmed carried the description of *handsome*. If Rodin needed a model to sculpt a one-year-old horse, it would be Affirmed.

Wolfson put a large amount of trust in James and often conferred with him, not only about Affirmed but other matters. James felt that Wolfson liked him because he was so independent and spoke his mind. One such time Wolfson asked James why an expensive yearling, which was a purchase and not a homebred like Affirmed, had his own pen away from the rest of the horses.

"So, I said, 'You know what that is, Mr. Wolfson? That's the rich white kid on top of the hill up there eating his steak and potatoes. And, in a few months, you'll send him down to Harlem and he'll get his ass kicked.' Nobody could tell me what to do because if I didn't see it work, I wouldn't do it."

James shook his head at what happened next.

"Mr. Wolfson knew what I was saying, and he made sure they turned that colt out to be a horse with the rest of them," he chuckled.

Affirmed never had such luxury. His stall was no different from any of the others. The farm was designed so that the homebreds were housed in one section of the barns and the purchased yearlings in another section.

"Nobody could see a streak of lightning in him," admitted James. "He was just a very docile, very quiet horse. One of the noticeable things about him was that things that got a horse excited did not bother him. Things would be going on in the barn, grooms would be walking through and horses would be going into the stalls, and he would be sound asleep. Lying down, flat asleep. You could hear him snoring.

"Come feeding time, all the horses would be banging on the tubs waiting to get fed and he'd be asleep. Some days you'd have to step over him to put his feed in the stall. He'd rise up maybe a few seconds after you left and he'd feed. And by the time you got done at the other end, he'd be back to sleep."

Affirmed's personality was so unusual, different from that of any of the other horses. It wasn't that Affirmed was lazy. At times, more likely he was bored. He was alert and aware of what was taking place around him and reacted to it. It's just that if he wasn't interested in what was happening, he would just lie down and take a nap.

Gauthier, the manager of Harbor View since 1971, also had a deep affection for Affirmed. He saw the newborn on the morning he was born in stall 80.

"Mr. Wolfson spotted him right away when he was a weanling," remembered Gauthier. "He saw Affirmed running along with a group of other weanlings and he picked him above the rest. While running in a field of eighteen or twenty others, he would always go to the front. Mr. Wolfson picked him out as the one which would be the best of the lot."

Wolfson's wife, Patrice, named Affirmed, and poetically so. She grew up in Queens, New York, in a horse environment with her father, Hirsch Jacobs, an outstanding trainer who is in the Racing Hall of Fame. She was a precocious child who loved horses. As a youngster, Patrice would do any number of chores around the stables and learned from her father the nuances of training horses.

The name History was the first choice bandied about by the

Wolfsons. But Affirmed was a lawyer's term Patrice had heard so often from the legal tribulations her husband had undergone over the years. She, more than anyone else, was fond of Affirmed, who would often lay his head on her lap.

"We watched, as time went by, how the colt became the leader of the pack, roughhousing with his playmates, yet coming over to the fence where we stood to gently nuzzle his admiring owners," offered Patrice.

"Affirmed was a smart horse with such a beautiful head," remembered Karla Wolfson, the wife of Louis's son Marty Wolfson, who began his career as a trainer back then and is now one of Florida's top three conditioners. "I told Patrice that Affirmed was a reincarnation of her father, who she was very close to," added Karla.

It was why Louis Wolfson looked upon the dawning of 1977 with high anticipation. Other owners might have, too. It's the nature of the sport. But for Wolfson, it was personal. He was on a mission, with his mantra being that it was not enough to own a thoroughbred; one also had to foal and raise one. He went about it with many detractors from other states attempting to discourage him in his quest.

That the horse industry in his home state of Florida wasn't looked upon with the same reverence as the ones in Kentucky and Maryland didn't deter him. Not until after World War II did horse farms begin to occupy the Florida landscape, and Wolfson was convinced he could carve out a niche in a sport that was rife with conservative tradition. The focal area was Ocala, in the north-central section of the state, where it was some ten degrees cooler than the heat and humidity of South Florida. That's where Wolfson began Harbor View Farm in 1960, and many detractors looked with a jaundiced eye upon raising a thoroughbred in a tropical climate, which nettled Wolfson. He was determined to show that horse breeding would be successful under his banner.

In a relatively short time, Wolfson had built his stable with older horses under the guidance of Burley Parke. As a trainer, he was somewhat different, soft-spoken, reserved, and polite in the Andy Griffith mode, but nevertheless respected by his peers. "I'm just an Idaho farm boy," he would often drawl.

He may have been, but when Wolfson hired him, he knew he had someone special, someone who could take Harbor View to the next level in building a champion stable. Parke had worked for John Marsh, one of the country's richest men, and won nine major Futurities from 1942 to 1944. Later in the decade, Charles Howard, who owned Seabiscuit, hired Parke to run his farm. Parke developed Noor into one of the greatest thoroughbreds of American racing, who beat the great Citation four times.

After Noor won the Hollywood Cup in 1950, Parke retired. Nine years later his brother, Ivan, convinced him to work for Wolfson. Parke returned to racing and increased the value of Harbor View notably with two horses, Raise A Native and Roman Brother. Unfortunately, on the way to becoming the two-year-old champion, Raise A Native tore a tendon and was forced to retire. And so did Parke soon afterward.

"Raise A Native was as good a colt that has come along in many years," remarked Parke.

Wolfson was hoping that Affirmed would be another Raise A Native. The trainer he now had to emulate Parke was Barrera.

Like Parke, Barrera, too, was different, only more so, an under-dog before he reaped noteworthy success in getting Bold Forbes to win the Kentucky Derby in 1976.

It took some doing. Bold Forbes was a strong-willed horse who tended to ease up in his races if nobody was challenging him. In training him for the Derby, Barrera cut two football-shaped holes in the colt's blinkers so that he could see other horses threatening to pass him.

Barrera's upbringing was in Cuba. His family lived near Ha-vana's Oriental Park Racetrack, and as a youngster he found work mucking out stalls and whatever else he could do to help his large family. He had a happy childhood. Not until years later did Barrera leave Cuba after the only horse he owned as a teenager was killed by a severe storm that ravaged the island. He didn't know a word of English when he headed in 1951 at the age of twenty-seven for Mexico City, where he would at least be comfortable with the language.

After a slow beginning, he found work as a trainer and be-came literally an overnight success by winning his first five races his first day at the track. However, it wasn't always that easy after that. One day, years later, Barrera had a disagree-ment with the racing officials and decided he had enough of Mexico. In 1960, he arrived in Los Angeles' Hollywood Park as the owner, trainer, groom, hot-walker, and one-man band with a cheap horse named Destructor and little else.

"I was practically broke when I arrived in America," remem-bered Barrera. "And, I could hardly speak a word of English."

Destructor won his first outing in a claiming race, but Bar-rera lost him when another owner claimed him, leaving Bar-rera horseless and penniless. Yet, a sympathetic Bill Winfrey loaned Barrera eight horses to get started again, and in 1971 he trained his first American Stakes winner.

Wolfson, who always insisted on exclusivity with his trainers, reached out for Barrera. But the compassionate Cuban didn't want to desert his ailing owner, Rafael Escudero. He wanted to remain with Escudero and a couple of other old friends from the bleak days when his shoes were worn and his bank account skimpy. Wolfson appreciated Barrera's honesty and even more so his allegiance to Escudero.

"He was my kind of man," claimed Wolfson. "When I was looking for a trainer, I remembered Barrera. I asked him to train exclusively for Harbor View Farm, but he told me he had one owner he didn't want to give up. The man had a malignancy and Laz was afraid he might die if he dropped him. I was so surprised with his loyalty and his feeling. I told him to take part of my horses if he wanted, and he did."

Wolfson now had Barrera to train Affirmed. Wolfson had purposely planned years earlier for foaling a homebred. On February 21, 1975, a thirteen-year-old modest broodmare named Won't Tell You foaled Affirmed, a chestnut son by Exclusive Native, a descendant of Native Dancer, the 1953 winner of the Preakness and Belmont Stakes. Wolfson had purchased Won't Tell You for only $18,000 in 1972, and except for Affirmed, she never foaled any notable horses.

When Barrera got him as a yearling, Affirmed had begun to develop a personality of his own. Along with his intelligence, he could be curious and quite often a ham when cameras were clicking around him. He was friendly and had a love for people and playfully nipped at them when they came close. He loved attention all right, but Barrera also found him to be relaxed and cooperative.

"Nothing seems to bother him," said Barrera, smiling. "He listens and does what you ask him to do. I can't ask no more of him."

By 1976, Wolfson could look back on eighteen years as an owner.

He began modestly in 1958 with the purchase of four thoroughbreds. The following year he expanded his stable to eleven. By 1960, he established the black and pink colors of Harbor View on a 478-acre expanse in Ocala with Parke, who had a reputation for judging horses, and began to purchase some good ones. One was Roving Minstrel, who cost $100,000 and became the winter book favorite for the 1961 Kentucky Derby. However, misfortune struck. In January of that year Roving Minstrel reared back and tumbled heavily to the ground. His career suddenly and unexpectedly ended with a cerebral hemorrhage.

At the Saratoga sales that summer, Parke bought a colt named Raise A Native out of Native Dancer for $39,000. Burley took personal charge of the well-defined chestnut, which began to attract attention with a series of impressive wins as a two-year-old. However, bad luck again surfaced. After a big win in the Great American Stakes on July 17, 1963, Raise A Native tore his tendon in his next start at Monmouth Park, which ended his career.

Wolfson was undismayed. Two years later, Parke closed a deal on a gelding named Roman Brother for only $23,000, who turned out to be the Horse of the Year in 1965. However, two years later Wolfson's legal troubles surfaced in the financial world, which created a setback for him at Harbor View. Wolfson had to spend considerable time away from horse matters to defend himself in the legal system and in an eventual court trial that resulted in his conviction.

Wolfson's financial empire, at one time one of the richest of any American, had dwindled in the nine years since he was incarcerated in a federal prison for a white-collar crime that had all the appearances of a trumped-up charge. He was targeted because of his acumen in acquiring corporations and generating huge profits with them. He was feared yet respected by the Wall Street barons and was looked upon as a corporate raider.

His menial crime was that he sold unregistered securities in one of his companies. It was manna from heaven for the Wall Street crowd and they didn't hesitate to alert the Securities and Exchange Commission. Wolfson never denied the charge and explained that none of the shareholders lost any money. He was sentenced to a year in prison, paid a substantial fine, and was released after ten months.

That's why Affirmed's prospects meant so much to him. He perceived them as vindication, but he would have to wait one more year to see if Affirmed would deliver. . . .

TWO

Louis Wolfson:
A Junk Dealer's Son

By the time he was forty-eight, Wolfson had control of several companies and was on the board of others. A regular at Hialeah and Gulfstream racetracks, not far from his sprawling Bal Harbour enclave that offered a panoramic view of Biscayne Bay, Wolfson decided it was a propitious time to enter the business end of racing as an owner. He nurtured an affinity for horse racing and the challenge it presented in winning. Not just winning, he thought, but in building a champion stable. In 1960, he opened Harbor View Farm in Ocala.

The 1960s were a period of challenge not only for Wolfson but all America. It was a time of hope, energy, and prosperity as the nation confidently evolved into its role as a superpower with military might and financial clout. What's more, the nation was effervescent with its newly elected president, John F. Kennedy. He was young, handsome, and his oratory rekindled the spirit of the country as President Eisenhower left office for a world of leisurely golf. "It's a time for a new generation of leadership to cope with the new problems and new opportunities," urged Kennedy. "There is a new world to be won."

Wolfson had already succeeded in the old world and was eager to invoke his sagacity for new opportunities and vigorously embraced racing. He acquired his mettle early in life as the son of a junk dealer who emigrated from Lithuania after escaping from the Russian army. Following the birth of their third child, Louis, Morris and his wife, Sarah, left St. Louis and settled in Jacksonville and made a meager living peddling papers, rags, bottles, and scrap metal from his junkyard while raising eight children.

Louis's older brother, Sam, approached him with an idea while Louis was still a senior in high school. Boxing was quite profitable in the pre-Depression South, and Sam wanted to utilize his younger brother's athletic prowess as a boxer. He gave Louis some boxing lessons, dubbed him Kid Wolf, and kept it a secret from family members. Although the prize money was minimal, Sam was banking on money tossed into the ring by spectators that could amount to as much as $5 a night.

Sam got Louis prepared for his first fight with a sparring session with a professional fighter no less, heavyweight contender Young Stribling, that paid $1 a round. Sam was stunned when Louis nailed Stribling with a right hand that floored him. Louis impressed a local boxing promoter, who quickly booked him for a bout at the Arcade Theater, Jacksonville's most prestigious arena. Both brothers were ecstatic and had illusions of grandeur in making boxing a career.

A large fight crowd turned out and Sam had thoughts of a

big payday, maybe $5 or $6. Kid Wolf looked impressive after the first round, but Sam had a worried look. He bent over and whispered in Louis's ear, "Finish this guy off. Pop's in the crowd. But don't let Pop see your face."

In the second round, Kid Wolf, keeping his back to his father in the second row, unleashed a powerful right-hand uppercut that lifted his opponent off the canvas, then coins began flying into the ring. Sam didn't stop to pick up any of them. Instead, he rushed his brother out of the ring, quickly changed clothes in a makeshift dressing room, and quietly returned home. Morris was waiting for them and sternly rebuked the pair. He instructed Louis to forget the boxing nonsense and concentrate on his studies so that he could attend college. Neither Sam nor Louis objected.

Wolfson's athletic prowess on the football field earned him a scholarship to the University of Georgia. Morris was pleased. Young Louis's biggest dream was to make All-American. He also confided to friends that he "had to make some money" and felt football would present the opportunity. As a sophomore, Wolfson's hopes vanished. In a 1931 game against Yale, he delivered a crushing tackle on Yale's All-American, Albie Booth. Slightly wobbly, Booth rose to his feet while Wolfson remained on the ground with a dislocated shoulder that ended his football dreams.

A year later in the wake of the Depression, his business career came into focus practically overnight. Together with his father and brother, they came up with $10,000 from family insurance policies and a $5,000 loan from an Atlanta attorney, Harold Hirsch, a Georgia alumnus who supported ex–football players. Wolfson's first corporation was baptized Florida Pipe and Supply Company, and it didn't take long to show a profit. He apparently inherited his father's eye for value. It presented itself twenty-five miles west of Jacksonville at Penney Farms, where J. C. Penney, a millionaire merchant and philanthropist, had built a retreat for retired clergymen.

The Great Depression forced Penney to cancel development of the property, which was an eyesore with large amounts of pipe and building material strewn along the roadside. Wolfson's genius for seizing a business opportunity became apparent. He was driving with a friend when Wolfson was taken aback by the waste. Minutes later, a party they were attending took on a serious mood. Wolfson asked Penney's son about the discarded material.

"What are you going to do with all that?" inquired Wolfson.

"We want to get rid of it."

"Do you want me to take it off your hands?"

"Are you serious about it?"

"Most definitely."

"You can have it for $250."

Wolfson shook hands on the deal and hurried back to Jacksonville to come up with the money. Several days later, the materials began arriving at his father's junkyard. Morris Wolfson became skeptical.

"Are you doing something illegal, Son?"

"Not at all." Louis then showed his father a contract, which allayed his fears. The youthful Wolfson's purchase later turned into a $100,000 windfall, and he was on his way to becoming a millionaire with that one single transaction.

"I felt that business was a field that had possibilities," remarked Wolfson after his initial successful business transaction.

He was so right. With the 40,000 percent financial bump he produced, Wolfson continued to accelerate Florida Pipe and Supply Company vigorously. With the clouds of war gathering across Europe and eventually spreading to the United States, he envisioned that the South, with its modest temperatures, would be an ideal region for military camps and airfields. Wolfson began increasing his inventory of pipes, valves, and sundry other building materials. A bad kidney and his damaged shoulder from his old football injury that caused him pain whenever he raised his arm were enough to classify him 4F. He remained at home to run the family business while his brothers went into the service.

Wolfson privately lamented about not being able to serve in the armed forces. He was a warrior, a former football player and boxer, who relished action. He harnessed his energy in the financial arena, and no one could accuse him of being torpid, especially after closing the biggest business deal of his burgeoning career. Wolfson was never one to sit on the sidelines and created his own action. In a stroke of genius that solidified his future, he generated enough publicity to make corporate America wince.

Who was this brash twenty-eight-year-old, a relative stranger to big business? Wall Street didn't embrace him but instead looked at him with a jaundiced eye. Florida Pipe and Supply wasn't even a footnote in the *Wall Street Journal*. Wolfson's strategy was brilliant. In 1946, he directed his action on two shipyards in Florida that were for sale at two ends of the state. One was privately owned in Tampa, and the other closer to home, the huge St. John's River Yard in Jacksonville, which the federal government had poured $19 million into to erect.

Wolfson attempted to buy St. John's in a negotiated sale. However, his offer was rejected by the Maritime Commission. They preferred closed bids on the property from experienced shipbuilders who would continue its operation and provide jobs for the local economy. Wolfson appeared on the dry dock with no knowledge of shipbuilding. But he moved fast and efficiently. Four days before the bids for St. John's were opened, Wolfson turned to the west and purchased the Tampa yard for $1.5 million. This superb transaction qualified Wolfson and his company overnight as a working shipbuilder.

Wolfson made his next move with the guile of a chess master. Some ten minutes before the bids were to be revealed for the St. John's project, a member of his Tampa operation submitted a bid. Wolfson's earlier offer under the Florida Pipe and Supply banner had been for $1.95 million. Wolfson's checkmate came into view. His Tampa Yards bid was for $1.92 million. His nearest competitor was $500 more. He successfully middled his opponent and became the owner of two shipyards as America and the rest of the world were emerging from World War II.

America was marked by change in 1946. Americans were beginning to travel again without restrictions and the threat of air raids from an ominous enemy on both ends of its shores. The populace was invigorated from the termination of the biggest war mankind had ever endured, but was still anxious about what lay ahead. Resilient Americans across three thousand miles of country who had overcome food and gas rationing and wartime employment were now bracing for life in postwar America. The transition wouldn't be easy. Thousands of families had lost loved ones in the war, which claimed over half a million lives. It was by far the most war casualties ever suffered in the history of the United States, more than the combined total of the Revolutionary War, Civil War, Spanish-American War, and World War I.

The year before was climactic as World War II came to an end. Within a month of each other, the Stars and Stripes were raised over Iwo Jima after four days of bitter fighting, and General George Patton let his tanks across the Rhine on bridges that were constructed in forty-eight hours. Both battles turned the tide of war in favor of the Allies.

In April, when the baseball season opened, three powerful world figures died within weeks of each other. Americans mourned President Franklin D. Roosevelt, who succumbed to a cerebral hemorrhage on April 12 at the age of sixty-three. Two of America's antagonists also died: Italian dictator Benito Mussolini was killed on April 28, and two days later Adolf Hitler committed suicide in a bunker in Berlin, which led to Germany's unconditional surrender on May 7. Three months later, after U.S. atomic bombs destroyed Hiroshima and Nagasaki on August 6 and 9, Japan capitulated on August 15. The tumultuous year culminated on December 21, when the sixty-year-old Patton died at an army hospital in Heidelberg from injuries sustained in a car wreck.

The gloom that hovered over America in the early days of 1946 was marked by labor restlessness. In January, eight hundred thousand steelworkers joined thousands of others on strike throughout the nation. Anxiety and capriciousness pervaded a thankful nation that had escaped harm's way and wanted to revel once again without the fear of war, which had left Europe barbarously scarred. The term *war brides* was introduced to America. Thousands who had married U.S. military personnel began arriving to a new life, leaving behind millions of displaced persons who were struggling to survive with nothing more than cartfuls of belongings they'd salvaged from the ashes of their destroyed homes.

The world was indeed changing. The United Nations met for the first time on January 10, just a week before Charles de Gaulle resigned as head of a French provisional government. Then, three days after the UN Security Council convened for its first session, de Gaulle resigned as president of France, on January 20.

Two months later, British troops withdrew from Iran according to a treaty, but the Soviets remained. On March 5, the world heard the words *iron curtain* from Winston Churchill, in his speech at Westminster College in Fulton, Missouri. England remained in the news. On March 10, British troops left Lebanon, and on March 22 it granted Transjordan independence. Finally, on the last day of the year, President Harry Truman officially proclaimed the end of hostilities in World War II.

In the next decade, Wolfson continued to prosper in the financial world. By 1955, he was the most powerful financier in the country, sharing the mantle with H. L. Hunt and Howard Hughes, in a rags-to-riches career as an industrialist, sportsman, and philanthropist. Wolfson's diversified business interests ran the gamut from shipbuilding to transportation to construction of bridges to newspaper ownership and finally to moviemaking in Hollywood, where he financed Mel Brooks's first movie, *The Producers,* which won an Oscar and later became a major New York play.

At one time or another, Wolfson tried to buy Montgomery Ward, American Motors, Republic Pictures, the Brooklyn Dodgers, Washington Senators, the Baltimore Colts, and Churchill Downs. Rebuffed in trying to purchase a major league franchise, Wolfson decided to build one himself. He turned to horse racing and in 1960 founded Harbor View Farm in Ocala, Florida.

By now, the junk dealer's son had become a national figure who would receive mail addressed to Louis Wolfson, Miami Beach, Florida. Handsome, nattily attired, he was often in the company of celebrities such as Frank Sinatra, Marilyn Monroe, Lauren Bacall, Barbara Walters, Larry King, Hedy Lamarr, Joan Crawford, Joe DiMaggio, Hank Aaron, Billy Martin, Mickey Mantle, Yogi Berra, Frank Leahy, Bud Wilkinson, Mel Brooks, and even a Supreme Court justice, Abe Fortas.

He was a doer, not a consumer. . . .

THREE

—— *A Heartbroken Man* ——

When a crestfallen Louis Wolfson walked out of a federal penitentiary on January 20, 1970, he was resilient in spirit. He had undergone an emotionally draining year in which his wife had died, his reputation was soiled, and his Harbor View Farm was in chaos. Although the penal institution in Fort Walton Beach in Florida's Panhandle was minimum security, that he wore prison garb the ten months he was incarcerated dwelled on him every day that he was there. He was now fifty-eight years old, still handsome with strands of gray in his bountiful hair. In the business world he was always impeccably dressed and an inspiring figure wherever he appeared. But prison! Wolfson was debilitated from wearing a grotesquely blue inmate #3362 uniform, which certainly didn't distinguish him from others and was far removed from the elitist demeanor he presented in the outside world.

Wolfson maintained his inner strength and resolve as the

patriarch of a close family who supported him with letters and
weekend visits. Mail call was the best part of Wolfson's day,
and he would eagerly wait for its announcement. His mail occupied most of his day, and he relished the hours of reading
and answering each letter. His family was his life, and the
lonely days in prison drew him even closer to them.

His oldest son, Steve, offered to move his family to Fort
Walton to be near Louis during his imprisonment. But he rejected the idea. "I don't want to uproot my grandchildren" was
Wolfson's terse reply. Instead, determined to keep the family
unified, Steve relocated to Miami Beach to be with his younger
brothers, Marty and Gary.

Wolfson's imprisonment was especially difficult for Marty,
a seventeen-year-old who had recently finished high school. He
was depressed to the point of being aloof and not interacting
much with other members of the family, namely Steve; Gary,
who was ten years older; and his married sister, Marcia, who
was too far away in New York. Marty's mother had died the
year before and now his father was gone. It was hard on a teenager who was withdrawn and alone. The void created by the
patriarch's absence spoke volumes.

Wolfson spoke with his family weekly and stayed busy in
his new environment. He worried about everything that didn't
have anything to do with prison itself. He had an open ear for
anyone and sympathy for those who he felt were wronged.
Wolfson would often ask Steve to help others in prison, while
all the while advocating prison reform. The magnetism that
he generated in the business world transferred to the dullness
of prison and its servitude existence.

"I was with Dad one day when one of the other inmates

walked by," recalled Steve. "He looked at my dad and remarked, 'If you would ever get a PR man, you could become president of the United States.'"

Wolfson didn't sleep much in the drudgery of prison life. Some nights slumber escaped him completely. His conviction, which he felt was inequitable to the point of being immoral, disturbed him immensely and ravaged his sleep. His name and reputation were tarnished, and it tormented him every day he was a prisoner. A white-collar-crime prisoner, but a prisoner nevertheless. He worried that it would be the way he would be remembered. He had accomplished too much and helped too many others only to be looked upon as a felon. He had been a giant in financial circles, humbled now in a prisoner's outfit.

Wolfson's daughter, Marcia, substantially helped fill the void in his life. They both needed each other, a despondent father, and a daughter, with a one-year-old son, who was getting a divorce. Marcia fled her fashionable Manhattan apartment with her son and her aide, Elizabeth, and camped out for the three months before Wolfson was released in a motel ninety minutes from the prison. At first Wolfson objected to Marcia's appearance. Yet, she convinced him that she had to get away from New York, and what better place than to be near him. For five or six days a week, they were together.

The federal detention center wasn't exactly a hardened one but was still classified as a prison. That word alone was debilitating to Wolfson and would indelibly appear in anything written about him. Yet, he made his temporary existence bearable. What helped was not being confined to a morbid cell, which would have suffocated him. Instead, he slept in a large, airy room that let in the sunlight, with sixteen beds aligned in a row in military fashion on each side of the chamber.

Marcia experienced a depressed father, yet at the same time a strangely affectionate one. Their relationship had vibrated with differences, but that all seemed long ago now. They were happy and enjoyed one another, and Marcia was never more joyful in rekindling the love she had harbored for her father that had been lost for years. They had quiet moments together sitting on the grass talking and laughing. Wolfson would wave one or two others over and introduce them to Marcia. A proud father indeed.

"I hear that you are thinking about getting a divorce," he remarked one day.

"Yes, most definitely," answered Marcia.

"Are you sure you want to do that?"

"Positive."

"Divorce is a serious matter, you know."

"I'm sure, but it's the best thing for me and Alan."

"Why didn't you tell me about it sooner rather than me learning of it from someone else?"

"Well, mother had just died and I didn't want to bring this all on you."

"But I have to know so I could help. Now, don't worry about anything. You and Alan will always be taken care of when I get out."

Some days Marcia would be in the kitchen cooking for everyone. She liked doing it and it was to some degree therapeutic. The inmates loved her sweet-and-sour meatballs, and she always made her father's favorite, chicken Parmesan. Those were happy days for Marcia, and whatever she and her father had quarreled about in years gone by was forgotten.

"Now don't get too friendly with the prisoners," warned a concerned Wolfson, always the father. "Remember, you're in a prison and not in a social world. Promise not to give your phone number to anyone."

Yet, Wolfson had compassion for all of them. He told Marcia that he would like to get jobs for every one of them. He would even help by giving them money to help get them started. She detected the glow in her father's eyes and confirmed that it was just like him to want to help others, just as she remembered. Marcia was proud of him.

"Dad got assigned to the laundry and took over from day one," said Marcia, beaming. "Just like it was his business. He took the system of tagging clothes, which consumed six hours, and reorganized it to incorporate only an hour. The warden was so thankful that he brought Dad outside into the sunshine and had him attend to the gardening."

Wolfson suffered and endured from an explosion of injustice. Marcia said that the joy of life for him was giving. He did so with no obligation. He was devoted to his loyal wife, Florence Monsky, and worshipped her. She never embarrassed him and he embraced her with all his strength. When she became fatally ill and died in 1968, he not only mourned her deeply but lost part of his soul from a marriage that had germinated thirty-two blissful years.

Wolfson had every reason to be indignant at being subjected to prison. He had been victimized by an obsolete rule regarding stock transactions that had never been enforced in financial circles. It had been a Securities and Exchange Commission regulation for as long as anyone could recall, and Wolfson's transgression was the first ever acted upon. His menial crime was selling unregistered securities in one of his companies. Wolfson admitted doing so, yet emphasized that none of the shareholders suffered any monetary losses. The SEC was looking for a fall guy, and the moguls on Wall Street had targeted Wolfson, who was depicted along with Howard Hughes and H. L. Hunt in a *New York Times* article as one of the three most powerful financial giants in America. The SEC charged him with failure to comply with SEC regulations. However, he was never accused of fraud.

His crime was selling unregistered securities, which meant if you owned 10 percent of a company, you had to file a registration statement. It was the first time in history that anyone had ever been criminally indicted for this.

Wolfson had a friend who worked for the SEC. "Tell your father they are out to get him," was the friend's warning. And they did. In September, Wolfson was offered an early release on his sentence. He replied that he would accept it only if the government admitted that they had railroaded him. They refused and Wolfson remained in jail until January.

After his death, in 2007, the indomitable *Wall Street Journal* defended Wolfson's innocence, which certified Wolfson's contention that he did nothing surreptitious. The article would, to some degree, have soothed Wolfson's hurt had he lived to read it. Still, he was tormented that he was convicted of a felony that he could never eradicate, and his pride and honor suffered immeasurably.

"I didn't use any fictitious name in selling the stock," Wolfson would say whenever he was confronted about his conviction. "No Swiss banks. When I made the sale, I reported it to the SEC. I'd have to be an idiot to do anything willfully wrong. There are more crooks on Wall Street than there are in racing."

"In one of the most disgraceful episodes in American legal history, Wolfson was convicted in 1967 of a trumped-up securities law violation (selling some unregistered shares) which should never have been subject to criminal charges," wrote Henry G. Manne in the *Wall Street Journal* in 2008. "A second case found him guilty of one of the government's all-purpose 'perjury and obstruction of justice charges.'"

"It was a horrible ten months and it ruined his life and changed him forever," pointed out Steve. "If you ever said the word *judge*, he'd bring out a stack of papers to show you how he was railroaded."

Wolfson's conviction numbed him. He isolated himself from corporate America by liquidating his empire and turned to philanthropic foundations and prison reform, having observed many injustices during his ten-month ordeal. He didn't wait long either. Two months after his release, he scheduled a press conference at the Robert Meyer Hotel in Jacksonville, where he was raised and where the family had a large presence in the community.

In part he stated:

After serving my full sentence, perhaps wiser, but with a feeling of sadness because of my deep concern, not for myself, but for our great nation, I have every conceivable reason to be scarred with bitterness, but I am not bitter. If I were, I would not be able to accomplish the goals I have long envisioned. If justice breaks down anywhere, it begins to break down everywhere. I envision an opportunity to battle for justice and to fight as I have always fought for the rights of every human being.

My conviction was unprecedented in judicial history. When the Court of Appeals gave a reversal in my case, I was tried a second and third time, after a 10-2 and 11-1 [vote] for acquittal; and the government threatened to try me a fourth time. I have evidence that the reason for this is the fact that I have spoken out and criticized the judiciary and the Justice Department.

I have found it was much easier to fight the Ku Klux Klan in Jacksonville, disguised with their hoods and white sheets, at a time when I had little or no financial means or influence, than it is to fight the elements that hide behind the guise of respectability and lack the courage to openly disagree with me. It is too late for me to change, nor would I be willing to do so, in my efforts to constantly fight any and all types of injustice wherever they raise their ugly heads.

The press conference was well attended. The magnetic Wolfson name attracted some two hundred observers to the venerable hotel. They each received a booklet written by Wolfson about the injustice of prison life. Some viewed it as self-serving, but newsman Charles Aldinger felt Wolfson's disclosure was sincere.

"In the rambling news conference, Wolfson led off with a statement where he attacked the American penal system and other laws in this country," said Aldinger. "As for his prison term, he said he spent five weeks working in the laundry and then he was appointed as a teacher.

"He said he was ashamed when prisoners insisted on shining

his shoes and pressing his clothes. 'I would never ask anyone to do that. In fact, I would ask them not to. I found out money is not very important to me. Now I want to help this country, which has been so good to me and my family.'"

Yet, he was still haunted by his conviction.

Over the next two years, Wolfson began liquidating his company holdings, retaining only a few of them. Racing renewed his vigor. He had to reapply for his licenses, which were relinquished following his conviction. On December 30, 1972, Wolfson's personal life changed dramatically. A widower for four years, he married Patrice Jacobs, the daughter of highly acclaimed trainer Hirsch Jacobs. It was a June-in-January union with Patrice being twenty-five years younger than Wolfson and a new beginning for him.

A horse lover like her husband, the two began to rebuild Harbor View Farm. A large amount of the racing stock had been disposed of at public auction following the revoking of Wolfson's racing licenses. Wolfson's two sons Steve and Gary had purchased some of the stock, valued at $1.655 million, at the auction to race under their stable, Happy Valley Farm. Wolfson repurchased them for Harbor View.

He was back doing what he loved most.

FOUR

Steve Cauthen: The Kid

He was known as the Kid. And he was every inch one. At six-teen and ninety-five pounds, a fuzzy-cheeked Steve Cauthen instantly became a phenomenon in his maiden year as a jockey. Cauthen came out of nowhere from the Kentucky countryside and assiduously alerted the racing world that he was someone special even with an innocent smile framing his beardless countenance. "Nowhere" was Walton, Kentucky, a tiny hamlet that is only a dot on a Rand McNally road map. But Kentucky was horse country, and his father, Tex, was a horseman who put his cradling son on horses when he was only a year old. In Tex's eyes, his little offspring was a natural. Like any father, he might have been overboard in his appraisal of one so young. But as time went by, little Steve fulfilled his father's expecta-tions in a way no one could ever have imagined.

Frank Tours, a respected racing official who worked the big tracks from New York to California, got a close look at the kid

when Steve was five years old. Tours was on assignment in Latonia, a small Kentucky venue some twenty miles south of
Cincinnati and forty miles north of Lexington. That's when
he first became aware of Tex's boasts about his son. At first,
Tours wasn't too enamored when Steve's name was mentioned
almost daily. Tours never showed much emotion and was never
known to get excited about anyone, from trainers, jockeys, and
even horses themselves until they proved themselves. But a
five-year-old?

Tours was surprised by what he saw.

"I was working at Latonia in 1965 when I was told to come
out to Walton and look at something unbelievable," recalled
Tours. "I was skeptical but I went. And I saw this tiny kid handling a thoroughbred in full gallop, sitting over him like a
regular exercise rider. I never forgot the name Steve Cauthen
after that. You don't forget a kid five years old who looks that
good on a horse."

Tex Cauthen made sure no one else would either. He had a
profitable business shoeing horses in Kentucky, with a following at the racetrack and nearby farms. He did everything the
storied blacksmiths did in the growing years of a young America. It was a noble profession, one respected by horsemen, and
it remained that way until the turn of the twentieth century
when Henry Ford introduced a four-wheeled animal known as
the automobile. The list of horsemen, who held shoeing in
high esteem, diminished with the advent of the automobile.

One of those was John Madden, who was known as the
Wizard of the Turf. Madden was one of the best, an owner who
bred five Kentucky Derby winners at the turn of the century.
Some held Madden's opinions in high regard. Madden suc-

cinctly observed what the automobile meant to him and its impact on blacksmiths.

"No foot, no horse," believed Madden.

Tex Cauthen was just as wise and at the same time honest. He was a dedicated horseman, and trainers sought him out for his services at a shoeing fee of $18. Smartly, they also reached out for his advice and any knowledge he would relate. That's how much respect Tex Cauthen had earned. One time a trainer walked his horse and showed him to Cauthen. The colt's legs were spread far apart and his toes were turned excessively inward. Cauthen saw a horse that looked unable to walk, let alone compete on a track.

"We couldn't straighten this dude out with a crowbar," mused Cauthen. "You sure you want me to bother shoeing him?"

"He's well-bred, so the owner has high hopes for him," the trainer responded. "As long as he feels that way, I'll keep collecting my eighteen dollars a day for training him."

"Then I might as well take my eighteen dollars for shoeing him," reasoned Cauthen.

Somehow, some way, the forlorn-looking animal raced for three years. His sole win came at a small-stakes race in Ohio. Cauthen, with his crafty shoeing that contradicted scientific laws, had every right to boast. But he never said a word.

But little Steve Cauthen, all seven years of him, was learning. Often he would awake early and accompany his father to the barns at five in the morning. He'd help his father until about eight o'clock, when he would get a ride to school. Around the barns, the youngster never got in anybody's way and hardly anyone ever noticed his presence. He just quietly went about doing what he was instructed to do, learning all the while. Tex innately felt that his son was born to be around horses and would one day establish himself as a jockey or a trainer. The kid had a natural affinity for horses, and his father encouraged him in every way.

Steve's love for horses was never more evident than when he once watched trainer Lonnie Abshire and his prize thoroughbred Slade. The temperamental horse was acting up in the barn and creating a commotion. Some of the stable hands refrained from volunteering to walk the highly spirited Slade, who kept vigorously pulling on his shank. It wasn't a pleasant sight, yet the one person who didn't draw back from the excitable Slade was young Cauthen.

Abshire looked down at Steve. "Hey, Steve, you got your riding boots on?"

"Yup," he answered unhesitatingly.

"You want to ride this dude?"

"Yup."

"Okay, boys, put the tack on him. You sure you can do it, Steve?"

"Yup."

Realizing what he was doing, Abshire suddenly stopped. Putting a seven-year-old kid on a high-strung horse wasn't right, he thought. He abruptly told Steve to forget the whole thing. But Steve didn't want to. He wanted to ride Slade. He kept asking, pleading, until finally Abshire gave in and nodded okay. Steve mounted Slade while Abshire held his breath. *What if this kid got thrown off and was seriously injured?* he thought. Calmly, Steve walked Slade around the barn. The big horse began snorting and baring his teeth as he threw his head back, giving all indications of rearing back and throwing his rider. It wouldn't require much of a surge to toss a little seven-year-old either. Abshire expected the worse. He kept his eyes focused, praying the entire time. He kept looking and looking and finally couldn't believe his eyes. The kid was laughing at Slade.

"I can understand how kids might be scared of some things in their lives," remarked Cauthen years later. "But it never did occur to me to be scared of a horse."

He never was. Five years later, when he was twelve, Steve told his father that he wanted to be a jockey. Tex understood. He kind of expected it. Tex wanted to be one himself when he was younger but never realized the dream. How could he tell his son no? Steve waited for his father's answer, and in a moment he got it with old-fashioned wisdom.

"I think it's a good idea," Tex replied to his smiling son. "I'll help you on two conditions. First, don't ever let it swell your head or change you as a person. And, second, promise that you'll give it up if you start to grow too big. The minute you have to start starving yourself to make riding weight, you'll have to look for something else to do with your life."

Tex continued, "If you're going to try it, you might as well try to be the best. There are a lot of fine points that some riders learn very late in their careers or never learn them at all. I can show you some of them. And what I can't show you, some of my friends probably can. Just pay attention. And be ready to work at it."

Not long after that day, Tex began helping Steve. The kid was already well versed in the rudiments of grooming and caring for horses from all the countless hours he'd spent around the stables. This precious time was priceless for someone so young. Steve embraced it and was ready for whatever his father or others would teach him. He was a willing, anxious learner. And learn he did.

One of the first techniques Tex taught him was the use of the whip. Tex thought it was an art, not something to pound a horse with. The motion is often misunderstood by racing fans, who are under the impression that the more a jockey hits his horse, the faster he will run. Yet, some horses won't react that way. In Tex's view, whipping is not a matter of demonstrating strength but a matter of timing, balance, and sensitivity between jockey and horse.

So, Tex showed his son at a young age the proper method of holding the reins and the whip, the art of transferring the stick from hand to hand without losing control of the reins. "Showing doesn't mean much," cautioned Tex. "You've got to do it so often that you can hit a horse just the way you want to every time without thinking about it."

Steve couldn't wait to try. After school, he would head for the family's barn and straddle a bale of hay. He would finger makeshift reins and pass his stick from one hand to the other, just the way his father had taught him, snapping down on the hay. He practiced this for days at a time until he could hit the hay in almost the same place every time. The youngster's relentless slashing shredded bales of hay. During one of his sessions, Steve looked around and was caught by surprise. His father had been watching him.

"What are you watching?" asked Steve. "Am I doing something wrong?"

"Nope," answered Tex. "I was just wondering if you'll ever be worth all those bales of hay you're beating to pieces."

"Sure hope so."

Tex was pleased. He detected how deeply his son wanted to ride, and Tex would think about anything or anyone that would embellish his son's education. It's just that Steve did more. Whatever he could come up with. Such as the time Tex took Steve to River Downs in Cincinnati. Tex led him to the track's starting gate. Tex felt that's where it all begins, where races are often won or lost.

By the time he was fourteen, Steve had developed a great feel about the intricacies of the starting gate. His father was right about horses getting off to bad starts. Some things, such as a jockey's not having his weight properly distributed, could cause his horse to break slowly. Once the starting gate opens, there is countless room for error on the jockey's part, or the horse may be off-balance, causing a delay in breaking out.

"I watched a lot of starts," revealed Steve. "I saw riders who, no matter what they did, never quite seemed to be tied on when the gates opened. Others managed to be ready and get off okay. And a few really helped their horses get out of there. They didn't use one trick. They knew their horse and they paid attention."

In 1974, there weren't any Triple Crown hopefuls at Latonia, and Steve was anxious to ride what was known as a breeze in horse circles. It's a practice run that trainers use to gauge a horse's progress prior to entering the horse in a race. Steve mentioned to his father that he felt capable of a breeze. Tex wasn't so sure. He harbored misgivings of entrusting Steve with a breeze at such a young age. Lonnie Abshire had no misgivings. He never forgot seven-year-old Steve and the fiery Slade. He helped Steve aboard his horse without any concern.

"Just let him go an easy three furlongs in about forty seconds," Abshire instructed him.

Steve performed perfectly. The horse ran easily and Abshire clocked him at 39.5 seconds. With that one ride, Steve became an exercise boy, the first step in becoming a jockey, and received other mounts from other trainers; quite an achievement for a starry-eyed youngster in junior high school. Gushing with confidence, Steve accelerated his learning. He began hanging around the clockers, which became a daily routine. He would ask and he would receive answers. Being an urbane, likable kid, the answers came easily. One summer, he watched hundreds of horses work out and estimated how fast they were moving. Then he would authenticate his guess with the clockers' watches. When summer was over, he didn't need to check the timepieces anymore. He knew how fast a horse was running, and one day he would utilize that knowledge when he became a jockey.

That time was approaching. Several months before his sixteenth birthday, Steve kept reviewing with his father everything he'd learned, making sure he didn't miss anything. He even kept looking at films of races that Tex got from his friends, notably at River Downs and Latonia.

Although River Downs was the bigger track, Latonia had a richer history, which Tex Cauthen was well aware of. The Kentucky oval opened in 1883 with a spring-summer program and a second in late fall. It was once considered one of the country's best venues for racing and attracted more than one hundred thousand patrons annually. Its jewel was the 1½ mile

Latonia Derby, which at one time rivaled Churchill Downs and the Kentucky Derby in winnings and prestige. The Latonia Derby was initially called the Hindoo Stakes, in honor of the great Kentucky-bred champion Hindoo. The first Latonia Derby was won by Kentucky Derby winner Leonatis in 1883. Other Kentucky Derby winners followed: Kingman (1891), Halma (1895), Ben Brush (1896), Lieut. Gibson (1900), Elwood (1904), and Sir Huon (1906). Young Steve was being groomed in rich Kentucky racing history.

On October 11, 1924, sixty thousand racing enthusiasts gathered to witness the third and final segment of the International Special races that sent French champion Epinard against America's top thoroughbreds. However, Sarazen emerged victorious and garnered Horse of the Year honors. Epinard finished second, as he had done in his two earlier races at Belmont and Aqueduct in New York. Unfortunately, financial woes during the Great Depression forced Latonia to close its gates with the season's last card on July 29, 1939. Twenty years later it reopened ten miles south under new ownership as the Latonia Race Course, and Hall of Fame jockey Eddie Arcaro, from nearby Cincinnati, got his start there.

All of this lore was not lost on Tex Cauthen. In his younger years, Tex traveled the horse havens in Texas, Louisiana, Oklahoma, Arkansas, and Ohio before settling in Walton. What convinced him was the bucolic rolling green countryside that offered tranquillity at the end of a day. In his mind, there was no better horse country than the area around Lexington, which was famous as a major area for horse breeding since the late eighteenth century. The fertile land was known for its deep limestone beneath the soil's surface, which contributed to a high calcium content in its grass, making for stronger bones and greater durability in horses.

Lexington was founded in June 1775 in what was then Virginia, seventeen years before Kentucky became a state in 1792. By 1820, it was one of the largest and wealthiest towns west of the Allegheny Mountains. U.S. senator and presidential candidate Henry Clay had an office in Lexington. President Abraham Lincoln and Confederate president Jefferson Davis spent a great deal of time there. Lincoln's wife, Mary Todd, was born and raised in Lexington. The couple visited the city a number of times after their marriage in 1842. But not until 1924, when Calumet Farm was founded, did Lexington enjoy the celebrity of modern times with its reputation for producing champion thoroughbreds.

Tex settled his family on a small farm in Walton, earning his reputation as an excellent blacksmith, never once imagining that one day his son Steve would make national racing history and add a chapter to Kentucky's racing history as a native son.

Ironically, on May 1, 1976, the day that Angel Cordero won the Kentucky Derby with Bold Forbes, Steve turned sixteen and was eligible for a jockey's license. Steve didn't know it then, but Laz Barrera, the trainer of Bold Forbes, would become an intricate part of Steve's life a year later. That evening at a birthday dinner with his family, Steve couldn't hold back his emotions.

"I thought this day would never get here," he gushed. "I'm ready to start, Dad. I'm ready to ride."

Tex nodded. Steve had trained diligently and absorbed more knowledge than others his age who professed a desire to ride for a living. Tex was proud of his offspring and had every right to be. Everyone liked the kid, and they demonstrated it by helping him any way they could without a whimper. Tex was proud of that, too.

"Hell, I knew he was ready," he claimed. "By the time that birthday came around, he'd been ready for a long while."

The kid now assumed the responsibilities of a young man. One grows up fast in racing. It happened on May 12 at Churchill Downs when Cauthen received his first mount. Symbolically, two years later, the personable Cauthen would be in the biggest race of his burgeoning career aboard Affirmed in the Derby itself.

"That was the track that was open in Kentucky at the time," pointed out Cauthen. "I had a hard time getting the mount that I got. It wasn't like everybody was rushing to get me a mount. My dad pretty much had to ask his trainer to get me one. And he did. He was just getting fit again and he let me ride 'cause he was only fit to go about three furlongs. But it was a chance to get in the race and get out of the gate for the first time."

The horse had no pedigree. Cauthen was riding a long shot named King of Swat shipped from Latonia from a $5,000 claiming race. Babe Ruth would have cringed at the 136-1 odds the horse carried to the starting gate. But it didn't matter to Cauthen. This wasn't a breeze but his maiden race, and that was his Derby. Cauthen didn't look up at the odds but instead appeared to be all business. If anyone appeared worried, it was his mother, Myra.

"Steve walked the paddock trying to look as calm as he could," she remembered. "But I could see something in his eyes and the way he moved. My own knees felt a little weak, and suddenly I knew Steve was feeling the same way. Sure, he had the training and experience to do good, but in that moment I forgot all that. I was a mother and Steve was a boy who had just turned sixteen. We were both a little scared."

But if Steve was scared through his mother's eyes, he certainly didn't show it when the starting gate opened. He maneuvered his horse easily into the middle of the track. He didn't display any inexperience as he positioned his horse near the leaders. Riding smoothly, Cauthen had King of Swat third, only a length behind the leader. Could this turn out to be the upset of upsets? Although he dropped to fourth at the half, Cauthen was only a half-length from the lead. Then, the expected happened. Like Babe Ruth after some beers and a bunch of hot dogs, King of Swat began to tire. Cauthen felt it and knew the result. There was no horse under him that could rally. Steve had no use for the whip, and all that remained was a professional finish on a long, long shot that came in next to last, sixteen lengths behind the winner in tenth place. Cauthen had no remorse.

"We all knew that he was only fit to run about a half mile, and the race was three-quarters so nobody expected him to win," disclosed Cauthen. "I rode him good and then he stopped."

"That's right," agreed his father. "You rode him fine."

Cauthen would get another chance later in the day. Unfortunately, he didn't inherit a solid horse. The only consolation was that the odds on Singing Saint bottomed out at 50-1 in a race that was much longer at a mile and a sixteenth. If anything, Cauthen would benefit from a longer ride and at the same time build his confidence, which is so vital to a sixteen-year-old. Steve rode well. He had his horse within a neck of the leader around the far turn. But, like King of Swat, Singing Saint began to fade. He ran all he could and finished sixth in losing by six lengths.

Five days after his Churchill debut, Cauthen was riding closer to home at River Downs, where he had spent many long hours. The move was directed by his father and with good reason. Steve was comfortable with the track, and Tex knew that the trainers were familiar with Steve. Just as important, the competition was less intense than at Churchill Downs. The two races that Steve had under his belt made for an easy transition to the smaller River Downs. Steve brought with him a ten-pound weight allowance he carried as an apprentice. The allowance was commonly known as a bug and is indicated in racing programs by an asterisk next to the jockey's name. The three asterisks informed bettors that Cauthen was a "triple bug boy," but he wasn't fazed by all that. He just wanted to ride, and for the next two weeks he carried that tag without giving it a second thought.

On May 17, the featured race at River Downs had a purse of $3,800, which by the track's standards wasn't exactly small. More significantly for Cauthen, it was the feature race, and he would get to ride a strong stretch runner in Red Pipe, who was assigned 113 pounds. Red Pipe's trainer, Tommy Bischoff, was Myra's brother, who was pugnacious enough to employ his nephew and his ten-pound allowance for the five-and-a-half-furlong race at 103 pounds. Bischoff calmly instructed Steve to let Red Pipe relax, then turn him loose and make his run at the top of the stretch. The kid did exactly as he was ordered and brought Red Pipe from out of nowhere with a masterful ride to win his first race by a length and a half.

"We were way out of it," explained the happy prodigy. "We must have been fifteen lengths out of it at the three-eighths pole. But when we hit the stretch and I finally hit him, the horse really charged. I knew he would get home in time. It felt good as I always dreamed it would."

There would be more dreams. Two days later Steve made a stretch run of his own by booting home three winners. The triple bug next to his name was removed and replaced by a seven-pound allowance—which was the price of his success. All apprentice jockeys who have never won a race get the benefit of the bug. The ten-pound allowance enables the apprentice to tote a lesser weight in his saddlebags than veteran jockeys until he wins five races. Then, he is assigned seven pounds until he wins thirty-five times. After that, the weight is reduced to five pounds and remains until a year after the date of his very first win.

At times, the lower weight helps a horse win a race that he's not expected to win. Horseplayers often make bets based on the allowances, which are indicated by asterisks in the racing program. Three asterisks mean a ten-pound allowance, two a seven-pound, and one a five-pound edge, and apprentices are often referred to as bug boys. The hot-riding Cauthen was a triple bug for only two weeks.

In racing circles he was quickly making a name for himself. Cauthen continued to win, and the kid, who was still a junior in high school, created a buzz around River Downs. Tex and Myra, along with Steve's two younger brothers, couldn't have been happier when fall came to the Walton countryside and the kid had to resume his studies. Cauthen's mounting success didn't inflate his head or lead him away in any way from the tenets his parents had instilled in him. For a youngster, he was mature for his age and separated his dreams from the reality that is life. In two months of racing, he had won twenty-six races.

"There isn't all that much money to go around in a place like River Downs," realized Steve. "Guys aren't racing for headlines; they're racing to put food on the table, fighting for everything they could get."

Anxiously, Steve waited for River Downs' 1977 summer meeting, which contained fifty-six days of racing. He knew after his apprentice year that he would generate more mounts. In his first year, he had ridden 157 races and won 26 of them, which didn't seem like much. But he had accumulated valuable experience for one so young and had distinguished himself more like a veteran jockey than an apprentice. Trainers observed his calmness, and he would attract more attention for his services in what would actually be his first full meeting as a jockey. Indeed, Steve began to get the best horses with regularity, and before season was over, the precocious seventeen-year-old made headlines. He established a total record with 96 winners that summer, and his total of 120 wins set another record for the entire season.

Tex had seen enough. He felt his son was ready for the larger tracks. He was thinking about New York and was told about an agent named Lenny Goodman. Tex found him at Saratoga and introduced himself on a sunny August afternoon to the biggest agent in the business outside the racing secretary's office of the century-old, storied course.

As always, Tex came right to the point: "My son is riding two horses today. He's the leading rider at River Downs, and I was hoping you might look at him and see what you think."

Goodman examined the program and didn't like what he saw.

"These are terrible horses," he lamented. "'He's got no shot to win but I'll take a look at him."

He did and Cauthen surprised him. Even though Steve didn't win any of the races, Goodman felt the kid was something special in the way he handled his mounts with strong, large hands. He met with Tex afterward as promised and informed him that he was interested in handling Steve. Like Tex, Goodman didn't mince words. He didn't have to. His reputation as a shrewd agent didn't allow for any wasted time.

"I like your kid, but we got a problem here," began Goodman after removing a cigar from his mouth. "He's sixteen. A baby. I can tell him what to do from the time he gets to the barns in the morning until the end of the last race in the afternoon. But when he leaves the track at night, where's he gonna go?"

"Steve's a levelheaded kid to begin with," answered Tex. "Don't worry. He's not going anyplace where he doesn't have somebody reliable to live with."

"Well, I don't have any room for him," insisted Goodman. "Where would I put him?"

"We'll have to find some place for him sooner or later. But there's no hurry. We'll go on back to River Downs and let him finish the meeting. Then we'll decide if he should go to Chicago or New York."

"Fine," agreed Goodman. "When you can work out the arrangements and you want to come to New York, just call me."

Tex walked away with Goodman's business card. But he had some thinking to do after the cool yet honest conversation with Goodman. Tex made up his mind on the way back to Walton. It was Chicago, and Steve would take correspondence high school courses with him along with his 24 percent winning average he compiled at River Downs. His mother made sure of the correspondence part while Tex took care of the rest. Paul Blair was the agent who would handle Steve in Chicago. He was a good one who had a reputation for developing apprentices, and he was glad to get Steve.

"I've had some good kids, but I can't recall a bug boy who ever rode as low on a horse as Steve," observed Blair. "He looks like part of the horse."

A 20 percent winning percentage at Arlington Park was considered good. Very good. What Steve did that first year was exceptional. Blair contracted him for 160 races, and Steve responded by winning 40 times for a percentage of 25 percent. He finished in second place in the jockey standings and repeated it when the race schedule shifted crosstown to Hawthorne Park. In the fall, Cauthen returned to Churchill Downs, where it all began for him. He continued to gain in stature as a solid jockey. At the track's close, Blair was heading for Florida and offered to take Steve with him. But the kid was yearning for New York. Tex made the call to Goodman, who piped, "Send him up here," and Steve arrived wide-eyed for the fall running at Aqueduct.

"I've done good everywhere else and I figured I might as well try the best," confessed Cauthen to Goodman. "If it doesn't work out, I can always go back to Kentucky or Chicago."

"It'll work out, but just don't expect miracles," cautioned Goodman. "I figure we can win maybe ten races a week."

"Whatever you say, Mr. Goodman."

"That's right. You do what I say and we'll do fine. And call me Lenny."

One of the first things Goodman did was to meet with Laz Barrera. He was excited about Cauthen and wanted him to get on board Barrera's horses.

"Lenny Goodman said there was a friend he'd like me to meet," said Barrera. "I thought it was his friend's kid or something, but Lenny said, 'Hey, this is my new rider.' I say, 'Oh, boy, you're going to go to jail.' He looked like he was twelve years old."

The union of a hot young jockey and a power agent burst on the Aqueduct grounds like Fred Astaire and Ginger Rogers. They were in harmony, this fuzzy-cheeked kid and a cigar-smoking agent who was every bit a Damon Runyon character. Goodman secured the horses and Cauthen won with them and began capturing the imagination of the bettors along with the trainers, who sought out his services. During a cold December period of three weeks, Cauthen showed his stuff. He won twenty-nine races, and even Santa Claus had to marvel at the kid's deft handling of horses. Cauthen became known as Stevie Wonder. New York loved him. After one of his wins, writer Pat Lynch remarked in the press box, "We're watching the coolest young rider since Willie Shoemaker," which was high praise indeed.

Young Steve Cauthen had arrived. He was for real. In the

eight months he rode in 1977, his horses won $1,244,423. He was a seventeen-year-old who rode as if he were thirty. He was that far ahead of the field. Cauthen continued to impress. In one afternoon at Aqueduct he won six races, tying one of the most prestigious records in New York racing. He had reached stardom.

"Are you tired?" he was asked at the press conference.

"Not when I ride six winners," Steve said, beaming. "I only get tired when I ride losers."

California trainers were calling for Cauthen, and Goodman hustled him on a plane to make his West Coast debut at Santa Anita. His appearance attracted 42,506 patrons, the largest assemblage of the year. They wanted to see the kid, much like a young heartthrob such as James Dean on the silver screen. Cauthen didn't disappoint. The *Los Angeles Herald Examiner* headline read, "Cauthen Captures L.A."

When 1977 ended, Cauthen had accumulated a miraculous 487 wins, the most of any jockey, all of whom averaged ten years older than him. Not since Bob Feller, a seventeen-year-old phenomenon, left his family farm in Iowa in 1936 to throw 100 mph fastballs for the Cleveland Indians, had the sports world experienced anything so absorbingly breathtaking as Steve Cauthen. His accomplishments were the size of a tsunami in winning the national riding title Eclipse Award and cashing in a record of $6.15 million in purses. What else could he do?

It was only the beginning. The best was only a year away, when he would embrace racing history. . . .

FIVE

—— *The 1977 Season* ——

When 1977 dawned, and Alydar was training under the watchful eyes of trainer John Veitch, the Markeys were in the autumn of their years, infirm and rarely seen in public anymore. Calumet's fortunes had evaporated to the extent that in 1976 Veitch had only nine horses to work with, and Alydar was expected to regain the stable its glory years. The Markeys had every right to feel that way. Alydar was the best-looking colt Calumet had raised in almost a decade. A solidly built chestnut, he brought joy to the Markeys whenever they felt well enough to watch him in his early-morning workouts. So when the racing season opened, Alydar was looked upon as survival for Calumet, while on the other side of the track Affirmed was the emblem of redemption for Wolfson, who had been away in prison, which soiled his reputation. The racing world had no idea that Affirmed and Alydar would develop an ineffable rivalry such as never before witnessed on American tracks.

The 1970s were unfolding into perhaps the greatest decade of American racing with such stars as Seattle Slew, Secretariat, Forego, Spectacular Bid, Ruffian, Bold Forbes, Key To The Mint, Canonero II, Foolish Pleasure, and Riva Ridge. Most horsemen felt that Affirmed and Alydar had the potential to join this elite circle of horseflesh.

Other quality two-year-olds, including Believe It, Nasty and Bold, Darby Creek Road, Sensitive Prince, and Star de Naskra, also drew attention. Alydar, with better bloodlines and Calumet's reputation, was given the edge by horsemen over Affirmed and less honored Harbor View, which had never won the Kentucky Derby, Preakness, or the Belmont, where champions live. That's what Wolfson wanted and that's what the Markeys wanted again, and both owners felt they had that chance with Alydar and Affirmed. It would all begin with the Youthful Stakes at Belmont Park on June 15.

Three weeks earlier at Belmont, before the Youthful, Affirmed made his first start under apprentice jockey Bernie Gonzalez. He was described by Joe Hirsch, the respected columnist of the *Daily Racing Form,* as a "good little horse." After the 5½-furlong race, he had a more ebullient opinion of Affirmed, who easily breezed to a 4½-length victory. "Any horse that can win his first race that easily is someone to watch," said Hirsch.

The Youthful was looked upon as an early test for two-year-olds, some of whom had won their maiden races, and it attracted a field of eleven hopefuls. Barrera was determined to win, and to improve his chances he replaced Gonzalez with the veteran Angel Cordero. Alydar went to the post as the 9–5 favorite with Affirmed the second choice in the betting at 3–1.

For most of the 5½-furlong race, Cordero had Affirmed lying in second place. At the top of the stretch he made his move and gauged it perfectly, and Affirmed responded to his jockey's urging. He caught and passed 45–1 shot Wood Native just before the finish line to win by a neck as Alydar finished out of the money, running fifth by five lengths.

In his third start, Affirmed met Alydar for the second time on July 6, in the 5½-furlong Great American Stakes, also at Belmont, in what would engender their torrid rivalry, which would thrill racing fans for the next two years. Despite having lost to Affirmed in the Youthful, the Belmont crowd made Alydar a 4–5 favorite while Affirmed was the surprising second choice at 4–1. Alydar's backers were joyfully rewarded. He overtook Affirmed as they reached the stretch and pulled away for a handsome 3½-length victory in 1:03:3/5, which was only a razor-thin three-fifths of a second off the track record. Alydar became the popular favorite across America and was being talked about in comparison with Calumet's great Citation. Alydar was so impressive in the Great American that the *New York Times* pictured it as "the days of wine and roses may now be on their way back to Calumet."

After three races, Barrera had enough of Eastern tracks. He decided to take Affirmed west to California, where he always preferred to work his horses. Even though he only scheduled one race for Affirmed, the six-furlong Hollywood Juvenile Championship, on July 23, Cordero decided to remain in the East, and Barrera contracted Laffit Pincay to ride Affirmed in the Juvenile. Pincay, who was a popular rider in California, was Affirmed's third jockey in only four races. Yet, a new jockey was no bother to Affirmed, who blistered his competition with speed to spare to win by seven lengths as a 2–5 favorite.

Barrera as yet had no thoughts about Cauthen, who was in command of the Eastern tracks while generating excitement and accumulating a fervent following with his teenage mastery. At one juncture Cauthen turned twelve winners in seventeen challenges. He drew raves when he won his first stakes race in his burgeoning career by guiding Frampton Delight, a 19-1 shot, to victory in the Gallant Fox Handicap. "Never has so much been done by one so young in such short time" was the two-line headline in the *Daily Racing Form*. Not until August would Cauthen unite with Affirmed for the first time in a relationship that would excite the world of racing.

In August, Barrera had returned to the East and began prepping Affirmed for the six-furlong Sanford Stakes on August 17 in Saratoga. Pincay had a previous commitment, yet Barrera was not the least bit dismayed. He reached out to Cauthen and the kid delivered. He outdistanced the field, but not without a struggle, for Affirmed's fourth win. Down the backstretch, young Cauthen had to hold tight to control his horse. When he finally got him straightened away, he maneuvered him down the middle of the track to an almost-three-length victory.

"He tried to bear out the whole trip," disclosed Cauthen.

When a horse bears out, it can create a number of situations. In running laterally, he could create a collision or fall off the pace by losing valuable ground.

Affirmed was attracting attention and more so Cauthen, who Barrera kept on his prize colt. In just three months of competition, Affirmed had taken races on both the East and

West Coasts and was lighting up the circuit, especially with Alydar around to challenge him.

Alydar arrived from New Jersey's Monmouth Park to engage Affirmed in the Hopeful Stakes, Saratoga's most prominent two-year-old race on August 27. The public remained loyal to Alydar, betting him at even money, while Affirmed went off at a 2–1 in the 6½-furlong jaunt.

In most of Alydar's starts, he had trouble getting out of the starting gate, which accounted for his last-place beginnings. Yet, he was a great finisher and that's why the public liked him, urging him on as he came charging down the stretch. Breaking from an inside post position, Alydar swerved to his right and bumped into Tilt Up, who in turn slammed into Darby Creek Road. Eddie Maple acted quickly and dropped Alydar back into last place in an effort to calm him down.

Affirmed not only broke cleanly but Cauthen kept him out of trouble by staying away from the rail, where the track was deep. Alydar rallied and caught up to Affirmed as they went into the stretch, and the excitement began to build.

At the eighth pole, Affirmed held a head's margin with Alydar driving hard to make his run. But Affirmed didn't buckle and distanced himself from Alydar to win by a half-length in the record time of 1:15:2/5.

The victory was especially memorable for Wolfson's wife, Patrice. Through all the glorious years with her father, Hirsch Jacobs, Patrice's favorite horse had been Hail to Reason, the great colt who sired many of Jacobs's stars after he retired. On his way to the two-year-old championship, Hail to Reason had also won the Hopeful in 1960, ironically, the year Cauthen was born.

"Congratulating Stevie made me think of those seventeen years," gushed Patrice. "I felt like a little old lady."

Cauthen was bringing it all together for her.

Affirmed's victory was personally meaningful for Barrera. It was strictly family. His brother Willy broke and galloped Affirmed, and his other brother, Luis, trained him at Belmont after the Hopeful when Laz returned to California. For almost two weeks, Wolfson, a strong family man himself, couldn't have been more pleased.

"Sometimes I think I must be crazy to try to run one stable in California and one in New York," joked Barrera. "I'm on the red-eye airplane all the time. Until 1976 I had never won a $100,000 race in my life. Then I trained Bold Forbes to win the Kentucky Derby and Belmont Stakes. It brought me a lot of joy and publicity, but this year may turn out to be a good one, too."

Alydar wouldn't go away. He was entered to challenge Affirmed two weeks later in the acclaimed seven-furlong Futurity Stakes. Veteran jockey Eddie Maple, riding Alydar, went after Affirmed. He got too close to Cauthen and crowded him. Each jockey had to use his whip on his mount's other side to avoid collision. Affirmed inched his way back into the lead and won a photo finish by a nose in another pulsating duel.

"Affirmed never gave up in the stretch even when he was behind," remarked Cauthen.

The 1977 fall season was just beginning at Belmont, and the Affirmed-Alydar rivalry was thrilling New Yorkers. The two horses were practically inseparable, slugging it out race after race in a rivalry rarely ever seen among two-year-olds.

Cauthen's hot riding created the buzz. He was on all the

national TV programs: the *Today* show; *Good Morning America;* the evening news with Barbara Walters, Chancellor-Brinkley, Walter Cronkite; and the *Tonight Show Starring Johnny Carson,* talking about his success and the rivalry with Alydar.

One night, Carson quipped to his audience about booking Cauthen as a guest, "I want to get Steve Cauthen on. We're trying. He's the only jockey in the world you can bet on to win, place, or break out. If he keeps going from the finish line to the winner's circle as he often does, the racetracks will have to hire crossing guards."

Affirmed and Alydar were set to resume their battle in the Champagne Stakes on October 15. Affirmed had won three of their four meetings, which caused Alydar's trainer, John Veitch, to make a strategic move. He sidelined Maple and replaced him with Jorge Velasquez. Not only that, he also decided to fit Alydar with blinkers.

"Maple was a good rider, but I thought that Jorge was maybe a little stronger and more aggressive," explained Veitch. "Alydar is a classic one-run horse, and it was a strong run. However, I concluded that to beat Affirmed we needed to make a strong rush at him."

It was cloudy and damp when the two prize horses reached a slightly muddy Belmont track. The Affirmed-Alydar competition was the highlight of the Jockey Club Gold Cup card before a packed audience. Their rivalry was already approaching the stimulating ones involving Citation, Seattle Slew, Secretariat, and Spectacular Bid. Affirmed-Alydar would become bigger.

When the two valued thoroughbreds broke from the gate, the sun appeared and dampened spirits were warmed as the railbirds gathered along the stretch. The winner could very well determine who would win the valuable two-year-old male championship.

Both Affirmed and Alydar stayed back as Sauce Boat and Quadratic battled for the early lead. As in their other outings, the race appeared to be another one-on-one duel between Affirmed and Alydar. On the final turn Cauthen made his move. He guided Affirmed between the pacesetters and reached the stretch with half-length lead. Alydar loomed on the outside positioned to make a run. He flew past Sauce Boat and Quadratic and approached the front-running Affirmed. In full gallop, in front of a wildly cheering throng, he caught and passed Affirmed a hundred yards before the finish line and a 1¼-length triumph. Velasquez had run a masterful race.

"My horse had plenty left but he was playing games with Darby Creek and he never saw Alydar until it was too late," explained Cauthen.

Cauthen also told Barrera that Affirmed wasn't comfortable with the condition of the track. Affirmed and Alydar were destined to meet one final time that year, two weeks later on October 29 in the Laurel Futurity at Laurel Park in Maryland. The race would most definitely decide the two-year-old champion, with Affirmed holding a 3–2 edge in their races. However, a week before the race, Barrera announced two conditions. He would not saddle Affirmed if it rained, and he maintained that it would be Affirmed's last race of the year regardless of who won. After that, he would ship Affirmed to California to begin training for the 1978 Kentucky Derby.

Alydar's big win in the Champagne was impressive enough to radically change his odds in the 8½-furlong Laurel. He had been the underdog with the bettors in both the Futurity and the Champagne. However, he was made a prohibitive 2–5 favorite at the Maryland track, while Affirmed went off as a 7–5. The closeness of the odds suggested the tightest race of all between the pair. There weren't any excuses in the track's condition, which was firm after being rolled by two ground-packing tractors. The weather was fair and the temperature a bit chilly on the last Saturday in October as anxiety peaked at post time.

Star de Nashra lunged out of the gate first and grabbed the early lead. Still, all eyes followed Affirmed and Alydar. Affirmed was running second but not at his usual position on the inside rail. It was Alydar in third place occupying the space with Affirmed outside. It was planned that way. Barrera had instructed Cauthen to maintain a better spot in which to view Alydar throughout and not get caught by surprise the way Affirmed did in the Champagne. At the stretch turn, Velasquez moved Alydar between Star de Naskra and Affirmed and assumed a slight lead. Cauthen, steadying Affirmed, kept close. Midway down the stretch, Affirmed holding fast, edged in front and rejected Alydar's challenge by a neck in his fourth victory over his archrival. The rivalry would continue to manifest next year and Barrera realized it all too well.

"There is never a disgrace when one of them loses," he proclaimed. "This is the sixth time now that they have run against each other, and it is the sixth time they both have run their race."

Barrera kept his word. Affirmed was finished for the year. He went to the post nine times and was triumphant seven. His only loses were close ones, both to Alydar. But Cauthen kept riding and kept winning. He finished his year as the most decorated jockey who ever rode and the most celebrated athlete of 1977. He adorned the cover of *Sports Illustrated* three times, which no one had ever done before; was on the cover of *Time* twice, and even *Newsweek* did a feature about the seventeen-year-old wunderkind, who had to catch his breath from endless television, radio, and print-media interviews.

Cauthen was a Madison Avenue darling with commercials for American Express and Trident chewing gum, an appearance on the Wheaties box, and even his own record album: ... *And Steve Cauthen Sings, Too!* He laughed about that one: "I knew I couldn't sing but I had fun doing it."

The shy youngster was named Sportsman of the Year by *Sports Illustrated,* the only horse-racing personality ever so named. The Associated Press honored him as Athlete of the Year, the only one such winner in racing's history.

"He had the Midas touch," claimed Laz's son Larry. "It was amazing to be around him."

Larry told about the time they both were having dinner at La Scala, a famous restaurant in Beverly Hills. The celebrities there that night included Cheryl Tiegs, Frank Gifford, and Debbie Reynolds, among others, yet everyone was seemingly pointing out Cauthen.

"It was like he was a rock star," exclaimed Barrera.

Cauthen certainly had enough winning purses to show for it. His mounts earned $6,151,750, exceeding Angel Cordero's previous $4,709,500 by more than 30 percent. Amazingly, he won 487 races despite missing about a month with a concussion, broken arm, and rib.

"What he accomplished is without the parallel, not only in racing but in sports," praised Joe Hirsch of the *Daily Racing Form.*

It was a phenomenal year for the Harbor View contingent. Cauthen won the Eclipse Award as Jockey of the Year, Barrera was named Trainer of the Year, and Affirmed collected Horse of the Year honors.

There was more to come. . . .

SIX

—— *The Derby and Calumet* ——

There is something about the outside of a horse
that is good for the inside of a man.

—Winston Churchill

In the spring of 1978, when the crepe myrtle was blooming, there was a feeling of excitement on Versailles Turnpike Road where the fabled Calumet Farm sits like a dowager queen on 762 acres of lush, verdant grass. The buoyancy was generated by Alydar, the burgeoning hope of Admiral and Lucille Markey to resurrect the eminence of Calumet, which had been tarnished for almost a decade. The devil's red and blue silks, which had glistened with its Derby victories in the years it dominated racing like no other establishment, were soiled. The farm was tottering on the verge of bankruptcy after Calumet earned only $87,725 in 1976.

The octogenarian owners, both in wheelchairs, were flush with hope that Alydar would win the Derby just as had Citation and Whirlaway, the stable's superstar thoroughbreds, and no one else in racing came close to the amount of horsemanship of the farm over the years. But it had submerged into disarray and the Markeys needed someone to reverse the decline, and in 1976 they put their trust into a young, thirty-year-old trainer, John Veitch.

At the time of their offer, Veitch was for all purposes, broke. In betting jargon he was literally out of money. Veitch was training during the winter season in New York with a modest number of four horses. Veitch was in debt. One of his clients offered him $3,500 to keep going. He accepted the tender, let a couple of his stable hands go to cut expenses, and took over the chores of feeding and hot-walking the horses. Being cold and broke left an indelible impression on Veitch.

"It was so cold one night in February, the pits," recalled Veitch. "It was two a.m. and it was cold as hell. I got up out of my warm bed to begin my chores. It was so cold the water pipes were frozen in the barn area. I tried pouring hot water on them, which didn't do any good. I finally gave up, gave the horses some feed, and went home to take a double shot of whiskey."

Veitch was at the lowest point of his career when he received a long-distance phone call a week later. The caller was Melvin Cinnamon, the manager of Calumet. He didn't mince any words after the opening hello.

"Would you be interested in training our horses?" asked Cinnamon.

"Certainly," answered Veitch without wasting a moment.

"Why don't you come down to Florida next week so you can talk with Admiral and Mrs. Markey."

"That's fine."

In the spring, Veitch went to Lexington to inspect the year-lings. As soon as he laid his eyes on Alydar, he was impressed by the way he was built and the way he moved. Those first weeks at Calumet were hectic for the young trainer, who had the pressure of taking over a declining operation that was erod-ing even more.

"When I first saw the horses, I was really upset," admitted Veitch. "I sold off ninety percent of the stable and started from scratch."

But he had Alydar and maybe no one else to start with, and Veitch wisely devoted most of his time to training him. Veitch thought that perhaps Alydar would develop into something between Citation and Whirlaway, Calumet's most celebrated champions.

After winning the 1948 Derby, Citation went on to win thirty-two of forty-five races, finishing out of the money only once, at the end of his four-year career. He was good as a certi-fied check with Eddie Arcaro aboard. They were a pair as smooth as the finest silk from China. Arcaro confessed that of all the great horses he had ridden, Citation was the greatest. "Citation was so fast he scared me," remarked Arcaro.

Whirlaway wasn't mean but was high-strung, and it took extreme patience for Jimmy Jones to train him. The savvy Jones observed that when Whirlaway was in the middle of the track, he appeared lost and it made him behave anomalously. On race day of the 1941 Derby, Jones placed on Whirlaway a one-eye blinker, which was designed to give unrestricted vision to his left eye while blocking his view to the right. It couldn't have worked better. Whirlaway won the Derby by eight lengths in the record time of 2:01:2/5, a mark that lasted for twenty-one years.

That was some of the glory that Veitch knew about Calumet that he was determined to restore. He brought Alydar along beautifully in his successful two-year-old season as a challenger to Affirmed. Some ten days before the Derby, he was brimming with confidence. That's how good he felt about Alydar.

"I just know Alydar can beat that colt when the conditions are right," remarked Veitch seriously. "He lost three times to him by the margins of a nose, neck, and half-length. Forget about the first race, the Youthful. Alydar had traffic problems and was green. Alydar beat Affirmed decisively in the Great American and the Champagne. I believe that the only way a colt like him can make good at Churchill Downs is to come from behind. I trained him for the late run."

Yet at birth, Alydar got the jump on Affirmed. A week before Affirmed was born, Alydar made his entrance on the Calumet countryside, on February 15, 1975, and with better bloodlines. The sire was Raise A Native and the mare, Sweet Tooth, and it couldn't have been more ironic. Both Affirmed and Alydar were chestnuts; both were homebred; both inherited on the male side of their line the quality of Native Dancer. It was surreal to some degree. Native Dancer was Alydar's grandfather and Affirmed's great-grandfather. Native Dancer's son, Raise A Native, was the sire of both Alydar and Exclusive Native, the sire of Affirmed. Biologically, Alydar and Affirmed were related. They were distant relatives running for the same goal—the Triple Crown, a story line no one developed before the Derby.

Veitch was focused with intensity on the Derby. "That's the one we want, and we want it for the Admiral and Mrs. Markey," he confessed. "For all their patience and for all they have given to racing despite all the years of disappointment, I hope that Alydar can bring them one more Derby triumph."

The last memory the Markeys had of a Derby win was in 1968, when Forward Pass was declared the winner when Dancer's Image failed a postrace drug test and was disqualified. Forward Pass went on to win the Preakness and run second in the Belmont, which brought joy to the Markeys for an entire year.

Lucille Markey philosophically looked at Calumet's dilemma: "You always seem to be at your lowest before you start up again. We have been through some lean years recently, but you don't give up in the bad times. Calumet has won eight Derbies, and if Alydar is good enough and lucky enough to win this year, I'd like to see it, but I can't go because I'm in a wheelchair, and if we win, I'd want to go down to the winner's circle and hug Alydar.

"Admiral Markey and I go out to the track in the morning whenever we can. The car is driven up to the rail and we sit and look out. I always loved horses. Of all the racetracks, I love Churchill Downs the best. The Derby is the race you always want to win."

But ten years in an elderly couple's life is too long. The Markeys could only wait and hope for Alydar now.

SEVEN

──── *Road to the Derby* ────

The year 1977 was a magical one in the kingdom of the horse. It was Aladdin on his magic carpet. Only Aladdin was Steve Cauthen and the carpet was Affirmed. It was a seventeen-year-old neophyte in the ancient world of horsedom where the rich harnessed power and ruled its existence. But Cauthen shook its environs as no one else ever before. A teenager who belonged in high school like every other kid in America. But Cauthen wasn't your ordinary boy next door. He was special and so was his horse. Together they were a summer symphony. Cauthen described it best when he said that riding Affirmed was "floating."

What Cauthen accomplished was unparalleled, not only in racing, but in any sport, and certainly more in one year than any other jockey in history. In one season he captured every national award there was: Professional Athlete of the Year by the Associated Press; Athlete of the Year by the *Sporting News;*

Sportsman of the Year by *Sports Illustrated;* and Big Sport of Turfdom by the Sports Publicists of America. Add a number of regional awards and it's easy to see why the baby-faced seventeen-year-old was racing's poster boy, appearing on the cover of *Sports Illustrated* twice, on *Time* and *Newsweek,* and on television it seemed every week. It was a lifetime for anyone else.

Cauthen rode like a thirty-four-year-old. He accumulated a remarkable $1,442,250 more than the record established by Angel Cordero Jr. a year earlier. He was Stevie Wonder indeed. And he did it all despite being sidelined for a month with cracked ribs and a concussion, suffered in a nasty spill during Belmont's summer season. Cauthen recovered at home in Walton and was cheered. He rubbed grease on his sore right wrist and won on the first horse he rode after the accident.

"I knew I would make it that first season at River Downs," reflected Cauthen. "It was nice to win races and confirm my confidence, but I felt from the beginning I could hold my own with the jockeys I was riding against. I was never apprehensive about that.

"The injury might have been one of the best breaks I ever got. If I hadn't had that rest, I doubt seriously that I could have continued the season and might not have had the opportunity to do as well as I did with Affirmed. The 1977 season was so great that it's hard to single out a highlight. But if there were any, the races I rode with Affirmed were the most meaningful to me."

The term *jockey* might not be quite apt in identifying Cauthen. Officially, some three thousand of them were licensed in 1977. Rather, Cauthen could now be described as a *race-rider,* the highest compliment, bestowed on the likes of Pincay, Shoemaker, Cordero, and Velasquez among others. Sammy Renick, a former jockey who has been around racing a lifetime of fifty years, was impressed with Cauthen.

"Getting Stevie Cauthen to ride your horse with a five-pound allowance is like having a license to steal, and trainers know it. Cauthen looks like the best young rider to come onto the racetrack since Willie Shoemaker in 1949."

At five feet one inch and ninety-five pounds, Cauthen was every inch a giant. Besides being beloved by the racing public, he was also venerated by his fellow riders, none more imposing an admirer than Cordero. He had been watching the Kid closely for a year as Cauthen was chasing his money record.

"It was early December in New York when I first saw him," recalled Cordero. "A friend of mine said, 'Watch this kid, he looks good on a horse,' and so I did. And he did. What impressed me was that he was too cool for a bug boy. Very calm on a horse. Beginners usually go crazy on a horse, but not this one. He behaved like a rider. He didn't go where he didn't belong like most of them.

"I didn't see any weakness in him. He's not real aggressive at the end of a race, but how much can you ask of a kid the first year? Everybody likes him. Nobody has anything bad to say about him. He's just not a smart aleck. I got worried about him when he was riding those twenty-three winners in one week, breaking my New York record of twenty-two. It's like being an actor with everybody after you, paying attention to you, asking you for time."

Last year was only the beginning. Cauthen had a lot more work to do in handling Affirmed in his crucial three-year-old campaign. Cauthen, too, had to deliver, perhaps not in the number of winners he produced the last year, but in reaching the Holy Grail for the crusaders of the sport, the owners, trainers, and every jockey who rode—the Triple Crown!

The mosaic for the 1978 crusade, to some degree, began to galvanize in October of 1977. When Alydar impressively won the Champagne Stakes at Belmont on October 15, track historians pointed out that the winner of the prestigious race for two-year-olds went on in twelve of the last fifteen years to emerge as the two-year-old titlist. When Affirmed was voted the crown instead, most pundits raised their eyebrows.

Yet, Affirmed's anointment was justified. In six meetings against Alydar, the Harbor View entry was victorious four times. What piqued the early Derby interest over the next months was that in the slightly more than five miles of racing against each other, Affirmed's margin of victory totaled some five feet! That's how close they were and why the May 6 Derby had every indication of being a classic Run for the Roses. Anyone who doubted that certainly didn't know racing.

There would be no more head-to-head battles between the pair until Derby Day itself. Barrera decided to prep his star in California, while Veitch took Alydar to Florida. Barrera always maintained a preference for Southern California. Being a Latino, he was comfortable around the area's large Latino population and never had to worry about any shortage of Cuban coffee.

The Chamber of Commerce always heralded the area as sunny California. For the most part it was. But they never made any mention of the torrential rains that greeted Barrera upon his arrival. From time to time they came, inundating the environs and creating horrific mud slides that took houses with them in their destructive paths.

The day Barrera and Affirmed arrived in California, it rained. It rained day after day after day for two solid weeks. The unsavory elements were getting to Barrera, who could only stare indignantly at the raindrops while sipping cup after cup of Cuban coffee underneath the shedrow while Affirmed looked on curiously, waiting to run. Barrera was beginning to worry how he could get Affirmed in racing shape for the Derby. Affirmed must have wondered, too, because he'd never been on the track to run a breeze since his arrival. All he could do was pace up and down the shedrow, and even to a horse that had to be boring.

In the early-morning hours Barrera would awake looking for a sunrise. There wasn't any. It would be this way, a hellish nightmare, for the next three weeks. How could it be possible to get Affirmed fit for his three-year-old embarkation and the pursuit of the Triple Crown?

Barrera had to improvise to get Affirmed some movement. He got Affirmed out of his barn between raindrops with light gallops around the barn area. It wasn't much, but it was something. Barrera, who was looked upon as one of the best trainers around, had another worry. The incessant rain might inflict a cold on Affirmed, which would sabotage the horse's training regimen. Barrera had to get ready for the Derby in adverse conditions, and the strong-willed trainer had the willpower to do it.

But could he? Affirmed didn't race in December. And Barrera wouldn't send him out on muddy tracks not only in January but February, too. Barrera also faced the difficulty of priming Cauthen for the Derby. As brilliant as the young rider was during 1977, Cauthen had never ridden in the Derby. Barrera needed Cauthen and Affirmed to harmonize together as never before.

While Affirmed finished his two-year-old season in the Laurel, Alydar went to the post one more time a month later. Surprisingly, Alydar disappointed and came in second behind Believe It in the Remsen Stakes at Aqueduct. The loss translated into a huge negative in the Horse of the Year determination, which many felt swayed the voting to Affirmed. The Woody Stephens–trained Believe It with Eddie Maples aboard was now projected as a Derby threat in a three-year-old field that was considered the best since 1957, when Gallant Man, Bold Ruler, Round Table, Gen. Duke, and Iron Liege were creating excitement.

Like Gen. Duke and Iron Liege, Alydar was Calumet-bred. He'd been an exciting horse who thrilled fans with his patented come-from-behind victories. Alydar was the big hope of Calumet owners Admiral and Mrs. Gene Markey, who were trying to win the Derby for the first time since 1968 when Forward Pass did it. The decade-long slump had tarnished the image of Calumet, and the Markeys were confident that this would be Calumet's year.

"Alydar has a strange running style," said John Veitch, Calumet's thirty-two-year-old trainer. "He throws his head to the right during the stretch. So far we haven't been able to figure out why he does it, but maybe he's looking around for horses to come up and challenge him. He won just about as he pleased and did everything that was expected of him. In the Remsen, it might have been a case of my just getting greedy. He didn't run like the real Alydar."

Amazingly the Admiral and Lucille Markey had never seen Alydar run at the track. Both were in their eighties and confined to wheelchairs. Their only look at Alydar had been through videotapes of the races, which Veitch dutifully provided for them.

"But they've been out to the barn in the mornings to look at him," disclosed Veitch. "When I was a youngster growing up on the racetrack, I remember Calumet Farm very well. At the time my father was training for C. V. Whitney and he had the second-strongest stable in the country through many of Calumet's best years. I'd sit in the Whitney cottage at Belmont Park and watch Ben Jones ride out on the track on his pony. He'd have all those outstanding horses in training, and they would go out to work out almost in waves. I got to look at those devil's red and blue colors over and over again."

By March 1, Affirmed still hadn't entered the starting gate in California. It was all Barrera could do to keep his wits and not throw a temper fit that Latinos are well-known for. The California rains had dampened his regimen for Affirmed beyond belief. When the rains intermittently subsided, he got in some what he considered good workouts for his horse. However, on the other side of the track, Cauthen had not seen any competition in 1978.

"Affirmed is one of the best horses I've ever put my hands on," volunteered Barrera following a workout. "That Laurel Futurity in 1977 was one of the most amazing races ever won. Anywhere! Anytime! Any country! Affirmed and Alydar hooked up and went after each other like a couple of fighting chickens, only there is no chicken in either one of them. Before the race both Veitch and I felt it would be a great race, but not as great as it turned out to be. Alydar sticks his head in front, then Affirmed. Then nobody is in front. When they hit the wire, Affirmed wins by a neck. I was happy and proud because he won, but I knew he had run up against a very tough racehorse. Alydar has been tough all along."

While Affirmed was waiting to race, Alydar had already won his first outing in Florida. Veitch was now grooming him for the noteworthy Flamingo and an expected duel with Believe It. Both had won their early starts at seven furlongs, but Whittingham's horse came away more impressively. Following his usual form, Alydar loafed early in the Flamingo before crossing the finish line in still another of his come-from-behind wins. The Flamingo often provides the Derby with not only the betting favorite but most times the winner.

Before the race, Veitch had a welcome visitor. Jimmy Jones, the old Calumet trainer who had retired fourteen years ago, walked by with a smile on his face. He liked what he had seen in Alydar up to now.

"It's a remarkable thing to see Calumet Farm run an entry in a big stake," Jones began. "During the big days of Calumet we always somehow got lucky and could throw a good two-horse entry in the big race. Citation and Coaltown were the most famous, but we had others.

"In 1957 we sent both Gen. Duke and Iron Liege to the Derby, and Gen. Duke was injured before the race. I thought Gen. Duke was one of the best horses Calumet ever had, but he never got to run in the Derby. We won the thing with Iron Liege, and he beat good horses like Bold Ruler, Gallant Man, and Round Table. Calumet Farm coming back with a Derby candidate after all these years is delightful."

Jones and his father, Ben, were the reasons Calumet had infinite success in the past. And now Veitch had a worthy Derby horse in Alydar.

If Alydar had a flaw, it was in breaking out of the starting gate. Veitch recognized the problem, but didn't have a solution. Alydar, a big, strong horse, compensated for his poor starts with a strong run to the finish line.

"Believe It was the horse to beat and I thought we could beat him," said Veitch. "If any horse can run faster the last eight than Alydar, then the other horse should win. Last year Alydar was the second-best horse to Affirmed. Between the end of a two-year-old season and the start of the three-year-old season, horses can grow quite a bit and mature.

"I think that has been the case with Alydar. He's grown about an inch and put on some weight. I think a couple of things might happen with him, and I hope I'm right about them. As distances stretch out, he should get better. Better and stronger."

Veitch walked over to his stable office and reached for the phone. He called the Markeys, and Admiral Markey answered.

"Did you see the race on television, sir?" asked Veitch. "Good. Congratulations, sir. He ran a fine race and he's about where we want him to be at this stage of things. . . . Thank you, sir. . . . Yes, I'm quite happy. I just hope we can stay happy for a little longer."

The Flamingo brought a lot of attention to Alydar, but Velasquez also had a share in the attention. He was a hot jockey. The Panamanian attracted a surge of interest that afternoon at Hialeah by winning five consecutive races, which no other jockey ever accomplished in the fifty-one-year-old history of the track. He was indeed an elite rider, and it earned him the track's jockey championship and he humbly gave all the credit to his horse.

"Alydar is the champ," he exclaimed. "I've thought so for quite some time. When the distances get longer, he'll get better. The Flamingo was an excellent race for him. He got the lead when he wanted to and then started to slow down at the end once he knew things were safe. I had to get after him a bit with the whip, but only a bit. This is my Derby horse. I guess this is the one I've waited for, and I've waited a long time."

The combination of Alydar and Velasquez was looming larger as a Derby threat to Affirmed, who still hadn't raced in Los Angeles. Some were concerned that Affirmed's slow start might limit his Derby chances. However, Woody Stephens, for one, disputed it.

"A lot of people think it's getting late in regard to running in the Derby," offered Stephens. "If you go back to last year though, Seattle Slew's Flamingo wasn't run until March 28. Before that he had only one race, and then only one more after that before he started in the Derby. In most cases, a trainer doesn't want too many races before the Triple Crown. A horse can't dance every dance. There is a lot of time left for other horses to come out and prove they are runners. Early March is no time to start to panic."

Veitch also weighed in, remarking, "There are two things to be concerned about. The first of course is Affirmed. He was voted the champion two-year-old of last year. He hasn't been able to get to his races yet but still was the champion. I have only the highest regard for him. The second thing is to keep Alydar sound and keep his mind about his business."

Veitch had one more race on his card, the Florida Derby. Alydar's performance left him in a playful mood. Veitch is jocular and often makes cracks about his head, which is mostly bald. He hadn't shown any signs of pressure about Alydar's success the past month and all the conversation surfacing about the Kentucky Derby and how his horse might be the favorite after what he'd done in Florida. His relaxed manner was never more evident than at the Florida Derby Breakfast the day before the race, where he was the object of photographers.

"Should I comb my hair?" he quipped with a smile. "Is my hair straight?"

Later that day, he approached jockey Don Brumfield, not in the winner's circle where he would have liked, but after Don dismounted on a Calumet horse he had failed to win on.

"Why did you get all that dirt on you?" Veitch said, grinning. "I told you not to do that."

"I didn't want to get dirty," said Brumfield, laughing.

Veitch was also a pleasure to Gulfstream Park officials with his accessibility.

"He's been amazing," exclaimed Al Cadeaux, of Gulfstream's publicity department. "He's handling the pressure real well. He was jesting with Velasquez before Alydar's mile workout and said that he wouldn't give him any instructions for the race and if he loses, he'll have somebody to blame."

Alydar was installed as a 3–5 favorite on race day, which didn't disturb Veitch at all. He knew his horse would be the hunted, and that, too, didn't bother him.

"Alydar is as good as he's ever been and he's trained well for the race," he said. "I expect him to run well."

And did he ever. More so than even Veitch expected. Alydar

ran the best race of his career by winning the $150,000 Florida Derby at Gulfstream Park in 1:47, one second off the track record. A glance at Calumet's record books revealed that Alydar's time was the best for one of the farm's horses since Gen. Duke won the race in 1957. It appeared more and more the way Alydar was running that this could be Calumet's year. His two-length victory over Believe It made a believer out of Maples. "He's one helluva racehorse," he exclaimed.

Woody Stephens, the trainer of Believe It, who finished second, shook his head over Alydar's performance. He had had a Derby winner in 1974 with Cannonade.

"I have to like Alydar to win the Kentucky Derby right now," he predicted. "Affirmed's been wintering in California. They had such a terrible winter out there, and I think Barrera has had to miss so many days of training with Affirmed.

"I don't think California horses compare with these kinds of horses here in Florida. There have been a couple of horses who came out of California and won the Derby, but more horses come out of Hialeah and Gulfstream."

The Florida Derby was Alydar's last appearance in the Sunshine State. Veitch was more than pleased with his horse's performance and so were the Markeys. Veitch was also appreciative of Velasquez's efforts. He won the Florida Derby while suffering from a sore hip, injured five days earlier when he was slammed inside the starting gate on another mount. When he dismounted from Alydar after his victory, he limped into the winner's circle. "I feel okay, not great, just okay," he said, managing to smile.

Affirmed finally got to the track and, in a month's work of four races, was triumphant in all. Yet, not without some concern.

He was unimpressive in the San Felipe Handicap. Cauthen had to repeatedly whip him down the stretch to keep him focused for a two-length victory. Had the constant rain hindered his workouts too much? Was Affirmed in shape for the Derby?

Barrera felt some consternation. In the morning workout before the race, he wasn't pleased with Affirmed's effort. Yet, he still voiced optimism.

"He's a short horse," he remarked. "He could get beat today if someone else becomes a tiger. I'm worried just a little bit. The San Felipe is just a small stroll in the sunshine. I'm looking down the road toward the Kentucky Derby. That is what matters. We're going to have to fight Alydar again like we did all last year. My horse won't meet Alydar before the Derby. But that day we put on the heavy gloves. It will be him and us. Today we just lace the gloves up and spar. Later on Affirmed will be ready to say *grrr*.

"He's a magnificent horse. Smart, real smart. In the afternoon before he ran the race, he lay down in his stall and slept. Only I walk around like a crazy man. Everyone asks, 'How's the horse?' I say he's good. Nobody asks, 'How's the man?' Me? I'm slowly going crazy with worry. I don't want him to lose."

Still, others wondered. Affirmed didn't show much speed in the race. He nearly created a pileup among five horses around the first turn and ran a confusing race despite alertly coming out of the gate. Something bothered him that sent him wide at the turn. He dropped back and was off the pace. However, Cauthen managed to settle him down and he finally grabbed the lead at the top of the stretch for the win. Yet, Cauthen was not the least bit upset.

"This horse knows exactly what he's doing," Cauthen sighed.

"I knew I could take the lead at any point. Affirmed took the lead at the top of the stretch and began to move out, but when he got to the front, he just pricked his ears and began to pull up. I had to keep after him. I didn't lose one ounce of my confidence in Affirmed by this race. He has been my Derby horse all along and remains so. The Derby has been my big dream. Now I found myself really getting excited about it. It's going to be coming soon."

Barrera knew horses. In 1976 he won the Derby and the Belmont and almost won the Triple Crown with a sore-legged Bold Forbes, who was patched up with spit and mucilage in the Belmont. Barrera's quest came up short by two lengths, but he did a masterful job in training Bold Forbes. Yet, he had a special feeling for Affirmed.

"Bold Forbes and Affirmed are totally different," Barrera stated. "Affirmed loves me. Bold Forbes once bit a hole in my chest. Affirmed is a smart racehorse. You can do anything with him. If a band came around the barn, he would dance for it. Any dance."

After three straight wins that began with a short allowance race of 6½ furlongs, the affable Cuban had Affirmed primed for the $175,000 Hollywood Derby. It would be his final race before the Derby, and this was one time Barrera was happy to leave California and the merciless rain that had annoyed him and left him grumpy at times. Several days before the race, Barrera experienced the scare of a lifetime. Affirmed was galloping along the backstretch when he broke loose from his handler, crossed over the dirt road, and almost got hit by a pickup truck.

By the morning of the Hollywood Derby, his fears allayed,

Barrera stood outside his stable office and began talking freely about some of his homegrown philosophy about pumpkins and horses, of all things.

"I hate the word *great*," he waxed. "Everything must be great these days. Great, great, great. If the man walks down the road with a pumpkin and you stop him and say, 'That's a good-looking pumpkin you have,' he'll get mad at you. But if you say, 'What a great pumpkin you have there,' he'll stop and talk. I don't think there are too many great pumpkins, and there are damned few great racehorses.

"But let me say this: Alydar is a great racehorse. Affirmed? He is far and away the smartest horse I have ever trained. The first time I saw him, I didn't look to see how big he was or how good-looking he was. My eyes went to his eyes and I said, 'There is something about you that I don't understand. You're smart.' I wasn't wrong either."

Veitch shipped Alydar as planned to Keeneland Race Track in Lexington, Kentucky, after the Florida Derby, but Barrera was firm in wanting to remain in California, and not because the winter rains were gone for good. His reluctance to go East for the Wood Memorial in New York before heading to Kentucky was perplexing to many. He had done the same itinerary with Bold Forbes two years before. As always, Barrera had the answer.

"It makes more sense to stay here," maintained Barrera. "If we went East, he would have a long trip to New York, and then a few days later another long trip to Kentucky. This way we can ship directly to Kentucky. In addition, the Hollywood Derby was worth twice as much money as the Wood Memorial, and he's already beaten the horses he'll be running against."

Affirmed won the Hollywood without being challenged. It

was his fourth straight win and bolstered Barrera's confidence even more.

"I couldn't ask for him to be doing anything in his workouts," said Barrera. "He came back from the Hollywood Derby great. Nothing bothers this colt, thank God. And I know what he can do. He doesn't have to go to the lead and win like a lot of people think he does. He can do anything. And that gives me a lot of chances to do different things with him in a race."

Before the Hollywood Derby, Barrera told Cauthen that the only way they could lose this race was to get blocked or get into some kind of trouble. He instructed Cauthen to go to the front and keep Affirmed in the clear. He also brought to Steve's attention that they'd been babying Affirmed too much. Barrera left Cauthen with one more thought, and that was to let the horse get used to being whipped.

"Affirmed was just playing," offered Cauthen. "He was flopping his ears back and forth in the stretch and looking around for someone to beat. I don't care what it looked like from the stands. From where I sit, it seems Laz is bringing him up to every race stronger than he was before. I think I can do anything I want with him when I have to.

"When I read the stuff about me getting spoiled, I just turn the page. It doesn't bother me. But what really bugs me is when people start writing about me like I was a god. I don't have any magic. I have to prove myself like everybody else, as a rider and a person."

Affirmed would run against Alydar again, and one or the other would have to prove himself. This time, in the Derby.

EIGHT

—— *The Derby* ——

If you're going to win one race,
it should be the Kentucky Derby.

—Jim Murray

—— DERBY WEEK ——

America was sprinting so fast in the sports universe, and Veitch wanted part of it. He scheduled one more race for Alydar nine days before the Derby itself. The Blue Grass Stakes at Keeneland in Lexington was a special race for all of Kentucky. Lexington sits 83.7 miles east of Louisville, and the denizens in the very heart of Bluegrass Country looked upon the race as their Derby. They have every reason to feel that way. It's where Calumet Farm is resplendent on top of a hill, where Man o' War is buried, and where thousands of potential Derby horses are foaled each year. Veitch was giving back by starting Alydar in the $100,000 Blue Grass, Keeneland's richest stakes race, at a distance of 1⅛ miles. He wanted to give home-state fans another look at Alydar before the Derby. He was bursting with pride from his horse's showing in Florida. More important though, on a personal note Veitch wanted the Markeys to see Alydar run for the first time in person. Calumet pride. Kentucky proud. That was Veitch. This time would be different. The Markeys were sufficiently ambulatory to be driven to the nearby track, which was a mile and maybe a furlong away from Calumet. Track officials had made arrangements for the Markeys' vehicle to be parked alongside the rail near the starting gate, and Veitch was confident about Alydar in a field of eight, none of which was considered a threat.

It was Alydar's first outing since the Florida Derby earlier in April. The personable Veitch refused to take credit for Alydar's strong performance that day.

"He's a good horse," he told the media after the Florida Derby win. "Anybody can train a good horse. Velasquez knows the horse and used excellent judgment. He's one of the best riders in America."

On this race day, Veitch appeared calm before a race that was important to Calumet. Almost too calm. Outside Barn 17, where Alydar resided, Veitch was quietly reading a book by British actor David Niven, somewhat appropriately titled *Bring on the Empty Horses*. Veitch was only concerned about winning horses and looked his sartorial best in a gray suit and a maroon polka-dot tie.

"I'm trying to win the Blue Grass today and it's too far ahead for me to think about," he replied when asked about the

Derby. "This race means more to Mrs. Markey than probably anything that's happened to her. She's in such good spirits. It means so much physically and mentally."

There wasn't any time left for David Niven. Veitch had to get Alydar ready. The trainer was in good spirits, too.

"I feel fine," he volunteered. "This is what it's all about. On a day like today, if you feel bad, you don't belong in the business."

Like Barrera with Affirmed, Veitch had a close relationship with Alydar. The horse acknowledged as much. Even Alydar's handlers realized it.

"He's a very nice horse to take care of," said Alydar's groom, Clyde Sparks. "A very low-key horse. You ask him to do something, and he goes on and does it."

Charlie Rose, an exercise rider, quickly agreed with Sparks: "Offhand, I don't remember any other horse as intelligent. Some things he's done are amazing. The way he recognizes John Veitch for instance. He'll spot him in a crowd. I've never seen a horse that'll recognize somebody by sight or by hearing his voice.

"But John will be down the other end of the barn and Alydar will hear him and know it's him. Photographers love him. He's alert and will put his ears up. He's a ham."

When the race began, Alydar hammed it up too much out of the starting gate. Maybe he felt the Markeys were close by watching him. When the gates opened, he just stood there, which gave the Markeys a good look at him. When he finally took off, he appeared to be running a confused race and looked like one of David Niven's empty horses. He ducked inward and dawdled a good part of the way. When Velasquez finally got him going, he flew past his opponents as if they were painted on a billboard. The 13-length rout was breathless.

After receiving the trophy in the winner's circle, Veitch, accompanied by Kentucky governor Julian Carroll and Velasquez, made his way to the Markeys' car, where the governor handed Lucille Calumet's trophy. It was serene, sentimental moment for the sport's most beloved lady.

Larry Barrera, who scouted Alydar for his father, wasn't overly impressed with the horse's easy triumph.

"He has a little bit of a belly on him, and a slow race isn't going to help him," observed Larry. "This was just a public workout for $100,000. There wasn't much behind him. Well, at least Alydar had a race over a Kentucky track."

Larry's father was expected to arrive in Louisville from California later in the day. While he was away, Larry had the responsibility of looking after Affirmed. It's a big one even for a veteran trainer, let alone a young one.

"I had to take care of it, so I did," Larry remarked. "It's a lot of responsibility, but when you're around it all your life, it's just a natural. All the time we're together the conversation is always horses. Everything he sees new, he points it out to me and explains it to me. Of course, I'd like to stay close to my father as possible."

After the race, Velasquez was asked if Alydar was the best three-year-old he ever rode.

"Is he the best one?" he repeated. "One, two, and three. But he's not the champion yet. He's got to beat Affirmed, and that's not easy."

What separates the Derby from the Preakness and the Belmont is Derby Week itself. It is unmatched. The weeklong celebration surpasses any other celebratory moments that the other two races contain. In most years, Derby Week is extended as much as three days by an influx of horse lovers who love to party and make the Derby the one race of the year they attend. The Blue Grass Stakes, a week before the Derby, is a premier race that attracts an influx of visitors to Louisville. The storied Brown Hotel is booked fully six months in advance, and it's easy to get absorbed into the party mood that is prevalent every night of the week. It is one reason acclaimed turf writer Joe Hirsch exclaimed, "I never met a Kentucky Derby I didn't like," and Joe was every bit a partygoer.

Veitch didn't have much time for unbridled fun and left that for all the racing fans to enjoy. For one week the revelry is somewhat in the aura of Mardi Gras in New Orleans. Only in horse country it is much more sophisticated and not as boisterous and repugnant with the smell of alcohol and debauchery of New Orleans. In Lexington, it emanates ever so quietly and makes its way to Louisville. This would be a special Derby Week with Kentucky-bred Alydar and Kentucky-born Steve Cauthen the prideful attractions.

For years, sports pride in Louisville was grounded in the manufacture of baseball bats known famously as Louisville Sluggers. It also revolved around quarterback Johnny Unitas, who found a haven in the University of Louisville in 1951 after being spurned by his hometown University of Pittsburgh. The Brown Hotel was known for its Hot Brown Sandwich, and the Seelbach Hotel, just a few blocks away, was referenced by F. Scott Fitzgerald in his bestselling book *The Great Gatsby*.

The Seelbach also had an ominous link to Al Capone. The Chicago mobster often met his associates during Prohibition in the secret room provided by the hotel. The creation of the old-fashioned cocktail by Louisville's Pendennis Club might have been inspired by Capone's visits.

The parties on Derby Day are endless. *Esquire* magazine called the Derby "the biggest party in the south." Locals believe that the Derby is every bit as exciting away from the madding crowd and more enjoyable in a living room. Jesse Baker, of National Public Radio, grew up in Louisville but gives her Derby party in Washington, D.C., where she lives. She vividly describes what it takes to have a successful party:

"As any Louisvillian will tell you, 'It ain't Derby without a mint julep.'" Yet, the same Louisvillians also will tell you that they won't touch the stuff the rest of the year. They prefer their bourbon straight up, without the syrupy, green sweetness that gives the drink its swampy amber coloring. But even the bourbon purist won't pass up a mint julep on Derby Day.

The drink did exist before the race. Mint juleps probably were first served in the early 1700s in Maryland, Virginia, and North Carolina. However, the first juleps weren't made with bourbon, but rum or rye whiskey. (Kentucky bourbon wasn't commonly distributed until later in the nineteenth century.) Legend has it that mint was planted outside the clubhouse of Churchill Downs in 1875 so the drink could be served at the very first Kentucky Derby.

The regal tapestry woven for the 104th Kentucky Derby was like no other in the Derby's majestic history. The story lines for the May 6 joust contained a royal number of subjects. There was Harbor View Farm with Louis and Patrice Wolfson looking for redemption, while the venerable Calumet Farm of the Markeys was seeking restoration of its once proud empire. The two trainers had widely diverse backgrounds. Lazaro Barrera, an immigrant trainer from Cuba's barrios, who came to California with a one-horse stable, was matching strategies with John Veitch, a college graduate of the highest caliber from Bradley University.

Then there were the jockeys. Steve Cauthen, a puckish kid who'd just turned eighteen, out of *Grimm's Fairy-Tales*, who transcended the racing world like no one before him, matching guts against Jorge Velasquez, a grizzled thirty-one-year-old veteran who began his career as a hot-walker in Panama, where he rode 347 winners in three years before taking his tack to New York at the age of nineteen.

Finally, there were the contenders: Affirmed, who liked to race in front, and Alydar, who excelled in running from behind, both from the bloodline of Raise A Native. No two horses in history were so evenly matched despite their distinctly opposite styles, which created the greatest duel under the sun ever on America's racetracks. Both were legitimate Triple Crown contenders, and it would all start with the Derby.

On Monday night, at a Knights of Columbus charity dinner at the Galt House, three of the Derby trainers revealed their thoughts, although not too deeply, about Saturday's race. Conspicuous by his absence was Barrera, who couldn't commit to the dinner because of his California stay. Veitch was there, and so was Woody Stephens, the trainer of Believe It, and Allen Jerkens, who handled Sensitive Prince, the other two notable contenders in the Derby. Yet, the only one to exude confidence in his horse was Veitch, in his first public statement of a week that would generate a barnful of speculation.

"This is a fine colt, a very powerful colt," he pointed out regarding Alydar. "We couldn't be more pleased with the way he's coming up to the Derby."

But he warned about being overconfident, and being the gentleman that he was, he subtly issued praise to his rival trainers so as not to arouse their dander: "There are other good horses in the race. The Derby is always a very, very difficult race to win."

Barrera, a day later, was more demonstrative about the race and all the conjecture it was creating, especially regarding the trainers.

"The trainers can't run," he emphatically remarked. "Being the best trainer in the world helps only when you have twenty-five cents and go downtown on a bus. If I didn't have a horse, if Woody didn't have a horse . . . there aren't four trainers in the race. There are four horses. Horse racing is ninety percent horse and ten percent jockey.

"Because of the rain in Santa Anita this winter, I had to rush Affirmed to get him ready. Instead of getting him ready in sixty days, I had to get him ready in forty-five days. But he's better than last fall when he beat Alydar four times and lost to him twice.

"This horse is a runner. Don't let him kid you. Anybody who wants to win the Derby has to run his eyeball out to beat him. This horse is completely ready. He doesn't need too much work now. You squeeze the lemon all at once and you got nothing left. There's not an ounce of fat on him and you can do anything with him. There can be three hundred people around watching him and he will take a nap in his stall."

Barrera himself couldn't be caught napping because he had a formidable trio of trainers anxious to challenge him. Veitch, who had Alydar fit by his own admission, had been looked upon the past two years as the savior of Calumet, a stable whose racing fortunes had been in decline. Stephens, a Hall of Famer, is among the top three all-time stakes winners. Jerkens is referred to as the magician for his penchant for pulling the upset and did so against notable thoroughbreds such as Secretariat, Kelso, and Forego.

All things considered, the Kentucky Derby is an extremely emotional experience for any trainer. The overwhelming media crush, which extends internationally, is a contributing factor. Barrera was the first to admit it, and he talked freely about the weeklong activity:

"There are so many newspapermen and television and radio people that the Kentucky Derby can be a very mentally exhausting experience. It was especially tough for me. I was born in Cuba and I never learned English in any school. So, when a question is asked, I first have to translate my answer in my head from Spanish to English before I can answer. Many of the questions that you hear are so stupid they are almost funny. They take up time, and I have always felt that it is part of my job to be nice to the press, to build up the race. It's part of our responsibility.

"Every horseman wants to win the Kentucky Derby. It is the dream we all dream about because it is the most famous race in the country. With Bold Forbes, I learned a lot of things that helped me later with Affirmed. He got down there to Churchill Downs two days before me. He was stabled on the side of the Derby barn closest to the street.

"There was a lot of noise and traffic on that side. People were having picnics, reporters were always hanging around. I saw the horse couldn't relax and couldn't sleep, so I moved him around to the other side. When I brought Affirmed down, he always stayed on the quiet side.

"All of the trainers waited to bring their horses to the track until around eight o'clock, when it was in good condition. But I always brought my horses out first thing in the morning, around six or six thirty.

"This way, I missed all the commotion of the other horses. Also, after eight in Kentucky, there are a lot of green two-year-olds, and there is a chance of a loose horse at that time.

"Maybe the most important thing I learned was to watch out for my horse when he was walking anywhere in the stable area or on the track."

Barrera experienced such a moment with Bold Forbes when he was prepping him for the Kentucky Derby in 1976. Bold Forbes was returning to the stable area when he stepped on a stone and injured his frog, which is the softest spot on the foot. Barrera's initial fear was that his horse would miss the Derby, which was two weeks away. His blacksmith had to cut off half the frog and part of the hoof to save the foot.

Following that harrowing experience, Barrera exercised caution by having two stableboys walk in front of his horses and pick up any rocks they found. Barrera loved his horses and would do anything to protect them from harm.

"I have carried over this lesson into my daily training," disclosed Barrera. "I now have a groom bring many of my horses onto the track in the morning, leading them on a shank. The horses behave better and it is safer.

"And in front of the groom and the horse, about two lengths, I have the pony. My instructions to the pony boy are to look out for any loose horses that might be coming toward them."

Yet, the oppressing media blitz didn't seem to affect Cauthen. He avoided most of it by continuing to ride in New York for most of the week. He was making his first appearance in the Derby and it was indeed special in his eyes. It was on Kentucky Derby day two years earlier when sixteen-year-old Cauthen became eligible to become a jockey.

"The Derby means so much to every jockey, but being from Kentucky it means just a little more to me," said Cauthen. "It's a great race just to ride in but I feel I have a real good chance this year. I've seen a few Derbies. I was a kid on the backstretch when Majestic Prince won. I don't recall much about the race except that my mother was given a rose off the winner's blanket. But I saw Cannonade win and Secretariat. I saw the last couple of Derbies on television.

"I've heard that the Derby affects horse and rider. But perhaps the effect won't be too much. We had people in the infield of Santa Anita this winter big days, and they made a lot of noise. It didn't seem to bother the horses very much. As for myself, I've ridden in some big races and managed. I hope I'll be able to manage on Derby Day. It's a difficult race to handicap. The two horses have such different styles."

His father, Tex, knew how special this Derby was. After only two years on the circuit, his son came home to ride in one. It had been a lifetime for Tex, who had been in racing all his life, never imagining that Steve's innocent wish back then, to get a jockey's license, would manifest into this day in such a short time.

"It was Kentucky Derby Day, May first," recalled Tex. "Still, he pestered the daylights out of me all day to take him down to Churchill so he could get his license. It took a lot of explaining to convince him there was no way to get near the track that day. It's a great thrill to have him riding in the Derby. The Derby is the horse race. I don't care if you've been riding fifteen years, it would be a great thrill to ride in it. But when you're able to have a shot at it after a couple of years, that's great.

"The Derby is kind of what he's been pointing to since he got going good. He'd hoped to come up with something that would have a shot. I suppose winning the Derby is important because it's something everybody thinks about forever. Sentimentally, it's number one. To the whole world, the Derby is it.

"You know what, Steve has changed somewhat. I think he understands a little better now how to cope with some of the things he doesn't want to do, like signing autographs when he's busy and talking all the time to the press. And I think he's learned to relax more. He's not as intense, which is good, because there was an awful lot of pressure for a long time."

Barney Nagler, the excellent New York columnist, was having lunch one day the previous week with Cauthen's agent, the high-spirited Lenny Goodman, in Mike Manuche's, one of the city's popular sports hangouts. In the opinion of many, Goodman was one of the best in the business and actually admitted that he signed Cauthen by a stroke of luck. However, for a day, Goodman had lost contact with his prize jockey, but located him the next day in Scottsdale, Arizona, of all places. Goodman, who was never at a loss for words, was in a talkative mood between his cigar and Nagler's pipe.

"Well, Steve's with Shoe and some of the other riders," revealed Goodman. "They had two days off, so Marge Everett asked them out to Arizona. Hollywood Park is her track, you know. She's a great hostess. Been nothing but kind to us."

Goodman spent the winter with Cauthen in California. Even though he was a New York guy all the way, he enjoyed it. Winning does that.

"The Kid won about seventy races out there," mentioned Goodman. "Could of won more, but when you're hooked in with a stable, you can't pick your spots like you might like. I got Steve last year in New York. Cordero had Affirmed. He rode him first, but then Cordero fell in love with a Darby Dan Farm horse, Darby Creek Road, so he got off Affirmed to ride that horse. That's how I got on him.

"Cauthen started at Churchill Downs. It's going home for him and on a great horse like Affirmed. The Derby is a hell of a match this year, Affirmed against Alydar. Alydar's a darn good colt. But Affirmed beat him four out of six times. That should tell you something. But Alydar had a hell of a winter in Florida. Alydar was real good winning the Flamingo at Hialeah and the Florida Derby at Gulfstream. John Veitch has done a hell of a job with Alydar.

"Listen, the Derby's a tough race to win. I won it before, so I know. I won with Hartack and I won with Baeza and now I'm going to win with Cauthen."

This year's Derby was most definitely a homemade Kentucky pie. Alydar was Calumet and Calumet was Kentucky. Cauthen was considered a local boy, one who left home and made astronomically good in New York and California and who would be a source of local pride if he entered the winner's circle with Affirmed. In Kentucky, the excitement would crowd the borderline of hysteria. Louisville during Derby Week is a city of passion and the horse has always had a great appeal there.

The state's pride was ebullient during the week's bustling activity. If one wasn't caught up in it, he or she was an unwelcome intruder who didn't belong in Louisville. Although he was far removed from being an introvert, Wolfson and his Doris Day–look-alike wife, Patrice, kept a low profile and preferred quiet dinners in contrast to what seemed like an eternity of parties. They left that to the Kentuckians and their guests.

"I don't need to stand around with a wineglass making small talk" was the way Wolfson, who was accepted only condescendingly by the horsey set, described his privacy. Wolfson was well aware of the stream of questions that would flow about his legal problems that resulted in his jail time, something that had been haunting him for eight years.

Still, he remained outspoken on racing issues that he considered vital to the sport's survival. He had no qualms about going head-to-head with leading politicians regarding New York State's multitude of racing problems and did so with uninhibited frankness. On occasion, his honesty had turned heads in the racing establishment, and they never forgot such criticisms. Once during this Derby Week he granted an interview with Dick Young, the acerbic, well-read sportswriter of the *New York Daily News*, who was covering his first Derby after some forty years in the business. Young quoted Wolfson as saying, "New York racing is the most dishonest or corrupt in the United States." It was there in print for the newspaper's 2 million readers to observe, and it naturally created shock waves not only throughout the state, but nationally as well. It certainly was a distraction, one he didn't need before the Derby.

Wolfson didn't address the incendiary column until he returned to New York, dispatching a letter to Young. In essence he wrote that he would never had made such a statement and had the highest respect for New York racing and that corruption in the state would be virtually impossible. Wolfson felt that in the commotion that accompanies Derby Week he had been misquoted and regretted that it occurred.

Regarding Affirmed's future, Wolfson reiterated that he would race as a four-year-old. Wolfson would race the horse not for the purses, but with the sport in mind.

"That's the trouble with racing," he remarked. "Good horses have been retired when they are three, and racing needs gate attractions."

The Affirmed-Alydar rivalry was a gate attraction and every bit more. They enlivened 1977 and added palpitation to the 1978 season with their spectacular wins. In fact, Wolfson became an admirer of Alydar's after the 1977 combat and sent out an offer to buy him through Leslie Combs, a Kentucky breeder. He remarked that he felt that Alydar was one of the best two-year-olds he had ever seen since his own Raise A Native.

"Combs offered six million dollars but they turned it down," Wolfson said sadly.

Barrera was also a big admirer of Alydar's, and three days before the Derby he was standing, seemingly relaxed, outside Barn 41, wearing a yellow HOLLYWOOD PARK Windbreaker with blue letters. A cordon of reporters looking to get one more angle to write about surrounded him. On this day he wasn't talking about horses but about baseball, which Cubans love. One writer asked Barrera, "If Affirmed was a baseball player, who would he be?"

"Joe DiMaggio," he answered without hesitation.

"Why DiMaggio?"

"Because he was the greatest baseball player of my time. He was my idol. Once I was in Cleveland and went to the ball game. I paid thirty-five cents and sat in center field. That day he hit three home runs and I caught two of the balls."

"What about Alydar? Who would he be?"

"I don't know if the owners of Alydar would like me to compare him with any baseball player. But, Allie Reynolds. Or, Roberto Clemente, perhaps."

Those were two star players that Barrera admired as a big baseball fan. Reynolds was a Yankee pitcher who was strong-armed, threw a mean fastball, and challenged hitters without ever once backing down against any of them. In Barrera's eyes, Clemente was the greatest Pirate of them all, an outfielder who displayed grace in everything he did—run, throw, field, and hit. That's how Barrera saw Alydar, who he felt was all of that to some degree, paying the Calumet thoroughbred the highest compliment for his heroic efforts against Affirmed.

Cauthen finally arrived in Louisville Thursday night, and on Friday morning he arrived at Barn 41 for a scheduled meeting. At least fifty reporters were gathered waiting to talk to him, but he only had time to answer a few questions, none more poignant than "What do you think about your first Derby?"

"I'm glad I'm in it" was all he had to say, then he headed behind closed doors to talk with Barrera and the Wolfsons. The session lasted about a half hour, and when Cauthen emerged, the reporters were still there waiting for him.

"Are you excited by this?" he was asked.

"No, not at all," replied Cauthen while heading to his limousine.

"If you're not excited, could you describe your feelings right now?"

"No, I can't right now. I gotta go."

The reporters looked to Barrera for help. There wasn't any. "I only put him on a horse. I don't tell him what to do," Barrera apologized.

"Are you worried about entrusting your Derby horse to an eighteen-year-old who's never ridden in this race before?"

"Worried? You are kidding?" Barrera snorted. "Maybe some people still don't understand. Steve Cauthen is no eighteen-year-old. He's an old man. Sometimes he makes me believe in reincarnation. Maybe he had another life, where he was a leading rider for fifty years. That's how he knows about this business. Maybe Steve is the thousand-year-old man. Maybe he came to us as a gift from another planet."

Almost lost in a weeklong revelry of the 1978 Derby was that baseball's Pete Rose reached a milestone by accumulating his three thousandth hit as a Cincinnati Red. A baseball romantic would look upon Rose's feat as the equivalent of assuredly winning the Kentucky Derby of baseball perpetuity. While Rose's journey was a long one of sixteen years, the Derby has been framed as the fastest two minutes in sports over the distance of a mile and a quarter. Pete loved the horses and would wager a hundred or two on a tip from one of his cronies.

Saturday at 5:38 p.m., the Derby would present many interesting possibilities, scenarios, and as many wonderful personalities and voluminous talk after it. No figure would be bigger before the race than Calumet's homegown Alydar, who had taken the Markeys on a sentimental, somewhat romantic journey. After its last Derby win exactly a decade ago, Calumet had submerged into financial morass so deep that rumors had swirled that the Markeys were considering selling the fabled farm. However, they persevered and with Alydar and Veitch had regained the luster that once was Calumet. An Alydar victory would be popular with everybody who remembered what Calumet had been and would hopefully be again.

The one horse that could ruin Calumet's homecoming was Affirmed. Like Alydar, Affirmed was unbeaten in four outings as a three-year-old. While Alydar was running wild in Florida, Affirmed was doing the same thing between raindrops in California. The only horse to beat Affirmed as a two-year-old was Alydar, who did so twice. A third time would be the charm for Alydar's loyalists. In Affirmed's four wins, his combined margin of victory was a skinny length. Yet, the sentiment that Calumet inspired could also be aroused by Cauthen, a boy wonder who came out of nowhere, the tiny Kentucky town of Walton, 82.7 miles northwest of Louisville. In the storybook season of 1977, Cauthen won 487 times and set a world record with over $6 million in earnings. Now, everybody knew him.

Affirmed and Alydar were enough to make that Derby a monumental event. However, if either of the favorites faltered, several others were capable of pulling an upset. Believe It, trained by Woody Stephens, one of racing's top conditioners, was impressive in winning the Wood Memorial before arriving in Louisville after his final prep race. And if it turned out to be a rainy Saturday, Believe It would welcome the mud.

Allen Jerkens had an unbeaten, although untested in six starts, contender in Sensitive Price. At forty-nine, Jerkens was the youngest trainer ever inducted into the Hall of Fame and carried the high respect of horsemen, who call him the Genius. Veitch always addressed him as "Mr. Jerkens." Wolfson refered to him as "the Magic Man" because of his remarkable feats in upsetting better horses with an underdog of his own. It was all out there.

The magic of the Kentucky Derby was thirty-six hours away.

——— DERBY DAY ———

What Affirmed and Alydar brought
to the table cannot be bought or
manufactured . . . the greatest
show in racing.
—Woody Stephens,
Hall of Fame trainer

On Derby morning a chilly sunrise crept over the stables where the trainers and grooms were busy with the final preparations for the late-afternoon race. Since daybreak, one could see the same routine that takes place on any race day—workouts, cooling off the horses, mucking out their stalls. Only this day was special. The Derby was the first ornament of the Triple Crown, with the winning horse having a shot at the jeweled crown.

It was a particularly Kentucky setting. Alydar was a Calumet-bred horse that the wagering public favored at 6-5, with Affirmed the second choice at 9-5; there was sentiment for the

Markeys from the blue-blooded horsey set, and finally people were euphoric over Cauthen, a pugnacious youngster from Walton who had just turned eighteen with the opportunity to set Derby history as the youngest jockey ever to win it. There were certainly enough trophies to go around from the Louisville Chamber of Commerce.

Veitch appeared calm and relaxed, reading a book, the same demeanor he exhibited before the Blue Grass Stakes. This time the book was *Going After Cacciato* by Tim O'Brien. Veitch also spent the hour before post time by watching television. He knew all about the glory that was Calumet and his role the past two years in bringing the famed devil's red and blue colors back into the spotlight and the match-race atmosphere between his horse and Affirmed.

"Are you nervous?" he was asked.

"No, I'm not nervous." He smiled. "But I'm getting more and more anxious."

"Any second thoughts about your strategy with Alydar?"

"I always do. Well, they're not second thoughts, but you do question yourself. Have I done too much? Have I done too little? But I'm very satisfied. Of all the horses, he should be the fittest. In the draw for post position, we got number ten. That's good. I wanted one of the four outside positions because Velasquez can pick his spot wherever he wants to be and keep Alydar free from trouble.

"Sensitive Prince drew the outside, and that makes me feel that he will have to go to the front. Affirmed drew post two, and that would indicate that he must run hard early and commit himself. If Raymond Earl, a thirty-to-one long shot on the rail, rushes for the lead, and he has to, then Affirmed might have to run a very fast three-quarter of a mile. I don't think Barrera likes the number two post for his horse."

Veitch, his hands in his pockets, which offered warmth from the chilly air, looked at Alydar, who walked by with his groom, giving a "Hi, Alydar" greeting that the animal recognized. They genuinely had a special relationship.

Much like Barrera and Affirmed. Barrera was talking with Cauthen in front of Affirmed's stall when the alert thoroughbred stuck his head out to see what was going on. However, he quickly lost interest and turned away. After the trainer and his jockey finished their conversation, Cauthen left with his father in Tex's Mercedes, which was a testament to the Kid's success, shared by the closely bonded family.

When Barrera was apprised of Veitch's remark about Affirmed's No. 2 post position, he shook his head.

"Look at the Hollywood Derby." He smiled. "That was my horse's last race. It was run at Hollywood Park and that's not in China. Who broke from number two? Affirmed."

Barrera was confident about Affirmed. Very much so. He had shared his feelings with Wolfson in one of Affirmed's final workouts. Wolfson and his wife were alongside Barrera observing the five-furlong jaunt.

"It's a perfect work, fifty-nine seconds," exclaimed Barrera. "It does two things. First, it puts some speed into him to get him sharp; second, the pressure comes off because the bees will stop buzzing.

"In racing, everybody trains everybody else's horse. I train my own and let people say whatever they want. A few days ago I worked Affirmed one and one-eighth miles in 1:56:1/5 and people said it was bad work. Well, it was one of the most brilliant workouts I've seen, because I started him in a place where he would have to go around a lot of turns. You can do anything with Affirmed. On the afternoon of his races, he goes to sleep in his stall when all the other horses are up and about and getting themselves on edge.

"Affirmed is his own main man. He knows himself, and by now I think I know him. When I won the Derby with Bold Forbes two years ago, it was different. Bold Forbes came out of Puerto Rico and I didn't get him until he had raced quite a bit. With Affirmed it is different. I have him all along. I think we haven't seen how good he is yet because you only can tell when another horse challenges him—and no one has challenged him this year.

"This is no pickin' chicken party. Believe It should run good, and I think that Darby Creek Road might be underrated. Sensitive Prince has won all six of his starts, and because Allen Jerkens trains him, the horse must be respected. I think Affirmed has to beat Alydar, and it could be just as simple as that.

"In any race luck influences the outcome. Affirmed and Alydar have always dominated their races and let the other horses fall far behind. A lot of people don't believe that Affirmed can be rated, but they are wrong about that. Affirmed can be rated and will be. Once you get to Kentucky, you have to listen to so much nonsense that your head gets full of bees. All I hear in Kentucky is that Affirmed cannot win the Derby because he was bred in Florida and raced in California this winter. Florida and California are part of the United States of America, aren't they? Affirmed has not been winning races in China."

Woody Stephens, who had been a trainer for almost forty

years, looked closely at his horse Believe It, who was expected to be the third or fourth favorite behind Alydar and Affirmed. He walked over to where his horse was grazing and relieved the groom who was attending him. Stephens would have loved a rainy day because Believe It performed better on an off track. But it wasn't to be.

The gates had opened at eight o'clock for the anticipated large crowd. An old man carrying a lawn chair secured a special spot in the infield for a close look at the eleven horses who would charge by him. One, a long shot, had the strangest name, Esops Foibles. There was no such person named Esops, but the name represented a group called the Employee Stock Ownership Plan. And probably a few employees in the country would make a $2 hunch bet on Esops, who was listed at 30-1 with five other field horses.

Mutuel clerks were at their windows at eight thirty, even though wagering didn't open until eleven. This would be the biggest betting day of the year with betting windows provided in the infield, and the clerks had to be alert for heavy action. At times a bettor leaves more cash than it takes to cover his bet. It creates a surplus that is called a drop. Most times the clerk succeeds in returning the surplus to the bettor. When the attempt is unsuccessful, the clerk deposits the surplus in a box. On a hectic day like the Derby, the clerks were expecting a windfall.

Among the early arrivals was the strongly opinionated sportscaster Howard Cosell. And where else would Howard be but among the flowers signing autographs in the tulip garden. He finished his last one politely.

"I've really got to go," apologized Cosell. "I'm exhausted and I won't have much left for the Derby."

By noon, most of the expected crowd of one hundred thousand or more had arrived. The Derby was more than just a race. It was a social event. The Derby is especially attractive for the ladies. It is every bit a millinery extravaganza. Large, over-the-top hats are the vogue. The floppier, the better, and the tackiest even more so. Derby hats feature feathers, gauge netting, gaudy fake flowers, and the works. Originally, the floppy hats were intended to shade the ladies and prevent too many freckles. That was then, many years before. Now the bonnets had blossomed into an ostentatious fashion statement often in the company of gentlemen in seersucker suits.

All of it presents an occasion for people watching, especially concentrating on celebrities. Spotted in the clubhouse were Bob Hope; Jaclyn Smith of *Charlie's Angels;* Heisman Trophy winner running back Paul Hornung of Notre Dame; University of Louisville football coach Vince Gibson; Tennessee running back Johnny Majors, who was the runner-up to Hornung for the Heisman; Seattle Seahawks defensive coordinator Jim Mora; John Forsythe of *Charlie's Angels;* Dick Van Patten of *Eight Is Enough.*

Louis Wolfson had no time for merriment or celebrity gazing. He, more than anyone else, had waited for Derby Day 1978. It occupied him for eight years, ever since he was released from prison in 1970. He wanted a Derby horse and he bred one three years ago. During that period his thoughts intensified. He knew he had something special in Affirmed, and winning the Derby would be the first excursion on the path to the

Triple Crown. Wolfson yearned for racing's crown jewel. It would cleanse his soul for his detractors and the ones who had adored him but disassociated themselves from him when he went to jail.

Yes, there was no bigger race for Wolfson. Mentally, he was ready for it. He had the horse and the best trainer and jockey on the circuit. Physically, too, he was sound. His thick, wavy hair had turned white, but he remained erect and handsome, belying his sixty-six years. He still cut an imposing figure and was always nattily attired, making him to stand out in a crowd in Kentucky far from his Florida waterside home on Biscayne Bay.

Wolfson, who remained low-key during Derby Week, was buoyant about Affirmed's chances in the race. He spoke about it several days earlier.

"If Affirmed is in front at the top of the stretch, you can put your binoculars down because Alydar won't catch him," predicted Wolfson. "I realize that sounds presumptuous, but that's the way I analyze the race. We have examined the six meetings between Affirmed and Alydar pretty carefully, and it looks to me like Affirmed digs in when things get toughest. Up to this point in his career, Affirmed has done everything asked of him, but I couldn't call him a great horse yet because the Kentucky Derby hasn't been run. Because Affirmed and Alydar haven't met since last fall, and each has won all its starts this year, people are very decided in their opinions. Well, here's mine. The critical point will come when the horses turn for home, and I think that you will see Affirmed leading at that stage. If so, I have to believe he will win. But he's running against an excellent field."

The unwavering Wolfson was never unsure of himself. He was a powerful figure in financial circles because of it and was now becoming a force in racing. Barrera had seen someone special in Cauthen, a shy seventeen-year-old who had the greatest year any jockey could have in 1977. Was he worthy enough to ride a potential Triple Crown horse? Barrera assured Wolfson that he was. Wolfson remembered his youth also, when as a youngster he rode Florida Pipe and Supply into a million-dollar bonanza. He never hesitated in endorsing Cauthen, not after listening to Barrera.

Racing was literally in the blood of Cauthen, the son of a trainer and blacksmith. He adroitly convinced everyone that he could ride without flaunting any of his God-given talent. Despite his youth, Cauthen was an exceptional rider with strong hands, the courage of a lion, and the instincts of a predator. He would need all three of his endowments to overcome the expected torrid stretch run of Alydar.

All winter long and into the spring, racing fans spiritedly debated who would be the favorite for the 1978 Derby. As two-year-olds, both Affirmed and Alydar performed masterfully and captured the racing crowd's imagination from one coast to the other with their stimulating duels. Affirmed had beaten Alydar in four of six challenges, enough to give him year-end honors and make him the winter book favorite for the Kentucky Derby.

But the strong local betting crowd established Alydar as the even-money favorite, with Affirmed behind at 7–5. Two others, Sensitive Prince at 6–1 and Believe It at 8–1, drew some interest. Wolfson understood why Alydar was the people's choice. Alydar was a Kentucky horse and Calumet was a Kentucky farm and there was enormous sentiment for Admiral Gene and Lucille Markey, two wheelchair-bound octogenarians who would watch the race on television in their Lexington home.

It was time for the race.

The clarion's call to the track brought cheers from the festive throng. It had been a number of years since there was so much excitement for a Derby, which was ignited by Affirmed and Alydar. If there was one horse in America, or Europe for that matter, that could beat Affirmed, it was Alydar, the best specimen of horseflesh that Calumet had produced in over ten years.

Webster's *New World Dictionary* describes a horse as "a large, four-legged, solid-hoofed animal with flowing mane and tail domesticated for drawing loads, carrying riders, etc." The horses in the Derby all carry the same load, 126 pounds. The one difference was that 96 pounds of Affirmed's burden was Cauthen. The rest was lead in the saddlebags, 30 pounds of it. In 1975, the Jockey Club registered 27,649 foals, yet only eleven made it to this year's Derby, one for every 2,513 registered three years ago.

Cauthen, the wonder child of his sport, just five days past his eighteenth birthday, was coming home to his native Kentucky. In 1976, when he was only sixteen, he had his maiden ride at Churchill Downs on a long shot that never got close to winning. Now he was aboard a champion thoroughbred with a robust chance to win the Derby and to prove to the racing world that he was a champion jockey despite his youth. All he would say in his youthful innocence was "It is a thrill to be here."

A gentle breeze of May enriched spring for the madding

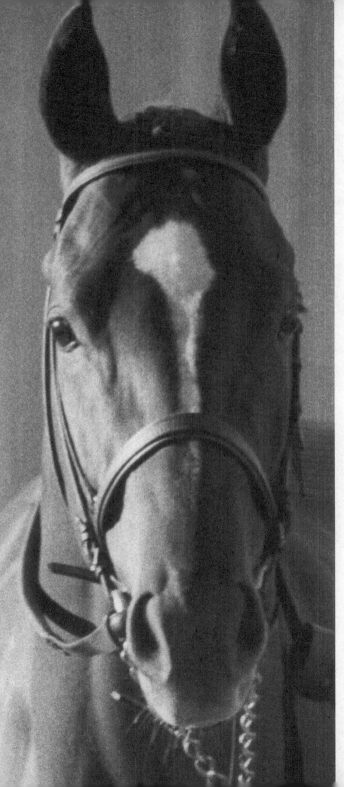

Laz Barrera
called Affirmed
"the smartest
horse I ever
trained." *(Katey
Barrett)*

Steve Cauthen, the eighteen-year-old wunderkid. *(Bill Straus)*

TOP: On March 18, 1978, Affirmed (second from left) won the San Felipe at Santa Anita. *(Katey Barrett)*

BOTTOM: Steve Cauthen rides Affirmed to an easy victory in the first leg of the elusive Triple Crown. *(Bill Straus)*

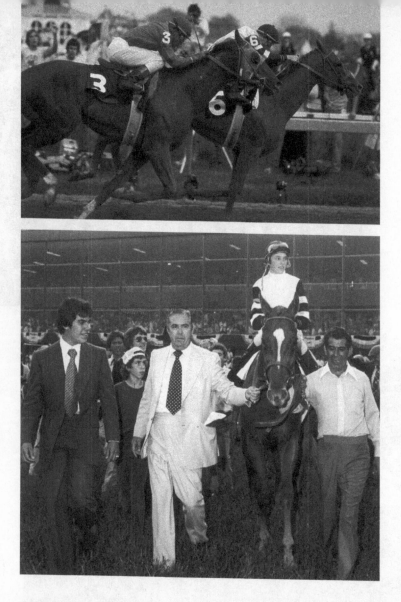

TOP: Affirmed (number 6) on the rail, wins the Preakness, the second jewel of the Triple Crown, by a head over Alydar. *(Gerry Cooke/*Sports Illustrated*/Getty Images)*

BOTTOM: Laz Barrera leads Affirmed and Steve Cauthen to the Preakness Winner's Circle. Barrera's son, Larry, is on the left, and Affirmed's groom is on the right. *(Jim McCue, Pimlico Race Course)*

Cauthen (right) using the left-handed whip on Affirmed for the first time in the Belmont Stakes, 1978. *(Bob Coglianese)*

TOP: Affirmed (on the inside) nudges his head in front of Alydar in the Belmont, winning the 1978 Triple Crown. *(Bob Coglianese)*

BOTTOM: Laz Barrera and owner Louis Wolfson share a worried look after a steward's inquiry disqualified Affirmed in the 1978 Travers Stakes at Saratoga. *(Bill Straus)*

Steve Cauthen and Affirmed began their climb for the Triple Crown by winning the Kentucky Derby, the Preakness, and the Belmont, with Alydar close behind. (Daily Racing Form/Keeneland Library/Peb Collection)

Laffit Pincay rode Affirmed to seven straight career-ending wins in 1979. *(Katey Barrett)* crowd in anticipation of the Affirmed-Alydar confrontation on venerated Churchill Downs. Esops Foibles was the first to be led onto the track, which had good footing for the race. Alydar followed him. So it went as one by one all the hopefuls came in full view of a frenzied crowed that numbered 131,004, the third-largest attendance in Derby history.

The Cauthen family was in a reserved clubhouse box. It was Myra's first attendance at a Derby since 1974, when she saw it from the backside. She was teary for the national anthem and freely cried at the playing of "My Old Kentucky Home" by the collective bands in the infield. When Steve appeared with Affirmed directly in front of her, she blew kisses to him in the parade to the post. She was indeed a happy and proud mother.

To Kentuckians, "My Old Kentucky Home" is as sacred as "The Star-Spangled Banner." The song brought tears to many in the century-old venue, enough to make Stephen Foster proud, and is revered by anyone born and living in Kentucky or who has moved away to another state. There is something moving about the age-old ballad.

At the starting gate everything appeared to run smoothly, until Special Honor began acting up. But, more significantly, Alydar demonstrated his stubbornness. It took three attendants pushing and another one pulling to get the Calumet horse into the gate. When Sensitive Prince went into the gate without any trouble in the No. 11 spot, starter Tom Waggoner immediately triggered the button for all eleven horses to get cleanly away from the clanking gates.

For some reason, Alydar wasn't comfortable with the track, Velasquez would say after the race. Something must have been bothering him. It could happen to any horse before any race.

Raymond Earl was the first to jump into the lead. He was pursued by Sensitive Prince, who ran by him at the half-mile juncture by 1½ lengths. Cauthen followed Barrera's instructions and had Affirmed third, six lengths behind; while Alydar lagged seventeen lengths in the rear before a stunned crowd. It would be quite a distance for Alydar to make up.

As Sensitive Prince began to fall back, Believe It took over the lead. At the mile marker, Cauthen pulled Affirmed even with the leader and bolted into a two-length lead at the top of the stretch. "Affirmed began to prick his ears like he always does, so I started hitting him," disclosed Cauthen later. Everything was working as planned. Finally, Alydar came into view. But was it too late? Driving the outside, he swerved into Believe It and lightly bumped into him at the sixteenth pole. The crowd's roar prompted Cauthen to look back. Seeing Alydar, Cauthen made use of his whip and thumped Affirmed six times on his right rump.

Velasquez was working hard. He made it an even dozen swipes on Alydar. Cauthen kept waiting for Alydar, and when he saw Velasquez urging him on, got Affirmed to resist any challenge that Alydar could produce, as both horses swept across the finish line at full speed. Alydar gamely tried to catch Affirmed from as far back as sixteen lengths, only to come up short by a length and a half. The Harbor View champion crossed the finish line at 2:01:1/5, which tied him for the fifth-best time in the race's history with Lucky Debonair in 1965. It was a bittersweet Derby, bitter for the Markeys and sweet for the Wolfsons.

The state of Kentucky also shared in the sweetness. A record $4,425,828 went through the mutuel windows with over

$2 million wagered on Alydar and Affirmed. Alydar attracted the most money, $1,501,236, while Affirmed accounted for $1,242,322. Either amount would certainly buy a lot of mint juleps.

Barrera reached the winner's circle as fast as he could from his box in the clubhouse. He happily grabbed the groom and then hugged Cauthen the moment he dismounted. Barrera then turned and extended his congratulations to the Wolfsons. He even had a hug for Kentucky governor Julian Carroll before being asked to the microphone.

"I hope to be with you a lotta years more," Barrera said. "Thank you to everybody, all the loving Americans watching on television. And to my grandson Mickey in Mexico City, Mickey, God bless you."

The jovial trainer was then escorted by security to the clubhouse and the postrace press conference. There were no tears for the emotional Barrera after the Derby, not like when he'd won the prize race with Bold Forbes in 1976. But, those had been tears of joy.

"Sometimes you get emotional and cry when everything comes to you because it's your life," expressed Barrera after Affirmed's 1½-length triumph. "I was confident. I knew he was going to win 'cause I know the way he trains. Cauthen rode the horse perfect. He was just where I wanted him to be. We didn't want any horse going to the outside on us. We wanted to keep the horse in the clear. He got to the lead, then, good-bye, baby.

"He's going to be proven the day we find a horse that makes him run fast. We can go five miles. I don't want to hear no more excuses. He showed we can go the classic distance. It doesn't matter if he ran in China. He's a good horse and I'm very proud of him."

Barrera had much more faith in Affirmed than in Bold Forbes because of the injury he'd sustained two weeks before the Derby and the trainer not knowing if Forbes could run the entire race or would pull up lame.

Affirmed improved when Barrera had him training in California. What was noticeable was that Affirmed got bigger by adding muscle. It didn't change his disposition at all. Barrera took it easy with him on some days and sped it up on others. Whatever Barrera asked, Affirmed complied.

"I was very confident I had a winner," disclosed Barrera about Affirmed. "I know my horse, and he is a very good horse, against the opinion of many here who don't think so because he ran in California. It doesn't matter if he ran in China, he's a good horse."

With his temper, Barrera could be irritable at times. He couldn't help but take a swipe at the detractors who thought that horses who ran on Eastern tracks were superior to the ones running in California because of the competition from better horses in the East. But, Barrera managed to maintain his restraint at a time of celebration.

"My horse trained better, he looked better. What did he pay?" Barrera asked.

He was told $5.60.

"My God almighty," Barrera said, swooning. He was relishing the moment. And he deserved every bit of it after being second-guessed repeatedly about keeping Affirmed in California.

"The war was over a long time ago," he boasted. "It was over when my horse won the Futurity. I didn't know if he would win the Eclipse Aware or not, but he did win it. You asked me if Affirmed and Alydar will ever run head-and-head or neck-and-neck again. Maybe so."

Barrera was later informed that Veitch claimed, "I still think Alydar can beat Affirmed."

Barrera countered, "If he doesn't get hold of the track with firm footing, he doesn't finish second. The only trouble he had was he couldn't get ahold of Affirmed."

There was one more place Barrera had to be, the Directors Room, where the winning owners sipped the congratulatory champagne, a smooth Piper-Heidsieck, a French import. Barrera, in a blue suit and shirt, looked every inch a director, rather than the most-talked-about trainer in America. And if he sounded a little cocky, so what? He'd answered enough questions during the week, some questioning his horse and others questioning his disrupted training of him in California. He disposed of a ceremonial sip of the bubbly and replaced it with a plastic cup filled with ice and ginger ale as he accepted a roomful of good wishes while watching a replay of the race.

The Derby triumph brought out thoughts of the Preakness. He was asked if he thought Alydar would make an earlier move in the Pimlico race. He gave a haughty answer, still flushed from his success in the Derby.

"Alydar can move from the front and we beat him," snapped Barrera. "He moved from the middle and we beat him. He moved from the back and we beat him. I don't want no more excuses. Veitch said my horse would lead and his come from behind. He forgot, I got Affirmed. Why second-guess me? You play with fire, you're going to get burned. They both are great horses. It's a shame they both got together the same year."

Wolfson, with his arm around his wife, smiled at Barrera and sipped champagne. There was plenty of time for smiles, and Patrice looked emotionally drained.

"I've had a couple of weeks of excitement and nervousness," she explained with a faint smile. "Now I'm going to relax. I think winning this has whetted my appetite, but I'm going to calm down."

As Wolfson stood hugging his wife, who was pertly huggable, he disclosed how he almost owned both Affirmed and Alydar last year when his horse nipped Alydar by a nose in the Belmont Futurity.

"We, Spendthrift Farm and I, tried to buy Alydar," remarked Wolfson. "I told Leslie Combs that whatever he paid, I'd take part of it. I knew he was a great horse. I thought he was the best I've seen since Raise A Native. After the Futurity, though, I knew we had a better horse.

"Until now, I thought Roman Brother was my best horse, but now I've got to say Affirmed is the best. I just liked his position throughout the race. When he went to the lead, he did it so easily. If I didn't breed the horse, there would be less feeling. I remember this horse on the farm as a foal and a weanling."

Wolfson was bursting with pride. He had accomplished what he'd started out to do when he began in racing. He expressed it to Kent Hollingsworth of the *Blood Horse:*

"A man can buy a champion, but it is not the same thing as racing one you've bred. I spent twenty years of my life to get this one. I brought him into this world. I bred and raced his sire. I raised him at my farm."

Wolfson then turned and gave a victory hug to Monteen Tomberlin, who was crying, and had been his secretary for forty-three years. He had enormous affection for her.

"She's the most brilliant businesswoman I've ever come in contact with," praised Wolfson, who was one of the brilliant financial minds of the twentieth century.

Cauthen couldn't have returned home to Kentucky a bigger winner if he had been aboard Man o' War. He'd convinced the entire country that he knew how to ride, not only ride, but win the nation's biggest race. Affirmed handled as easily as a stable pony for him, and his Derby debut was every bit as eye-catching as Lady Godiva's ride at Coventry. Affirmed relaxed under Cauthen's perfect ride, which was as smooth as the silks on his back. All by an eighteen-year-old. He did it all with calmness and poise, which he later displayed at his press conference.

"Surprisingly, it went a lot like I expected and he was calm and relaxed when we went to the post," revealed Cauthen. "Like he always is. The crowd was tremendous but it didn't seem to bother him. At the break, I was just laying off the number one horse. Sensitive Prince came to me at the first turn and I had made up my mind to let him go.

"I just let Affirmed settle and he settled good on the backside. At the half-mile pole he started gradually easing up toward the front. He got to Sensitive Prince at the three-eighths pole. Then, when Believe It came to me, we moved together to the head of the lead.

"When Affirmed had opened up a couple of lengths, he started pricking his ears like he always does. That's when I hit him to keep him on his business. He had a habit of waiting for the competition. That's why he didn't win the Hollywood Derby by much. He wanted more competition.

"Most of the time races don't shape up the way you figure, but this one did. I figured those two horses would go to the lead and I figured they'd stop. I know my horse. I know how he runs and I knew he would run easy. He was just waiting for the main competition. By the time I saw Alydar, I knew I had him beat!"

"Could you have run a better race?" someone asked.

The coolheaded Cauthen answered with a question: "Whattaya want? He just won the Kentucky Derby."

It was time to end the press conference.

Cauthen's father confirmed that his son was unmoved by the pressure associated with his first Derby. And Tex wasn't surprised by it. Cauthen had slept for two nights on the floor of the hotel room the Cauthens shared. A Derby jockey doing that? Even Affirmed had some soft straw under his body.

"Steve was himself last night," claimed Tex. "He slept and then he complained when I woke him up. How normal can you get?"

As normal as any teenager even to the point of forgetting his goggles and having to borrow a pair from ex-jockey Don Brumfield. Nothing seemed to upset Cauthen. He went into the biggest race of his young life with someone else's goggles and never once thought anything about it.

There was no press conference for Veitch. Only tears when the race ended and left an empty feeling for anyone involved with Alydar.

"What are you crying about, Margarita?" inquired Veitch.

"I'm so sorry, John," replied Margarita Velasquez.

"That's all right, Margarita."

Veitch's conference was with the Markeys. He dutifully called them in Lexington when he retreated to the barn area. It was a long walk for him this time.

"I talked to Admiral and Mrs. Markey," he made it known. "The Admiral says, 'John, don't worry about a thing. He just got himself too far out of it and couldn't make it up.' They were disappointed but they told me not to be. They were more concerned about me and how I was feeling."

Then Veitch talked about the race he'd been so confident of, the Derby, which he'd said he felt Alydar, so fit after the Blue Grass Stakes nine days earlier, would win.

"He ran a good race but he just got beat," observed Veitch. "Nobody likes to lose, but people take things differently. I think you would have to take victory well and not get yourself all screwed up when you lose, and a trainer is going to lose a lot more races than he wins.

"I know myself the next time we can't be anyplace as far back as we were in the Derby. I knew going down the backstretch that we were in serious trouble, but I thought that we were moving good through the stretch. Affirmed was the best horse in the Derby. Whether he will be in the Preakness and the Belmont, nobody knows. We'll have to wait and see. But Alydar will try Affirmed again in both races."

Lou Rondinello, Darby Creek Road's trainer, expected this to happen.

"I'd say the rivalry between Affirmed and Alydar is still on," he claimed. "Alydar had a legitimate excuse in the fact that Velasquez said his colt couldn't get hold of the track. But

Alydar was closing with a rush. While my horse ran a good race to be fourth, he was still beaten by seven lengths."

One trainer who was feeling worse than Veitch was Jerkens, who was known as the great upsetter. He was totally perplexed by his horse's sixth-place finish and showed it by kicking the cement wall in front of Prince's stall.

"I don't know why Sensitive Prince ran so poorly," he remarked quizzically. "God, he was beaten by fourteen lengths. Maybe I made some kind of mistake that I'm not aware of yet, but I don't think Sensitive Prince fooled me. I know he's a good horse.

"The Preakness? Not until I find out what went wrong in the Derby. It could be best to stop on him now and then come back later on. This Derby was a complete mystery to me. We certainly wasted an awful lot of time by coming to Kentucky."

It was quite a while before Velasquez said anything. He carried the disappointment of defeat across his face and didn't say anything about the race until he was toweling himself after a shower in the jockeys' quarters. He knew he had to talk. Losing jockeys are part of what happened.

"Well, it's over," he lamented. "The horse just couldn't get started. He never got the track under him. For a long time I thought he was going to be off the board. I imagined 130,000 people booing me, losing with the Kentucky Derby favorite. Then finally he started to go in the stretch. Maybe next time it will be different."

Later that night, Louis and Patrice Wolfson didn't have any wild celebration. Instead they celebrated Affirmed's victory with a quiet affair with their friends in the Tudor Room of the Executive Inn. The occasion was marked by a large candle stuck into a cupcake. Not for Affirmed, mind you, but for Barrera's fifty-fourth birthday the next day. Cauthen was there, but Affirmed remained in his barn, perhaps too tired to party. "The war is over," proclaimed Barrera. "We have the better horse."

Barrera was a talker who mixed his Cuban Spanish with English in a syntax that was at times humorous. He wasn't talking about his birthday. He was talking about Cauthen, whom he regarded as a reincarnation of a supreme jockey.

"This boy, he must be from another time, maybe one hundred years," Barrera gushed. "He came from space on a flying sausage."

Thanks to Cauthen, Walton was now the biggest little town in Kentucky. One signpost on a city limits read *Walton, population 1,600.* Another said. *Walton, birthplace of Steve Cauthen.* There was even a tavern now called Steve's Pub. Only Cauthen would have to wait three years, until he was twenty-one, to legally order a drink.

NINE

The Preakness

*If you had to name the five greatest
horses in history, Affirmed is
right up there with them.*
—Laffit Pincay,
Hall of Fame jockey

The Preakness has been held on the third Saturday in May
ever since 1873 at the Pimlico Race Course in Baltimore. Still,
quite a number of influential horsemen would argue for a
change in the calendar. Barrera for one. His contention is that
the Derby, Preakness, and Belmont are too crammed into a
short span. The astute Cuban feels that three strenuous races
within six weeks is much too taxing on the horses. He would
prefer more time between each event to help the thoroughbreds present their best form late into the season. Although
the three races are grouped together, each has a distinct flavor
and personality all to itself.

While the officials at Pimlico try hard every year to establish the Preakness as racing's premier event, no other race in America has the allure of the Kentucky Derby. Since the Derby is the beginning of the Triple Crown procession, the Preakness is the precious stepping-stone to the elusive bauble and a harbinger for the Belmont. Yet the Derby and even the Belmont don't have the audacious history of the Preakness.

The Preakness is older than either the Derby or the Belmont. It was first contested in 1870, yet its inception was spawned three years earlier by a charter that established, of all things, the Maryland State Agricultural and Mechanical Association (MSAMA). It was a significant year in young America back then. Georgia was the last Confederate state to be readmitted to the Union; President Ulysses Grant met with Sioux Chef Red Cloud; the United States Postal Service issued its first postcard; construction began on New York's Brooklyn Bridge and the city introduced the subway transit system.

The MSAMA objective had nothing to do with horse racing. It was established for leading farmers around the state to promote Maryland's agriculture and livestock, specifically through a series of state fairs. However, it failed. The last fair occurred in 1871, much to the dismay of MSAMA. However, they judiciously developed a land-saving strategy the year before. In 1870, MSAMA began leasing its property to the Maryland Jockey Club. That enabled the group not to default and surrender their property to the City of Baltimore. On October 25, 1870, the first race held at the Pimlico Fair Grounds under the Maryland Jockey Club took place. Ironically enough, a horse named Preakness won.

The origin of the name Preakness began with a northern

New Jersey tribe of Indians known as the Minisi. The area they inhabited was known as Pra-Qua-les, which meant "quail woods." The name somehow evolved into Preakness. In the winter of 1776–77, General George Washington, who had his Continental Army headquarters there, described the area as "Prekiness." Almost a century later, Milton Sanford, an owner of thoroughbred horses, named his two farms, one in Paterson, New Jersey, and the other in Lexington, Kentucky, Preakness. In Jersey, there remains a town called Preakness.

Maryland governor Oden Bowie was the biggest benefactor in promoting thoroughbred racing in his state. A passionate horseman, he was one of the distinguished, and conveniently wealthy, guests at an elegant dinner party sponsored by Sanford at the Union Hall Hotel in Saratoga. At the conclusion of the dinner, which apparently went well, one of those in attendance, John Hunter of New York, proposed that the evening be commemorated by a stake race in the fall of 1870 for three-year-olds to be called the Dinner Party Stakes. Bowie was the first to endorse the idea. He stunned the guests by announcing a $15,000 purse, then suggested that the race take place in Maryland. At the same moment, he pledged to erect a new racetrack to host it, Pimlico Race Course.

When Sanford, who acquired a large amount of his wealth selling blankets in the Civil War, purchased a colt for $2,000 that was bred in Kentucky, he named him Preakness, after the little community in New Jersey. As he grew into a three-year-old, he was looked upon unflatteringly as a "cart horse" because of his ungainly appearance. But Preakness fooled everyone who attended the Dinner Party Stakes on Pimlico's inaugural race day. Ridden by the highly regarded English jockey Billy

Hayward, Preakness easily came across the finish line first. It was his one and only race of the year. He retired from racing to allow him to fill out his large frame.

Man o' War's presence in 1920 at the forty-fifth Preakness did more to establish the magnitude of the race than any other event. Samuel D. Riddle, who owned the magnificent horse, bypassed the Kentucky Derby, announcing that Man o' War would make his first start as a three-year-old in the Preakness. The revelation excited the Baltimore countryside. Thousands, estimated at more than twenty thousand, appeared at Pimlico to watch Man o' War work out days before the race. People were elbow-to-elbow striving to get a glimpse of the two-year-old champion of 1919, who won all of his nine races that year by large margins. He began his three-year-old campaign with a 1½-length victory.

Man o' War in the Preakness elicited this endorsement by the *Morning Telegraph:*

"In naming his Man o' War, 2-year-old champion, for the Preakness of 1920, it was inferred that Samuel D. Riddle discriminated it as a superior breeding potentially to the Kentucky Derby of then-current racing.

"Mr. Riddle evinced no interest that Autumn and Spring in anything but the Preakness, so that stake was scheduled to become preeminent among early-season fixtures of American racing largely through its choice as the setting of Man o' War's three-year-old debut, and none gainsay that Man o' War in winning the Preakness not only revealed himself as America's premier thoroughbred and potential sire, but elevated the Preakness to equal billing in stakes prominence."

Not until 1940 was it decided to drape the winning horse in

a garland of black-eyed Susans, the state flower. Thus the Preakness is referred to as the Race for the Black-eyed Susans. However, the flowers never come into bloom until late June or July. Chrysanthemums or daises with a pinned black center were the substitutes five years after the Preakness was televised for the first time.

Affirmed had won the Derby fairly easily but would need a stronger effort to win the Preakness. Because of its sharper turns, the Preakness is a challenge for both horse and jockey. After the Derby, Barrera declared, "The war is over." But it wasn't. In reality, it was an armistice after the battle of Louisville. Two weeks later it was the battle of Baltimore. Yet, there was something about the Preakness after its century-long battle to survive. It is looked upon by many in the sport as the most important of the races simply because only one horse comes out of the Derby with an opportunity to annex the Triple Crown. Cauthen, Barrera, and Affirmed were projected to be in the spotlight for an entire week. But Cauthen would be riding in New York most of the week, while Barrera was left to handle the media barrage.

Affirmed, too, had been in New York and didn't arrive in Baltimore until Monday. That was the game plan Barrera enacted, and he leaned on experience in making it. He shipped Affirmed directly to Belmont after his Derby victory instead of sending him to Baltimore.

"I can fly a horse to New York from Kentucky in two and a half hours rather than van him down to Maryland in four and a half hours," explained Barrera. "It's less commotion. It is much better than vanning him all the way from Kentucky to Maryland when he is dead tired after a tough race.

"I do a little something different in the van. I make the van a stall. I have only one horse on it. I have to so that he can walk around, and if he wants to, I have it set up so that he can lie down. It's very comfortable when he gets there, he had been rested."

Barrera was doing what he did with Bold Forbes two years earlier when he galloped home first in the 1976 Derby. The Cuban isn't one for change if whatever he decided was working to his satisfaction. In his mind, the transporting of Bold Forbes worked out it and would do the same for Affirmed.

"By the time a trainer gets to Pimlico and has listened to the questions, he gets psyched out," contends Barrera. Everybody talks about how the Preakness is shorter than the Derby and how the turns are shaper. This is true. But there is no time left to shorten up a horse's training and put more speed in him.

"Many trainers make a mistake and panic and try to change their horses too much. At this time the only thing a trainer can really do is to hold his horse at a peak and get him to relax and feel comfortable."

Veitch, for one, wasn't looking for advice before the Preakness. In the week following the Derby he received a voluminous amount through the mail. What more ironic that a "Dear John" letter.

"I'll bet you I received three hundred letters last week criticizing Jorge Velasquez's riding, criticizing my training," snapped Veitch. "One guy wrote that in the Preakness we should take Alydar right out and never look back. The Admiral got a telegraph from somebody who suggested we give Jorge Velasquez back to Panama and keep the canal.

"Some of them were addressed to the Dumb Trainer, care of

Belmont Bark. You don't even open those. Those kinds wait for you with a lead pipe outside a saloon on some dark night and, whammo."

One annoying topic that Veitch handled professionally concerned Velasquez. Many faulted him for his ride in the Derby, but Veitch staunchly supported him.

"With Jorge being the good rider that he is and the horse being so far back in the Derby, it was only natural for people to say he screwed up, that he got overconfident and let Affirmed slip away," acknowledged Veitch. "But the track surface at Churchill Downs changed from the time of Alydar's last workout and the day of the Derby. They rolled the track and he couldn't handle it. Jorge knew he was too far back, but there was nothing he could do about it. I certainly can't fault him."

When asked, Velasquez didn't shy away from any questions regarding his ride. He's always been a popular interview with the writers because he always makes himself available, this time on a phone call from Aqueduct in the middle of the week. He still had bad memories of the Derby and had felt confident that Alydar would provide him with his first victory in the classic. It wasn't meant to be.

"He broke good and I tried to save him some ground going into the first turn," began Velasquez. "And he wasn't doing no running at all. I had to hit him two times, tap him on the back shoulder, about the middle of the first turn. When he got to the backside, I was still trying to make him pick it up, make him go on.

"By the time we got to the half-mile pole, he was so far back that I felt that I wasn't going to be on the board. Then, all of a sudden, about the three-sixteenths pole, he started picking it up. And when we got to Believe It, we kind of brushed him lightly—very lightly—and he took off running again. Then he got serious and he was running. But it was too late. The race was over.

"I hate to get beat with an excuse. I don't like to come up with an excuse after I got beat. But certainly, in the Derby, I don't want to be that far out of it. It was not my fault. It was the horse's fault because he didn't want to pick it up and I'm trying to make him pick it up.

"With the kind of horses he was running against, and by him being so far back like that, he has to be a good horse to make up so much ground like he did."

By midweek, rain was becoming a concern. After four days of heavy precipitation, the track was muddy and looking ugly. It must certainly have evoked memories of California for Barrera, but he wasn't saying anything. He had enough of the wet stuff during the California winter to last him a lifetime. However, Barrera could take some solace in the weatherman's forecast for a sunny Thursday, which would bring good weather with it. In any event, Pimlico's excellent drainage would ensure a fast track for Saturday.

Veitch believed track conditions could be a factor. He was prepared for whatever the weather dictated, and it didn't seem to bother him.

"If the track is muddy, horses who race on the lead would tire," analyzed Veitch. "In all likelihood, Affirmed will go to the front at the start and Cauthen will attempt to control the race while saving his horse as much as possible. This will put a great deal of pressure on Velasquez, who will have to gauge how much horse he has left under him at every stage.

"We certainly want Alydar closer to the pace than he was in the Derby, no more than three or four lengths back at the three-eighths pole. I hope Affirmed and Alydar hook up at some point and drag each other over the finish line. We beat Affirmed twice last season by flying past him with a big move, but Alydar is bigger and stronger this year. He's grown enough that I feel our colt can wear him down in a drive. I think we can look him in the eye and win."

All the prerace hyperbole was directed at a two-horse duel, as it had always been between Affirmed and Alydar ever since last year. If any horse was conceded a slight chance to overtake both favorites, it was Woody Stephens's Believe It. He held his form all year and even looked better than he did a month earlier. A Stephens-trained horse is most always a dangerous animal.

"These three horses are not going to be too far apart at any stage of the Preakness," reasoned Stephens. "The race could be more exciting than the Derby. Post position could be a factor in determining who is on the lead. A horse who draws number one might very well want to keep the rail all the way and might be in position to protect his lead."

Barrera experienced a scary bit of the midweek blues when he received word that Cauthen had fallen off his horse at Belmont. Barrera didn't hesitate in reaching for the phone and calling Steve's agent, Lenny Goodman. After speaking with the fast-talking Goodman, Barrera was relieved.

"He told me it's nothing," related Barrera. "They took pictures. You know how I know it's okay? If it wasn't, three hundred jockey agents from all over the country would phone me by now."

On Thursday, Barrera's mood was upbeat. In the drawing for the seven-horse field, Affirmed came up with the sixth post position, which thrilled the unflappable trainer to no end.

"Beautiful," he exclaimed, with delight spreading across his ruddy face. He outwardly loved the spot Affirmed drew. Barrera explained that he was happy to be on the outside, where there were fewer chances of another horse hitting him at the start and throwing him off his stride. He also noted that with a small field Affirmed could either take the lead from the start or relax and wait to make his move.

"But I'm not going to say how I'm gonna run," emphasized Barrera. "It's not fair to me. It's not fair to my horse. He might lay third or fourth. If he goes easy to that position, that's okay. But if you have to run him, you change your style on him after you teach him so long to rate him and bring him from behind. You'll see how he's going to run Saturday."

Outside of the horsemen, the biggest worrier about the rain was Chick Lang, the general manager of Pimlico. Lang, a former trainer and jockey agent for Bill Hartack, had been in racing all his life, beginning with a father, who was a jockey. Lang was predicting a record turnout of eighty thousand for the Preakness, which would be grossly diminished by a wet Saturday.

"I don't know that I'd go so far as to say I'm the world's biggest weather worrier, but I do think about it a lot," he admitted. "We've had a tremendous advance sale. Every seat in the grandstand and clubhouse has been sold on a renewal basis since January. But the infield is where we get the crowd, and even a forecast for poor weather can hurt us there.

"I love the Preakness and I always want the weather to be

beautiful so everybody who comes out to the race can enjoy it the way I do. There's only one Preakness, too. There isn't even another race with its name. You might say the Preakness is more important than the Kentucky Derby because there isn't a Triple Crown winner unless the winner of the Derby can prove himself in the Preakness."

Lang was making a valid point about the importance of the Preakness and not trying to conjure hype for the event. After the Derby, everyone knows what horse is the one to beat, and every entry in the Preakness is out to beat the Derby winner. It's one of the reasons why there had only been ten Triple Crown winners in over one hundred years of racing.

Although Barrera often refered to Cauthen as being "one hundred years old," fuzzy-cheeked Steve was on a storybook script that could be finished with his being the youngest jockey to win the noble Triple Crown. Hall of Famer Eddie Arcaro was a strong supporter of his. The Master, as he's saluted, thought the Kid was something special. Garnering this salute from Arcaro, perhaps the greatest jockey on American turf, was gospel. It was from a jockey whose record in the classics is unparalleled: five Kentucky Derby winners, six Pimlico victories, and six Belmont triumphs.

"He's way in front at his age compared to where I was at eighteen," began Arcaro. "I think I rode about seventy winners with the apprentice allowance, and many of those were at Sportsman Park competing against ordinary riders. In about two-thirds of a season as an apprentice in 1976, Cauthen rode 240 winners, his mounts earned over one million dollars, and many of those came in New York, riding against top jockeys."

Arcaro liked what he saw in Cauthen and took the time to

explain why he was so good from a jockey's viewpoint. There was none better than Arcaro to break it down:

"First of all, Steve seems to know a lot about pace. Look how nicely he rated Affirmed in the Derby off that fast early pace. Most kids his age don't know nearly that much about pace, if anything.

"Second, he has a good seat on a horse, good balance. Jockeys these days are riding with much shorter stirrups, and balance is more important than ever. Cauthen is not all over a horse. He's very quiet in the irons. He's not pulling on the reins, depending on them to stay in balance. He's got great hands, sensitive to his horse's movements."

Arcaro had closely followed Cauthen. It was, to a degree, a bit of sentiment. Cauthen broke in at River Downs, just as Arcaro did, and both were from the same area near Cincinnati. Like Arcaro, Cauthen was a cool rider who didn't display any emotional outbursts, remarkable from one so young, especially if something didn't go right at the start of a race. He was almost the mirror of Arcaro, who down deep was pulling for the kid from his own backyard.

"He came along at the right time. Racing needed a star to focus attention on our fame and away from the topics such as falling attendance in New York. He's been like a breath of fresh air in the spring, and he's handled himself very well in the face of terrific pressure. Most important, he's an asset to racing, and I wish him well with Affirmed in their bid for the Triple Crown."

At Friday's annual Alibi Breakfast for the media, the working press dined on strawberries and eggs while washing it down with Black-eyed Susans, something resembling a mint julep, at the Pimlico Clubhouse. Once gastronomically satisfied, the writers turned to Velasquez, asking him about restating Alydar's alibi.

"Well, I guess it was not his day," answered the popular Panamanian. "He was not together in the early part of the race. I hate to make excuses after we got beat, but he was not himself. I hope it works out better tomorrow. I can only try my best. I cannot jump off and carry him."

There were no alibis from Barrera. He had the winning horse in the Derby and was confident about the Preakness. Not only that, but he exuded unabashed confidence about winning the Triple Crown, even though he had been striving to temper his enthusiasm all week. Was the colorful Cuban imbibing too much rum?

"No one knows how good Affirmed can run," commented Barrera. "He certainly hasn't been tested to the limit this year. He was an easy winner of the Santa Anita and Hollywood derbies in California, and I thought he was an easy winner of the Kentucky Derby, too.

"Alydar tested Affirmed last fall in the Hopeful, the Futurity, and the Laurel Futurity, but this year, Affirmed has been the best by far. I think he'll win the Triple Crown.

"My colt has developed beautifully over the winter. In one respect, the rain may have been a help, for he had more of an opportunity to grow than if he had been in serious training since January first. Affirmed is a much better horse this season, and since he was an outstanding two-year-old last year, you know what I think of him now."

Veitch, too, wasn't hesitant in expressing confidence in Alydar. He noted that his horse had lost five times in seven starts against Alydar:

"We've been beaten only a total of two and a half lengths in those five races we lost to him. Until the Derby, the total margin in four of the losses was just a length. That's not much. We're in good condition. The horse has kept his condition these two weeks since the Derby."

Veitch explained why Alydar had trouble in the Derby and didn't run his race. He also admitted a mistake on his part:

"The Derby was basically a matter of handling the track. The reason he had so much trouble was that I didn't train him very much at Churchill Downs. If you recall, he won the Blue Grass Stakes at Keeneland by a rousing thirteen lengths, and I wasn't anxious to overtrain him.

"I think he can beat Affirmed. I thought he beat him decisively in the Champagne last fall at level weights. He blew right by him and was going away at the end. It was a muddy track, too. Alydar doesn't need a fast track. He just needs one that he's trained over. Then he can get maximum benefit from his strong finish. If the pace is realistic, Alydar will be right there. We intend to hang closer to the lead this time. No more than four, five, six going down the backstretch, and be right on top of the lead horse into the stretch."

Down deep, Veitch felt he could beat Affirmed. It sounded as if he was fantasizing.

─────── **RACE DAY** ───────

The racing gods were kind. Saturday morning blushed with sunshine. In the early-morning hours, it was welcomed by the stableboys, grooms, and trainers, and it showed in the roseate beam of their faces. There would be no rain today. There would be a fast track for certain and no excuses for the seven hopefuls in the Preakness, which was the shortest of the Triple Crown races at 1³/16 miles.

Affirmed hoped to move a step closer to becoming the eleventh Triple Crown champion in history, and he won in Kentucky to get this far. Would he be able to handle the sharp turns of Pimlico with an eighteen-year-old on his back? Would he jump into the lead or let the others set the pace? Racing dogma contends that front-runners have the best opportunity to win a race. In the last sixty-eight runnings of the Preakness, twenty-three victors led all the way, twenty-nine came from off the pace, while eighteen came from the rear.

Veitch didn't subscribe to any of the math. Being a college guy, he did his own.

"I'm not concerned with anything here than I was in Louisville," he said. "All the Triple Crown races are distance races. This one is just one-sixteenth shorter, that's all. I think all that stuff about the sharper turns is overrated, too. You know how it goes. One knowledgeable horseman says something and everybody believes it."

Sitting on a folding chair in front of his barn in the early afternoon, Barrera had his own theory: "You know, all these horses came here for the Preakness to correct the mistakes they made in Kentucky. Me, I didn't make no mistakes. We don't have no mistakes to correct. See, Affirmed is like an old man nodding off.

"Look down the other end of the barn. Alydar is being walked around and around. He's nervous and been walking forty-five minutes or more. Affirmed no walk. He does a doze.

Me, I cannot doze. I live to sit here and talk to people who stop by.

"The days of big races are long ones. You come to the barn at six in the morning, and if you win, you don't leave until nine o'clock at night. But you sit here long enough, you might learn something."

Barrera was at ease and doing more talking now than earlier in the day. He appeared more relaxed at ten o'clock. In the early-morning hours he was somewhat subdued while having breakfast in the barn area with Jimmy the Greek and Hank Goldberg.

"Laz was very low-keyed and the Greek was hoping to get some reinforcement from him regarding the bet he had made on Affirmed," disclosed Goldberg. "He didn't get any. Jimmy was forlorn until he looked around and spotted Wayne Lukas. The Greek immediately got up and approached him. Unfortunately, Lukas didn't have much to say either. Jimmy was exasperated. He had been worried about Cauthen's fall and got nothing from Laz to offer some confidence on the large wager he had going."

Cauthen had finally arrived at noon from New York and headed straight to the jockeys' room. He appeared unfazed by the importance of the Preakness, devouring a big lunch, then immediately taking part in a card came. After a couple hours, he would take time off to race before the Preakness, win, then return to the jockeys' quarters.

"Do you expect to set the pace today?" he was asked.

"It depends on what the other horses do," he replied. "I guess I might take the lead or just lay off the pace. What counts is that with Affirmed, it won't matter."

By now every car and every bus in Baltimore and its environs was heading in the direction of Pimlico. Chick Lang got his wish for sunshine, which he knew would generate a history-making crowd for the 103rd running of the Preakness he loved so much. And he knew the hot-dog and beer sales in the crowded infield would manifest in big dollars. On the wall in the press box hung a quote from the works of the late Tom O'Reilly, who wrote for the old *Morning Telegraph* until his death in 1962. This quote was written in 1959:

"Baltimore is one of my favorite towns in America. For me it has everything. A fellow with even a soupçon of imagination should never be bored there. It is indeed a fitting background for one of the greatest horse races on this continent—the Preakness."

Perhaps O'Reilly was fond of a couple of Preakness traditions that the Derby didn't have. One of the most alarming was a painter standing on a ladder next to a pole at the start of the race waiting to paint the winning stable's colors immediately after the horse crossed the finish line. Another tradition was the playing of the state song, "Maryland, My Maryland," as the horses paraded to the post. The glaring difference between the playing of this song and the playing of "My Old Kentucky Home" was that they cried in Kentucky during Stephen Foster's sentimental ballad.

The handicappers concluded the 1978 Preakness would be a two-horse race between Affirmed and Alydar with Believe It somewhere behind. Pimlico oddsmaker Earle Hart charted the numbers as Affirmed, 6–5; Alydar, 7–5; and Believe It, 5–1. By post time on Saturday, the odds would change. Affirmed was at even money, Alydar remained at 7–5, and

Believe It rose to 8-1. The remaining four rivals were at double-digit figures.

Veitch's confidence in Alydar was unwavering, and he wasn't at all concerned about the odds. Even though the race was being projected as a match race between Alydar and Affirmed, Veitch wasn't buying it.

"I think that anybody who'll say that it's going to be a match race doesn't know anything about horse racing because you never know on any given day when some horse will jump up and give a super effort and beat everybody," offered Veitch. "Of course, on past performances they go to the post and they load them in that gate, but past performances are behind them.

"My horse developed beautifully this season and is a better horse now than he was last fall. If the pace is realistic, Alydar will be right there."

Stephens had his thoughts about the race, and down deep one got the feeling that he believed Believe It had a chance.

"These three horses are not going to be too far apart at any stage of the Preakness," predicted Stephens. "The race could be more exciting than the Derby. Post position could be a factor in determining who is on the lead. A horse that drew number one might very well want to keep the rail all the way and might be in a position to protect his lead."

The horse who got the No.1 post in a drawing the day before was Noon Time Spender, a 15-1 shot. The drawing is a process much like bingo. The names of the entries are placed on a big board ranked by the money they've won, for the media to easily see. A track official, most often the racing secretary, draws numbered white balls, 1 to 7, from a bowl. Nothing scientific about it at all. Simply, it's the luck of the draw, and the trainers have to live with the result.

But Barrera figured that Stephens's horse would set the early pace.

"Woody Stephens tried his horse from behind in the Derby," recalled Barrera. "He got to my horse and my horse ran away from him. He has to do some changing. And the change I'm expecting him to do is to send his horse to the lead."

Barrera also pointed out that Veitch's idea of running closer to the pace in the Preakness might backfire on Alydar.

"He may lay third or fourth," suggested Barrera. "If he goes easy to that position, it's okay. But if you have to run him, you change your style on him after you teach him so long to rate him and bring him from behind. If you have to keep punching him to keep him close, that could be a very dangerous thing because probably he no gonna have no kick in the end."

Barrera had other problems. After Cauthen finished riding in the fifth race before the Preakness, he still hadn't seen Barrera, who was waiting to talk to him by the barn. The look on the trainer's face translated into anger in the early-afternoon sun.

"I'm mad at Stevie," he snapped. "He don't even call me yet. I wanted him out in the barn this morning so we could discuss how the race might run. He should have come here last night. Instead, he comes today. When you go out to the paddock to saddle the horses for the race, there isn't enough time to talk.

"All week I see things out here I feel I should explain to him, but in the paddock we have not time to talk. I want to talk to him at least ten minutes, because if you run a business you like to talk to the people who work for you. The Preakness is a big race. You've got to be careful. One mistake can cost you the race."

Barrera tempered his anger and collected his thoughts. He cared a great deal about Cauthen.

"Don't misunderstand. I like Steve very much and feel like his second father. But I don't want this to happen again. I will discuss the problem with his father in the nicest way possible."

This was as personal as Barrera got with a reporter. His attention then turned harmlessly to Gino Alongi, a twelve-year-old kid who wanted to be a jockey. The boy in all his innocence wanted to know about people who bet large sums of money at the racetrack. Barrera, the father figure that he is, patiently explained it to him.

"Some men have good luck and some have bad," began Barrera in a story-tone monologue. "Bad-luck men never seem to get rid of it. I once heard a story about a man named John Smith, and he has very bad luck. Even if he bet on a horse to show, the horse finishes fourth. His friends no want to go to the races with him because he is such bad luck.

"Then, John Smith isn't seen at the racetrack for several days and his friends get worried. They go around the hotel he is staying. John Smith is not around and nobody knows where he is. The friends look all over and then go to the mortuary and ask, 'Maybe you got a man here named John Smith? He's very unlucky. He could be here.'

"They open a drawer in the mortuary and see a body, but it is not John Smith in the drawer. Number two is not John Smith either. Nor in three. They pull open drawer four and find John Smith lying there. One of his friends looks at the body and say, 'John Smith, even here you finish out of the money.'"

When Cauthen finally showed up at the barn, he huddled with Barrera for only about three minutes. The crafty trainer was expecting more time with his cherub-faced jockey but there wasn't any. It was time for the paddock, and it would be a far different one this time for Barrera, but it didn't concern Cauthen. Laz's son Albert, a trainer, would saddle a horse named Track Reward, which upset Laz. He had strongly urged his son not to waste his horse in the Preakness, a race he didn't have a chance at winning. The irony of it all as it played out was that Track Reward, a 12–1 pick, was just two spots away from Affirmed in the No. 4 spot, too close for Barrera's comfort. The possibility of Track Reward luring Affirmed into a speed duel troubled Barrera.

Before the horses moved to the track, Barrera learned that two bettors earlier in the day had bet $60,000 on his horse to win. His eyes flashed with alarm.

"That's crazy," he exclaimed. "Anything can happen. Once in Mexico City, there was a three-horse entry and the horses figured to finish one-two-three. People placed big bets on the entry because you got all three horses running for you for the same price. The gate opens up and two horses in the entry slam together and fall down and the third horse stumbles over the two on the ground."

In past years, the Preakness had been a stumbling block for many of the Triple Crown contenders. Nine horses who looked unbeatable after winning the Derby tasted defeat in the Preakness, which eliminated them from winning the Triple Crown. That was the bugaboo hanging over Affirmed. And in the shorter Preakness, with its sharp turns, Affirmed under Cauthen would have to run a different race. He is a more versatile horse than the headstrong Alydar, who had established a pattern of coming from behind for his wins. Like a counterpunching boxer, Affirmed could do anything and had done so efficiently. Their contrasting styles highlighted their heated duels.

Veitch was right about Alydar. Leaving the paddock in full view of a record 81,261 horse lovers, the largest crowd ever to watch a sporting event in Maryland, Alydar looked superbly fit and appeared every bit ready to run the race of his life. As usual, Affirmed also looked in great condition and as always had a relaxed demeanor. In his Florida winter, Alydar was unbeatable. He showed awesome bursts of speed that blew away his rivals. It was Florida weather in Baltimore with no hint of rain. On this abnormally hot afternoon for the third week in May, the sun was sending the temperature into the high eighties. All seven horses cooperated and entered the gate without any mishaps. A hush momentarily descended on Pimlico.

The record crowd roared with the opening of the gates. The horses sprang smoothly with no entanglements. They were closely bunched at the start, and as Barrera expected, his son's colt, Track Reward, assumed the early lead. Believe It didn't move out as was anticipated, and Affirmed moved up alongside Track Reward. Using his instincts, Cauthen urged Affirmed into the lead. It was a vital decision in Cauthen's thinking, and it bolstered Affirmed's chance of winning while it was still early in the race. No one wanted to set the pace, and Cauthen wisely decided to take charge. He was aware that Alydar wasn't far behind as he had been in the Derby. Before Alydar made his move, Cauthen wanted to open up a lead.

That's exactly what he did. Affirmed wasn't challenged and remained in front and enjoyed a length's lead after six furlongs. Noon Time Spender, an atrocious 81-1 shot, had the temerity to test Affirmed, as Believe It remained third. The three leaders remained that way as they vacated the backstretch and glided into the far turn. Until now, Velasquez had kept Alydar under restraint, only 4½ lengths from the smooth-running Affirmed with a confident Cauthen on his back.

When the horses reached the top of the stretch, Cauthen looked back for Alydar, who began making his move on the backstretch. He wasn't sixteen lengths behind as in the Derby. He was a slim 1½ lengths back after passing Noon Time Spender and Believe It. With the crowd's noise rising in decibels, Cauthen knew it was the beginning of Alydar's charge. The spectators whooped and hollered as the horses approached the stretch. Velazquez rated Alydar evenly and got him closer to Affirmed, only a length behind. A roaring crowd anxiously awaited the ending. All the way to the finish line the two fought for the lead with legs flying, never more than a half-length apart.

Alydar kept coming but Affirmed resisted and remained in front. His pride and tenacity kept him there. Cauthen had him placed perfectly throughout the race. Affirmed was moving crisply. Cauthen went to his whip to keep him focused. The duel was on and Cauthen hit Affirmed with ten measured, right-handed strokes. Velasquez, too, went to the stick, ten times on the right side and two more on the left. Alydar inched a little closer, but that's all. Cauthen put away his whip and went across the finish line with a hand ride and a neck ahead of Alydar. As good as Cauthen handled Affirmed in the Derby, he exceeded it in the Preakness with a superb ride.

"I can hardly believe what I saw," exclaimed Lang. "I was standing in the infield near the finish line, and I swear, as he bore down, Affirmed had his teeth bared like a fighter moving in for the kill."

Barrera had saddled his first Preakness winner. But the jubilation it afforded was abruptly tempered. Security guards ushered Cauthen from the winner's circle to the press area, completely ignoring Barrera. When Barrera finally reached the press-box elevator, the door was rudely slammed in his face. It riled the hot-blooded Cuban so much that he never waited for the elevator to return and missed the press conference. It was inexcusable that the winning trainer wasn't made as much a priority as the jockey. As he addressed the writers in the press conference, Cauthen was unaware of what had happened to Barrera.

"I was waiting for Alydar," confessed Cauthen. "When he came to me, I set my horse down at the head of the lane. Velasquez set his horse down and my horse beat him. In the last few jumps, Alydar might have gained a few inches, but my horse was still running. He wasn't going to pass us up. I guess he gained a few inches when I hand-rode him at the end.

"Alydar ran a better race than he did in the Derby. He came to my horse at the head of the stretch. In the Derby, he made his move late. Today he ran game. They stuck together and he had no excuse. If Alydar was another horse, his heart would be broken now. He's run into Affirmed all these times but he keeps trying to win."

Cauthen ran a perfect race. The Kid was coming of age. He certainly didn't look like an eighteen-year old but every inch a veteran in winning the two biggest races of his life. He was two-thirds of the way to the Triple Crown, and his ride today impressed Danny Wright, who was on board Cormorant to a fourth-place finish in the Preakness the previous year.

"If he was a better horse, Alydar should have beaten him when he caught up in the stretch," analyzed Wright. "But the best one came in first and the second-best came in second. The Kid may look like a choirboy, but he deserves everything he's got in racing. You can't be jealous of him. He does things right, and every other jockey has professional respect for him. He's got a lot together a lot earlier in life than most jockeys. Steve Cauthen arrived young with great instincts and nobody begrudges him anything."

Velasquez, too, delivered a good race. There was no questioning his handling of Alydar this time. There wouldn't be any more letters in Veitch's mailbox or any phone calls to the Markeys, who suffered a second straight disappointment. But in horse racing, it's often the better horse who wins. And that had been Affirmed. Alydar came closer in the Preakness, but not enough. Maybe against another horse, but not Affirmed.

"Man, I'm hot, hotter than the horse," quipped Velasquez. "No excuse. Today he was trying. I was where I wanted to be and I thought I might win. But I also knew that Affirmed likes to wait for other horses when he gets ahead. So I knew that I'd have to battle him. And I did, but we got beat.

"Mr. Veitch had him ready for the race, he broke sharp, he handled the track well, he was well placed, he had a beat on

Affirmed, and when I asked him to respond, he responded.
The other horse just won.

"I was where I wanted to be. Didn't want him to drop back
like he did in the Derby and then people criticize me because
they thought I took him back. That's bull. I didn't take him
back. He took himself back. He wasn't trying that day. But today he was trying. I got beat."

Veitch remained upbeat and wanted another shot at Affirmed. He knew he had Alydar primed and he showed it, and
Velasquez rode him beautifully. Veitch had no excuses and
didn't talk about any. Being a student of history in college, he
could surely visualize that the Affirmed-Alydar battles were
becoming a sure piece of thoroughbred history.

"I just wish my horse's neck was a little bit longer," he said,
smiling. "It was a true test. It was a good horse race. When you
come this close, you can't give up. Jorge rode a perfect race and
the horse ran a perfect race, I thought. He outgained us there
just at the very end. But when you come that close, I ain't afraid
of him. We'll catch him someday. When you get beat like
that, there's no telling every time you meet who'll come out
on top.

"Affirmed is a very, very tough racehorse, and there's no telling how far he'll go. We just didn't make it today. Maybe next
time we will."

There wouldn't be a next time for Believe It, who finished
third in a credible performance. Woody Stephens intended to
keep his horse away from both Affirmed and Alydar. Earlier in
the year he felt Alydar had the edge over Affirmed.

"I can't beat them," admitted Stephens. "I've always said
they were tough, and if they made mistakes, then maybe I

could get there. To me, Alydar wouldn't have beaten Affirmed if they went around again. I'm going wherever they ain't. So long, Affirmed. Bye-bye, Alydar."

His jockey, Eddie Maple, felt the same way. Maple was on board Alydar three times the previous year before he was replaced by Velasquez.

"It starts to fall into a one-two-three category," explained Maple. "My horse is a good horse. A very good horse. But as far as Affirmed goes, he's the head of the class of a bunch of very good horses.

"Alydar is too good a horse in one respect not to give him another shot in the Belmont. But, then, he's too good a horse not to be knocking out first-place money somewhere else."

Immediately after the press conference, Cauthen left to catch an airplane to New York. He never took the time to see, much less talk to, Barrera. That, too, hurt Laz. An hour or so later, Barrera had cooled down by his barn, but there was still anger in his words.

"It went exactly the way it should have," he claimed. "When they turned for home, I knew Affirmed would win. I've been telling you all week he would." Then Barrera's anger surfaced. "I always try to be very good to the writers, giving them plenty to write about in the papers. But now all I read is Stevie wins this, Stevie wins that. I think I deserve more respect than that.

"Another thing. I see all the riders here at the barn this morning, talking to their trainers. But, Steve, he no show up until the race starts today. I'm going for one of the biggest races in the world and my rider isn't here to go over strategy with me.

"I only had three minutes in a crowded paddock to talk to my rider. I don't know if I should blame Steve, because he is so young, or his agent, Lenny Goodman. But I do know that even if he is a star, he should have been here earlier with me."

Saturday night in New York, Cauthen was apprised of Barrera's acerbity and quickly fashioned an apology toward the person he looked upon as a second father.

"I feel terrible about this," sighed Cauthen. "Laz has been like a father to me and I would never do anything to upset him. Everything happened so fast at that elevator, and I never realized he'd been left behind.

"And if I'd known he wanted me to go to Pimlico earlier, I would have. I thought we both know Affirmed so well there was no need to talk about the race. But, if he'd asked me, I'd have been there. I'll tell you one thing; I won't make a mistake like this again."

Sometimes a good night's sleep after a feel-good day is the best sedative. After he had his morning coffee, Barrera revisited the previous day's tempest.

"I didn't mean to blast Steve like the stories say," retracted Barrera. "I'm not mad at him. I love him like a son. In California this winter we weren't winning many races. I said to him, go and get some other mounts. But he said, 'No, I'm sticking with you.'"

"That's how close we are, and nothing like this will come between us. It's just that you maybe get one chance in your life to win the Triple Crown, and you don't want to ruin it with some little mistake."

It didn't appear that losing it would happen with Affirmed, Cauthen, and the guile of Barrera. Yet, Veitch was intent on getting another shot at Affirmed in the Belmont. He kept telling himself he could win. He was obsessed.

TEN

The Belmont

Been around racing fifty years,
but Affirmed and Alydar in the Belmont?
The best horse race there's ever been.

—Woody Stephens,
Hall of Fame trainer

The vestiges of late spring with the approach of summer presented a myriad of scenarios in the sports world. But that sunny New York day in June, it was all about Affirmed and Alydar. They had now run a total of 7⁹/16 miles against each other. After six victories, Affirmed had a cumulative margin of 2½ lengths over his stubborn rival. They had practically run as one, especially so in the Preakness, and even before they had a look at one another in the Belmont, the pair had become the greatest two-horse rivalry in racing's storied history.

Joe Hirsch, the dean of the nation's turf writers, framed the race perfectly: "One of the greatest rivalries in the history of thoroughbred racing will be recorded when Affirmed goes after a sweep of the Triple Crown against Alydar. Fans throughout the country are excited at the ninth meeting of Affirmed and Alydar, a rivalry that may be without parallel in the sport."

Even Cauthen was adding to the prerace hype across the country. Early one morning, Cauthen was up before the sun to do a live television appearance on the *Today* show and had no qualms about his horse.

"Affirmed will run his race, don't worry about that," he assured the viewers. "He always does."

A confident Barrera boldly predicted an Affirmed victory in an interview with Tom Cunningham of the *Albany Times-Union* after Cauthen finished his TV gig. "It will be his easiest race," gushed Barrera. "If he isn't in shape, then there is no horse in America that is in shape."

Barrera didn't hide his feelings in the interview. Inwardly he felt Affirmed could have won all nine races against Alydar.

"In his first race, when Affirmed came out of the gate, it hit him," explained the likable Cuban. "He split his lip and knocked a tooth out. And, in that race, he spotted Alydar five pounds.

"In the Champagne Stakes, my horse was between Darby Creek Road and Sauce Boat, battling for the lead, and never saw Alydar on the far outside. If he had, Alydar never would have gone past him."

The New York Racing Association experienced the great anticipation of Affirmed's challenge for the Triple Crown. The NYRA received more press requests than at any other Belmont. Any media type who could spell *horse* applied for a credential. Over one hundred were allocated and track officials had to improvise special seating to accommodate the overflow of media.

At one time it was possible to tell the time of year by the games that were being played. But the tentacles of television, needing programming, spoiled all that with sporting events overlapping one another. Only the sport of thoroughbreds remained constant, and that's all the horse lovers care about. The Kentucky Derby arrives on the first Saturday in May, followed by the Preakness exactly two weeks later, and finally on another Saturday, three weeks after the Baltimore classic, comes the Belmont. It's been turf gospel for as long as anyone can remember, and Affirmed and Alydar were ready to add chapter and verses to the most anticipated Triple Crown ever. Yet, for someone who had relished considerable success in Triple Crown competition as it was presently conducted, Laz Barrera was not exactly enamored with the arrangement. And Barrera, a sweet, insouciant person, freely spoke about it.

"There is too much pressure on the horses," protested Barrera. "And too much pressure on the trainers. If you ran cheap horses three times in five weeks, everyone would say you're ruining the horse. Now we are racing the finest three-year-olds in the country three times in five weeks and sandwiching in two trips, one from Louisville to Baltimore, and the other from Baltimore to New York."

Barrera always felt that the horse was more important than any jockey. He believed it was up to him to train a horse to perfection for a race, especially since the racing season had become longer.

"When the concept of the Triple Crown came into being, there wasn't nearly as much racing as there is now," pointed out Barrera. "There was no major winter racing. They were trained to the classics. Maybe they had a prep race and maybe they didn't. Now you start your horses on January first, and you give him a prep race after prep race before the Kentucky Derby. Look at Affirmed. He ran in the Santa Anita Derby and the Hollywood Derby with only two weeks between.

"I've been lucky with my two colts, Bold Forbes and Affirmed, but a lot of other colts have been worn out and injured because of this speedup and the pressure of the Triple Crown races. I've been on the go with Affirmed since the first of the year, and it's been a grind. It's wonderful to have a fine horse, but I'll be glad when it's over this weekend."

Barrera knew Affirmed was a special animal when he first laid eyes on him as a two-year-old. He felt it the moment he looked into the horse's face and tenderly grabbed his bridle. The chemistry between trainer and horse was manifested that instant, and it was left to Barrera to turn Affirmed into a champion. In the two years, which is an eternity in racing circles, he had done just that. Affirmed had been crowned two-year-old king and was looked upon to becoming the three-year-old one if he could complete the Triple Crown with a victory in the exhausting Belmont Stakes, a mile-and-a-half challenge that was had been a graveyard for so many others seeking racing's biggest nirvana.

Barrera had had good horses and bad ones, which so often define a trainer's skill, but nothing quite like Affirmed. Barrera recognized his greatness and never babied the prize of Louis Wolfson's stable. In 1976 and 1977, Barrera brought home winning purses that totaled $5,246,546 and in both those years took along the Eclipse Award as Trainer of the Year. In

1976 he had an opportunity to pursue the Triple Crown with Bold Forbes and came ever so close. But after winning the Kentucky Derby, Barrera had to patch up Bold Forbes's legs for the Preakness, which resulted in a third-place finish. Barrera never quit on his horse and entered him in the Belmont Stakes and won it with Angel Cordero steadying him across the finish line.

But 1978 would be different. He felt it and down deep felt that Affirmed would make it happen. In all his intense engagements with Alydar, Barrera's confidence in Affirmed never diminished. And now before the biggest of the races, it was unwavering.

"It will be these two horses again," he said flatly. "It was those two horses last year and it's been these two horses all along. And Affirmed has always had a little edge on Alydar. He's showed it at two last season and he's shown it this year. Affirmed is a great horse. His record will tell you that. He is just a little bit better than Alydar, and he has to be because Alydar is an extraordinary colt."

The intensely anticipated duel between Affirmed and Alydar was expected to magnetize a record crowd at the Long Island track and the race named for August Belmont, who was instrumental both as an owner and a breeder in establishing thoroughbred racing as a big-time sport in New York. From the time that it opened on May 4, 1905, Belmont has remained the largest track in the nation. The first Belmont Stakes took place in 1867 at Jerome Park in the Bronx, not far from where Yankee Stadium is today. It remained there until 1890, when it was transferred to Morris Park, then remained there until Belmont Park's grand opening.

Grandstand seats were priced at $2 and field seats for 50¢, and an estimated three hundred bookmakers were on the grounds to handle the action under a caste system. The eighty most honorable bookies occupied the first ring. Behind them were a hundred lesser bookies, and one hundred twenty of the lowest group grabbed the best spots in front of the stands. They were a licentious bunch known as hurdlers because these guys commonly hurdled fences and disappeared into the woods to escape paying off big bets.

When antibetting legislation was passed in the New York Senate, Belmont was forced to shut down for two years before it reopened in 1913. While racegoers liked the beauty of Belmont, horsemen didn't like the racetrack at all. Races were conducted clockwise after the custom in England, and not until 1921 did Belmont convert to conventional counterclockwise racing.

When Belmont was under reconstruction from 1963 to 1967, the race was held at Aqueduct. Its traditions have undergone changes. For decades, the theme song at the Belmont was "The Sidewalks of New York." It was replaced in 1977 with "New York, New York," to attract younger fans. That same year, the official drink was changed from the White Carnation to the Belmont Breeze, which the *New York Times* reviewed as "a significant improvement over the undrinkable White Carnation despite the fact that it tasted like refined trash can punch."

Barrera knew all about trash cans, having been raised a block away from Oriental Park, a racetrack built on land that once belonged to his grandfather. As one of twelve kids, he had to work hard to help bring food into the house. And he did so with pride. He walked the horses to cool them down after a workout seven days a week for a pittance of $3. He kept 50¢ for himself and gladly gave $2.50 to his mother.

It was as if Barrera had never left his native Cuba. In the fifteen years since he'd left Castro's island, he still talked with the emotion of the years he spent there. His memories were deep and he still maintained a love for its land and people. His full name is Lazaro Sosa Barrera, but he was affectionately called Laz by everyone in racing's kingdom. Despite his success on any number of ovals around the country as well as in Cuba and Mexico, he was low-key, and ruggedly handsome, which belied his fifty-three years, and was a Casey Stengel–type character with stories flavored with metaphors in broken English. Well respected as a trainer, he had paid his dues along the way, even to the point of being broke.

"I remember the first time I went to the track," he remarked one day outside his barn office. "I was maybe four or five. It was Cuban Christmas and it was being celebrated at Oriental Park. The children were given gifts and a man gave me a new baseball. I never had a new ball before and I rubbed it and looked at it like it was something made of magic. Everyone watched the races and I played with the ball."

Barrera's eyes lit up as he continued talking about his youth. At sixteen, he applied for a trainer's license and became deeply involved four years later by spending $50 to buy a horse. Although he experienced a period of bad luck, it nevertheless changed his life completely. He was relaxed now, sitting by the barn waiting for the race, and enjoyed looking back at his career.

"A hurricane hit Cuba," he noted. "The track was destroyed and had to be rebuilt. My horse got all cut up by flying glass and he could never run, so I set off for Mexico City. Training in Mexico was tough. If you didn't do well for an owner right away, you hear the sound of the vans backing up to take the horse away. At one time I had seventy horses to train and had the best owner in Mexico to work for. He loved me. He would call me in the morning and say, 'Laz, please don't eat breakfast before I get there. I want the joy of eating breakfast with you. I'll cook for the grooms and all the help.' He would say that I was working too hard and we should fly to Acapulco to rest. I would tell him the only reason I was tired was because he kept me up all night. We would go to Acapulco and get in great games of dominoes, and we'd win because I could really play dominoes."

Barrera was in a sentimental mood. He never forgot his early travails in racing and quite often reflected upon them.

"I had another owner in Mexico City and he thought he knew everything," Barrera continued. "The first five horses I ran for him won, but the sixth was beaten by a nose at the wire. This crazy man runs down from the stands and wants to beat up the jockey. I told him I wouldn't train for him anymore and I went to the stewards and told them so, too. They said, 'He has you under contract, and if you don't train for him, you cannot train here.' I said, 'The hell with this,' and went to Cleveland, Ohio, and became a jockey agent."

Barrera only stayed in Cleveland for a year. He returned to Mexico City and resumed his career as a trainer. Barrera and Affirmed were at the door of history with a sensational eighteen-year-old jockey. Yet on the biggest day of his turbulent life, he wanted to look back.

"Racing is such a strange sport," he said, shaking his head.

"In 1951 I flew out of Mexico City with twenty-seven thousand dollars in hundred-dollar bills in sacks. I was going to the United States to buy a horse named Crafty Admiral for an owner who wanted the horse returned to Mexico City. Crafty Admiral was for sale for twenty-five thousand dollars and been a good two-year-old. We got to Miami and it looked like the sale was all set, but the veterinarian wouldn't okay it because he didn't think the horse was sound."

It was quite a predicament for Barrera. Maybe another trainer would have taken a chance and bought the horse and earned a commission. But Barrera was just too honest.

"I didn't know what to do, but I didn't want the plane to go back empty so I filled it up with hay and straw and we flew back with no Crafty Admiral," revealed Barrera. "Later he was sold for less than twenty-five thousand dollars and went on to be an excellent horse. If he had raced in Mexico, he probably never would have been heard of and might have broken down.

"You see, if Crafty Admiral had gone back to Mexico City with me, I would not have Affirmed today. There probably wouldn't be any Affirmed today because Crafty Admiral became the sire of Won't Tell You, Affirmed's mother!"

The vicissitudes of racing made this the most improbable Belmont of them all: an astute businessman in Wolfson, who had extended his principles in the business world to raising horses; a Cuban refugee who had demonstrated a genius in overcoming adversity; and a tender eighteen-year-old jockey, the son of a small-town blacksmith, who appeared to have an innate gift for riding horses like no one before him. They were like a bunch of nobodies challenging the reputation of Calumet.

Veitch, too, looked back at history, which came naturally for him ever since his college days in Peoria, Illinois. He and his horse were intricately responsible for this duel, and even though they were coming up short at the finish line, he had never wavered in his high regard for Alydar. He made a remark after the Preakness that wasn't one of surrender: "Remember, the South won the first battles in the Civil War, but the North rose in the stretch and won going away."

Belmont was indeed north. And the battlefield would be one and a half miles of dirt. Racing Secretary Tommy Trotter suggested that six horses would enter the race. "There are always a couple of horses around whose trainers think they can go a mile and a half," reasoned Trotter. "Six, that's a nice round figure."

None of it would alter the equation. It would remain Alydar vs. Affirmed. When the entries were closed, Trotter missed by one. Five horses were officially in. Besides the logical two, Darby Creek Road, Noon Time Spender, and Judge Advocate got their names in the program and the tout sheets. Woody Stephens didn't want any part of it with Believe It, while Judge Advocate was a surprise entry that stimulated questions at the press-conference breakfast of "Who?" When the post positions were drawn, a tone of incredulity came over the microphone. Alydar got the No. 2 post and next to him was Affirmed at No. 3. They couldn't be any closer to each other if they shared the same stall.

Veitch was now the center of attraction for the media and was one up on Barrera. Only Alydar should do as good on Saturday. He would have a new look to produce a much needed victory. Veitch revealed that Alydar would run the Belmont without blinkers, after wearing the half-cup oculars with slits on the side in the first four races as a three-year-old. Veitch also admitted that he had been thinking about the change for quite some time. Veitch, a gracious loser against Affirmed, had always been honest and accommodating to the writers.

"Actually, I first gave thoughts to taking the blinkers off before the Kentucky Derby," disclosed Veitch. "But he already won four in a row and I can just imagine the field day people would have if I had done it and he ran poorly. They would have crucified me. He's very much the professional about his work now and he really doesn't need them anymore.

"When you're running short races, blinkers can be useful for giving your horse a little more sharpness. But the Belmont at a mile and a half is something else again. When you're running the distance, you want your horse to be relaxed and run freely without restraint. If not, then he's not going to have anything left at the finish."

Veitch then explained his strategy for the race, which he was confident about. "I'm not planning to get hooked up in a speed duel. But if they try to run the first half mile slow, they'll have to be going head-to-head with Alydar. Stamina will be important, and I think my horse has the strength to wear the other one down at a mile and a half. I'm sure they'll drag each other quite a ways."

Barrera remained low-key. And he took that approach with Affirmed after the Preakness, not working him hard but restricting him to long gallops. He wasn't the least concerned about Alydar's equipment change and used some homespun philosophy to explain it.

"The loser has to change," snorted Barrera. "You win, you

cannot change anything. My horse is gonna go slow the first part. The last part of the race will be fast. I'm not worried. My horse can do anything."

The amiable Cuban was hinting at pace. With such a small field and an uncrowded track, post position was not a factor. There was no question that the race would result in another tenacious match race between Affirmed and Alydar, with stamina, and not necessarily speed, determining the outcome, allowing the Harbor View star to hold off the Calumet ace. Barrera had no concern even regarding Cauthen's judgment in the longest race of his young career.

"He is very good at judging pace," remarked Barrera. "I think Alydar will be lying third or fourth and then come to me in the backside. And then, they're both going to go."

Goodman was delighted that Veitch had decided to pull the blinkers off Alydar.

"This is not the time to experiment," he exclaimed between puffs on his ever-present cigar. "They're groping and they don't know where to reach."

John Russell, the trainer of Judge Advocate, was an Englishman who thought American. He offered an opinion about Alydar's blinkers, which he felt contributed to the horse's losses in the Derby and Preakness.

"A horse can't see much off to the side through those slits," he remarked in an unmistakable British accent. "Alydar finished way out in the middle of the track, and he may have lost contact with Affirmed down on the rail."

When asked about his horse, he was brutally honest in admitting that he was entered just to pick up a check. Dry British humor was in his answer. "He is bred to run the distance.

The only question is how long it is going to take him to run it. And what better to find out than in a hundred-thousand-dollar race?"

Two days before the race Barrera appeared so relaxed that he didn't hurry to leave the press conference. Instead he hung around talking to a few friends and was content to tell stories, none of which concerned Affirmed. Winners can do that easily enough. This one was about a habitual bettor he knew in California, and he told it in his best Stengelese:

"This man in California, he is betting like crazy. He is walking around with all kinds of information under his arm, like he don't have no place to go, and when he is betting, he is losing his shirt, which he don't have. So, this friend of is, who has a big factory, he says to him, 'Look, I give you a job, twenty-four thousand dollars a year, which is big money, only you don't go to the racing Saturday and you don't go to Caliente on Sunday.' The guy said, 'No Caliente on Sunday, I don't take the job.'

"So, the guy who owns the big factory says he knows a big psychiatrist. He says he is confident the guy will get help, maybe. So, the guy goes to see the psychiatrist, who says, 'What's it all about, what about this racing?' "

Once more, Barrera was waxing about his past. He was a colorful storyteller, comfortable in relating his experiences.

"Well, the guy says, 'You don't see racing before? It is wonderful. You come with me.' So, they go to Hollywood Park and they put forty dollars together and they bet, and that day the patient picks six winners, they make three thousand dollars. What happened now is, the psychiatrist gets a load of this, he can't stay away. Now he's at the track every day with all kinds of information under his arms trying to beat the horses. The patient, I think, is cured."

Veitch with a number of writers around him at the other end of the room was absorbed in talking about the race. Trainers are a rare breed and unlike any others in sports. They carry a large responsibility for horses like Affirmed and Alydar, who are inordinately fragile and emotionally demanding of constant attention.

"Somebody pointed out to me that no Triple Crown winner has ever won the Preakness by so narrow a margin as Affirmed," related Veitch. "So, maybe that will take a little bit out of Affirmed. Maybe he'll just run one tough furlong too many, and in the Belmont Alydar will finally catch him. Alydar will be Affirmed's shadow.

"Everybody realizes now that the Derby was not a characteristic race for Alydar, that he didn't run to form, and they realize that in the Preakness more pressure was against Alydar more than in any of the races in the series. It is a little bit conducive to speed horses.

"The Preakness is like a watershed after the Derby in that a lot of horses that ran in the Derby that had speed but wouldn't go the distance weren't there to occupy a horse like Affirmed. So, Affirmed was going to get his way in the Preakness. The speed horse, if he is a good horse, will get his way in the Preakness more than in the Derby or the Belmont."

Veitch may have been frustrated about the two races, but he seemed upbeat about Alydar's chances in the Belmont. He didn't hesitate talking about it.

"In both the Derby and the Preakness I was disappointed. I was very impressed with Affirmed and also I was very impressed with Alydar's courage in the Preakness. I've been thinking of how I can get a neck closer. Stamina was always Alydar's strong card, and coming from behind, going a mile and a half, it minimizes the advantage of a speed horse like Affirmed.

"Maybe we'll catch him a little bit before the stretch, something like that. We'll probably be better off if we can wait until the last eighth, but I think we'll be wearing him down a little before that. If we don't really hook him until the last eighth, and if he should have anything left, it might be difficult to overwhelm him."

Affirmed was so good and so was Alydar that the margin between them was minimal. The only dimension Alydar lacked was Affirmed's speed, and the gutsy competition between the two had given the sport such a lift and even won the admiration of rival trainers. One, at trackside Friday, was Allen Jerkens. He'd already formed an opinion about the next day's race, and Jerkens was an excellent judge of horseflesh:

"It's amazing to me that Affirmed and Alydar are still going strong after such hard campaigns at two. It's also amazing they could have run so many close races together. In all my experience around the racetrack, I can't recall a rivalry like it.

"Affirmed is one of the best three-year-olds I've seen. He does everything so easily. He's got speed but can be rated. I ran against him in the Kentucky Derby and was impressed. Horses like Alydar, who are trained to come from behind, usually prefer to race that way. You can't push a button and have them up with the leaders. If you keep nudging them, you run the risk of taking something out of them so that they don't have their customary late punch."

Whether he won tomorrow or not, Barrera was having a

more ostentatious career than any of his American peers had ever experienced. That's speaking volumes for a once down-and-out trainer from Cuba, through Mexico, and finally in America. His stable of horses, and they numbered fifty, through May 25 had earned $2,013,947, a million more than his closest competitor, Charlie Whittingham. Already in 1978 he had accumulated twenty-one stakes wins, a prodigious accomplishment any trainer would relish over two years. What would tomorrow bring? Since 1948, only eight horses had won the Derby and the Preakness, but only Secretariat and Seattle Slew were good enough to take the Belmont.

"On Belmont day my ulcer will bother me again and the blood pressure will go up," confessed Barrera. "When I get up in the morning and look in the mirror, I'll say, 'Lazaro, you are having a big year. You should be proud. Laz, why aren't you smiling?'"

That would easily happen if Affirmed beat Alydar again.

—— THE RACE ——

The early-morning mist on the tenth of June was rapidly evaporating under a brilliant sun. It would indeed be a perfect day for racing. As usual, Barrera was an early visitor to his stable. The night before he hosted a barbecue for some thirty-five family members, and before it ended, he excused himself early and went to bed. There wasn't anything left for him to do with Affirmed. He had worked him easily all week and was pronounced fit by Barrera. The meticulous conditioner just wanted to see if Affirmed was at ease, something that he couldn't say about himself while waiting for the late-afternoon race.

"It's tough on your stomach, your mind, your nerves," diagnosed Barrera. "You say you should look in the mirror laughing in the morning, but you don't. You can't."

Affirmed's barn was quite a distance from Alydar's. They would get together later in the day. Barrera purposely wanted it this way. It had nothing to do with Alydar himself. Rather, Barrera was concerned about congestion around the stable area, which he wanted to avoid. It happens at times and Barrera had experienced it more than once.

"You remember last year when they packed so many cars in the stable area that Seattle Slew almost couldn't get through to the track?" growled Barrera. "My barn is so far from the track here I can't help worry about something like that. But if I send Affirmed over to the paddock too early, I risk getting him upset in the big crowd. Those little things, even with a great horse like this, they stay on your mind.

"Stevie will be on top galloping easily today. It's going to be my easiest race."

That said a lot. More than a prediction—a statement. While much had been made of Cauthen's youth, being overlooked was Cauthen's precocity in managing 1½-mile races. He demonstrated as much the previous fall in quite a few big races. He won both divisions of Belmont's Manhattan Handicap, won the Washington, D.C., International at Laurel, and earlier this spring at Santa Anita took Noble Dancer II, a 10–1 shot, across the finish line first.

"There are three important points to consider in riding races at a mile and a half," explained the Kid. "First, you should

know your horse. You've got to know what he can do and what
he can't do. Second, you've got to be able to judge the pace. I
practiced it a lot, even before I began riding, and experience
has given me more background. Third, you've got to ride your
own race to a considerable degree.

"Of course, if certain projections fail to materialize, you
may have to improvise, but essentially you've got to plan your
race and stick to the game plan."

Veitch was feeling every bit as confident as Barrera. He galloped Alydar in the early-morning hours while Barrera was
content to simple walk Affirmed on the shaded paths around
the stables. Two trainers, two different approaches. Vietch con-
tended that his horse needed to be occupied, and this morning, despite the significance of the race, was no different from
others.

"He's happiest when he's doing something," claimed Veitch.

Alydar had done better on this track than any other track.
He's beaten Affirmed twice on this racetrack. It's a mile and a
half with wide, sweeping turns. It doesn't give any horse, particularly a speed horse such as Affirmed, as much as advantage as sharper turns do.

It would be more about stamina this time than anything
else, whichever one had it, because Affirmed couldn't run that
fast in the first part of it and hope to last in the second part.
Alydar would have to be able to overcome him in the stretch.
But there was an important difference. There would be fewer
horses running this time than in the Derby or the Preakness.

There was no shadow anywhere over Belmont by ten o'clock,
three hours after the gates were opened to greet an expected
multitude of over eighty thousand people. By early afternoon

the hope for a record crowd dissipated. The Long Island Rail Road had experienced a large equipment failure that shut down service from Penn Station for the rest of the afternoon, and race lovers were loath to seek other modes of transportation. The highways would be jammed enough without absorbing an extra legion of automobiles. The ones who stayed away were satisfied with watching the Belmont on television in the comfort of their own homes. Offtrack-betting emporiums were also a neighborhood alternative.

The Belmont's record crowd was registered on June 5, 1971, when 82,694 fans filled the park to discover if Canonero II, a popular champion, could achieve the Triple Crown, only to witness his shocking finish out of the money as Pass Catcher won. That's how debilitating the Belmont can be, an exhausting journey for any thoroughbred. Since Citation in 1948, only Secretariat in 1973 and Seattle Slew in1977 had prevailed over the torturous route to achieve immortality. Secretariat, with a tsunami thirty-one-length victory is remembered most, and his prodigious record remains unchallenged.

That was part of the history that Affirmed and Alydar faced. In the weeks following the Preakness, the import of the Belmont escalated daily, and support between the horses showed only a modicum of difference. Both were heavily favored, Affirmed at even money and Alydar at 7–5, with only a hoof's length separating the two. It was theater, and the audience for the Belmont couldn't wait on the biggest stage of the Triple Crown.

Tony Triola, the maître d' at the clubhouse, knew better than anyone else what to expect weeks before the defining Saturday in June. He was inundated with requests for reserved seating that far exhausted his accommodations. It was a special Belmont indeed, and he relished the moment as never before.

"I've been begging everybody to cut off the reservations, because the demand is bigger than we had for Secretariat or Seattle Slew," bellowed Triola. "I'm overchairing everything now, turning four-seat tables into sixes and sixes into eights. I'm even setting up private buffets in some of the executive offices."

Since Belmont's record crowd, offtrack betting had victimized racetracks in all parts of the country, not even sparing the majestic Belmont. Nevertheless, on a pleasant, summery seventy-one-degree day, Belmont was as flush with celebrities as Triola had envisioned. His VIP list included, among others, New York governor Hugh Carey; Pete Rozelle; Washington Redskin quarterback Billy Kilmer; Wellington Mara; Phil Rizzuto; Al Rosen; Robert Sarnoff with his wife, opera star Anna Moffo; John and Dan Galbreath of Darby Dan Farm; Pittsburgh Steelers owner Art Rooney; Jimmy the Greek; and Louis and Patrice Wolfson; while Yankee owner George Steinbrenner entertained a party of friends.

The enticement of consecutive Triple Crown winners, which had never been accomplished, along with the cachet of the anticipated Affirmed-Alydar duel, which was acknowledged as the biggest in racing history, escalated the fever-pitch excitement. One of the more important figures was Perry Duryea, the minority leader of the New York State Assembly and a viable candidate for governor on the Republican ticket in the fall. He was a vital proponent of legislation to help racing. And where better than a racetrack to trumpet his message:

"The bill to assist New York tracks, now under consideration in Albany, has a few kinks that need working out. However, I am confident that it would ultimately pass and a likely target date is the week of June nineteenth.

"Both from an economic standpoint and as a sport with great appeal, racing is very important. Historically, New York has received more revenue from racing than any other state, and racing has attracted many tourists to our tracks here in the city, and upstate in Saratoga.

"Of late, we have faced competition from neighboring states including the Meadowlands track in New Jersey. We have to take whatever steps necessary to preserve our racing activity in New York at the strongest possible level."

Duryea received a strong endorsement from Governor Carey as they dined together in the VIP lounge.

"We are going to do it," assured Carey. "The legislation will be passed, and we will help thoroughbred racing. Not to do it would be irresponsible."

Sonny Taylor, one of the three judges assigned to the Belmont, has witnessed his share of big races. He was ready for the Belmont, calm and reserved with his valuable experience over the years.

"What I look for in a winning horse is fluidity of movement," disclosed Taylor. "I mean, the horse just seems to flow. If the horse has it, you spot it right away. Belmont puts you in mind of a racetrack. It's simply the best in the country."

Affirmed had the flow that Taylor looked for. Barrera felt that way about his horse and didn't mind answering questions several hours before the big race.

"Have you ever had a smarter horse?" he was asked.

"Not like this one." Barrera smiled without a second's hesitation.

Barrera spoke proudly about Affirmed in mentioning the seven races he won in nine starts as a two-year-old. The only two races Affirmed had lost in his last fifteen starts were to Alydar, and Barrera explained why. In 1977, in the Great American Stakes, which was held at Belmont that July, Alydar was given a five-pound weight advantage. The extra weight bothered Affirmed. He cut his lip in the starting gate, lost a tooth, and finished 3½ lengths behind the Calumet horse. In the Champagne Stakes that October, Affirmed was in a battle for the lead with Darby Creek and Sauce Boat. He didn't see Alydar, who charged past him on the outside for a length-and-a-quarter victory.

"He knows better now," emphasized Barrera. "Watch his ears in the stretch."

He explained to his listener that now when a horse comes up and charges at Affirmed, the smart colt gets the attention of Cauthen to the threat by pointing his ears. Barrera amplified his explanation by wiggling his fingers back and forth.

"A horse comes up on the outside," said Barrera, pointing his right finger. "'Hey, Stevie, a horse is on the inside,'" and Barrera demonstrated by pulling his finger back. "'Stevie, look.'"

This edge that Barrera brought to the track endeared him to Wolfson. In his eyes, Barrera was everything, and if anyone could deliver the Triple Crown, it was the likable Cuban. Wolfson needed the elusive relic to restore the image of Harbor View Farm, but more important, at least to him, his own. He still harbored a distasteful feeling of the time spent in jail eight years earlier that changed his personality. He was a star attraction to those who sought his company then, but now looked the other way. That Louis Wolfson served a term in prison would always be perpetuated in his biography. He hated the thought of it. The Triple Crown was his Holy Grail, one that would wash away to some degree people's misgivings. This was a special Belmont indeed.

Wolfson was a bit edgy the morning of the race. He went to sleep with the sobering thought that his dream of a Triple Crown might not come to pass. What disturbed him somewhat was that perhaps a rift had festered between Barrera and Cauthen ever since the Preakness that no one suspected. The jubilation then was tempered when Barrera was upset after the race at being ignored by the media, who swarmed around Cauthen as he headed to the press-box elevator, which would transport him to the interview area on the suite level high above the track. Barrera was visibly upset at being ignored, shoved aside by the track police while the elevator door was slammed in his face. If there was friction between the trainer and the jockey, it would only spell doom. Wolfson ruminated on the thought the entire morning.

However, he later learned that Cauthen had appeared almost every day of the week of the Belmont at Barrera's barn. Cauthen wanted to certify that there would be no further misunderstanding regarding the Preakness affair, and he did. There was no closer owner-trainer bond in racing than Wolfson-Barrera. They went back a long time from when Barrera was under contract with another owner. The stable was attempting to sell Wolfson a stakes horse for $200,000. If the sale was consummated, Barrera would benefit from a $20,000 commission, a good sum of money for Barrera, who wasn't earning big dollars then. When the deal was about to be completed in principle, Barrera quietly told Wolfson that the horse was unfit and not worth the money.

"I never forget that classy, self-sacrificing gesture," said Wolfson. "The first time I needed a trainer, I offered the job to Laz. He turned me down because he had a special loyalty to the man he was training for and didn't want to leave him. But I kept trying, and finally I was fortunate enough to join with a great trainer, and a great man."

Another area of concern also involved Cauthen. A year earlier, on the same Belmont track, he'd survived a tumultuous fall, and only the plastic riding helmet that hugged his head prevented a serious injury. Bay Streak, Cauthen's horse that day, was running without strain when his leg suddenly snapped. Bay Streak stumbled and then fell with Cauthen still in the saddle. Jorge Velasquez, driving his mount behind Cauthen, didn't have time to pull away and collided with Bay Streak. It left Cauthen motionless on the ground. When he was attended to while lying in the dirt, medics discovered a puffy eye, a slashed nose, and a bleeding right hand. Cauthen was immediately vanned to Long Island Jewish Hospital, where he remained for two days with a broken arm, two broken fingers, a fractured rib, and a concussion. Those close to him held their breath as the kid returned home to Walton to recuperate with a cast on his wrist. He vowed he would ride again. And soon, too. He did so six weeks later. That was the memory he was taking into the Belmont, and Wolfson could only hope that Cauthen wouldn't be thinking about the fall. He certainly remembered it though.

"The ribs hurt the most," he recalled. "And the rest of me,

well, I was trying to figure out just what happened. It was confusing for a little while but not scary."

The precocious youngster wasn't being arrogant. He was a youngster, and obviously a bit naïve. He didn't show any signs that he was affected by the fall when he returned to riding and now not before the Belmont. He was just a kid who had been riding for two years and wanted to keep doing so for as long as he could. He looked at his tumble as just a fall that could happen to any jockey, and Cauthen accepted it as part of the business. Eddie Arcaro, considered by many to be the top jockey of all time, endured a number of spills in a stellar career that produced over forty-seven hundred winners. Yet, he even carried the fear that weighs in a jockey's mind.

"There were plenty of times when I was afraid," confessed old Banana Nose, who had a near fatal spill on the same Belmont track. "Every day something would come up that would give me a scare. But I figured when I signed my name to be a jockey, death might be a part of it."

Tex Cauthen was well aware of Arcaro and how he, too, got his start in the Latonia–River Downs corridor and rose to the top of the jockey world. When a trainer had a good horse, he wanted Arcaro on him. Over the years, Arcaro got his share of them. What Johnny Unitas was to football, Arcaro was to horses. A horse advanced several lengths with Arcaro on his back. It was not considered wise to crowd him on a turn or get too close to him in the stretch. He could do anything on horseback that Jesse James or the Lone Ranger could.

In 1941, Calumet had a headstrong horse that could run with the wind. But he was temperamental and not many jockeys could handle him.

"You couldn't keep him between the fences," observed Arcaro. "He'd get five lengths in front and then head for the grandstand. He'd pull you off his back."

Calumet's trainer, Ben Jones, picked Arcaro to ride Whirlaway. The owner, Warren Wright, didn't. Jones threatened to quit if Arcaro wasn't allowed to ride the horse, and only then did Wright acquiesce. The strong-willed Arcaro took charge and drove Whirlaway into one of the great Kentucky Derby finishes of all time by eight lengths. Arcaro had tamed the Calumet star and won the Preakness handily by 5½ lengths, then won the Belmont just as easily.

"It's a question of who's going to be the boss," explained Arcaro simply.

In the 1950s, when he was aboard the great Nashua, Arcaro never had too many kind words for the champion thoroughbred. It didn't sit well with trainer Sunny Jim Fitzsimmons.

"Why do you keep knocking the horse when all he does is win?" asked Fitzsimmons.

"Because he ought to be fifteen lengths better than he is," snapped Arcaro.

Cauthen remained amazingly relaxed before the biggest race of his young life. He approached the Belmont with the same mind-set he possessed in the Kentucky Derby and the Preakness. He wasn't thinking about the Triple Crown but was concentrating on one race at a time. After he won both, the Triple Crown was there, and that's when Cauthen realized it, when he was getting ready to go to the Belmont paddock and unite with Affirmed.

Jimmy the Greek was already there. This race meant more to him than anyone else except perhaps the Wolfsons, Barrera, and Cauthen. Nobody knew about the $100,000 bet the Greek had made on Affirmed to win the Triple Crown. Like Affirmed, he was two-thirds of the way to winning his humongous bet. If it was going to be Affirmed's day, it would be his, too. And the Greek, who loves a good time, would party for a month eating gourmet meals and drinking good booze, which he shares with his friends, who know him as Demetrios Synodinos out of Steubenville, Ohio, who made it big.

"I was at the track when Riva Ridge won the Belmont," he was saying earlier in the afternoon. "For some reason or another, Riva Ridge never got the credit he should have gotten, as good a horse as he was. I would rather bet on Riva Ridge than Secretariat, Penny Tweedy's next horse. Riva Ridge was actually overlaid most of the time he ran. Secretariat took the country by storm and his prices were far shorter than they should have been.

"This day in the Belmont, I start looking at the board where Riva Ridge was three to two to win. I looked at the place price, and holy Moses, he's thirteen to ten or seven to five to place. I said to myself, 'Oh, gosh, that will change.' New York tracks get a tremendous impact from offtrack-betting shops around the city, with something like a million and a half dollars on a big race. Most of the OTB players played Riva Ridge to win, and the pie-in-the-sky bettors played the long-shot horses to place. A price of three to two to win and thirteen to ten to place is something like a three hundred percent overlay. He should have been three to five to place, returning sixty cents on the dollar. Here, he was returning a a dollar-thirty to a dollar."

The Greek had a quick mind for numbers, and with the amount of betting he did, he had to.

"I had five thousand dollars in my back pocket so I gave it to a friend, Mike Pearl, and sent him to the hundred-dollar place window with instructions to buy fifty tickets on number three [Riva Ridge]. The horse paid four dollars and sixty cents to place, and I won six thousand five hundred dollars, more than double what the horse should have paid. I had to go for the overlay."

The Greek was charismatic and was recognized anywhere he went, especially in Las Vegas, where he spent most of his time. He was a big guy who dressed well, often with a large gold chain visible around his neck that hung halfway down his chest. His appearance with Brent Musburger and Phyllis George on Sunday's CBS's *NFL Today* show was a must-see for pro football fans and had the high ratings to show for it. The national exposure projected the Greek's image in every living room and bar in America and magnetized him as a cartoon character. He had been a popular TV personality ever since the show first debuted in 1975.

Jimmy loved the horses. He made no secret about that. The hundred grand he wagered on Affirmed wasn't anything out of the ordinary for him. Some years earlier, he had placed a $50,000 bet on Tom Fool to win $10,000. That's how sure he was about the race and didn't hesitate in laying out the money.

"In 1959, I could have darned near retired from what I stood to win on Sword Dancer in the Kentucky Derby," said Jimmy. "I had taken up odds up to fifteen to one in the Winter Book in Caliente, on down to three to one, and by the day of the race, I had bet a total of nearly twenty thousand dollars across the board. In the stretch, Sword Dancer lost by a nostril in a photo finish to Tomy Lee.

"Though I made out on place and show, clearing nearly ninety thousand dollars, I had figured to win fifteen times that much. The kicker was that while Sword Dancer went on to be chosen Horse of the Year, Tomy Lee was to win only one more race in his career, an overnight in California."

At times the flashy Greek didn't have patience, but he did believe that it takes patience to develop a great horse. He contends that it can't be determined in two or three races. But, when it does happen, it could be money in the bank for those along for the ride. A bettor looks anywhere for inside information, but sometimes that can backfire. It happened to Jimmy in a classic experience and he didn't mind talking about it.

"In 1949, I was at a dinner party in Fort Lauderdale, attended by Jimmy Jones, the trainer for Calumet Farm," related the Greek. "The year before, they had won the Triple Crown with Citation. Now they had a Winter Book favorite for the Kentucky Derby.

"But at the party that night, Jimmy Jones let a bomb drop. 'Blue Peter won't be ready for the Derby,' he revealed. 'He hasn't been running up to expectations.'

"Now Fred Hopper had a horse called Olympia, and with Blue Peter out of it, I knew Olympia, listed at ten to one in the Winter Book, looked as the favorite. The price figured to drop to maybe three to one. 'We'll have Ponder ready,' Jones casually remarked, 'but it will be June before he's even close to his best stride.'"

Getting information like that was priceless. The Greek knew which way to go now.

"I sympathized with Jimmy, but when he said that, I mentally scratched Ponder. After dinner, I couldn't get back to Twenty-third Street in Miami Beach fast enough, rubbing my hands all the way. Everyone there had an opinion on the Derby. Twenty-third Street was a supermarket for people wanting to bet horses. That night I must have laid fifteen thousand dollars on Olympia for the Derby with odds of up to twelve to one.

"I watched the odds drop on Olympia with the inner contentment of a man who put his money in gold bullion shortly before the market crash of '29. Olympia went to the post as the favorite, at four to five, with Eddie Arcaro in the saddle. Olympia broke out in front and stayed there for a mile but finished sixth, barely in time to hear the last chorus of 'My Old Kentucky Home.' Naturally, you'll never guess which horse won— Ponder! And I didn't have so much as a bus token bet on him."

Cauthen looked as calm and patient as a trout fisherman in a Colorado stream as he paraded Affirmed in the paddock, which was bulging with admirers both for him and his horse. What Calumet was to racing, in a short time Affirmed and his teenage jockey had meant to Harbor View Farm. Horse and jockey had brought Louis and Patrice Wolfson out of the backstretch and into racing's elite in just two short years. Once in the starting gate, Cauthen and Affirmed were an irritant to other owners and horses.

The Kid was on the cusp of immortality as he along with Affirmed mesmerized the country in the quest for the Triple Crown. The mere possibility of it was a mega-attraction and in what bigger metropolis than New York.

The fuzzy-cheeked Cauthen's unflappable serenity on a twelve-hundred-pound animal had created success in a turbulent sport. Across Kentucky, he was already cheered as a homegrown icon despite his age. And he was twenty minutes from his final journey with Barrera's message: "Pace makes the race."

Alydar, too, was worthy of applause. He received a generous amount, which brought a smile to Velasquez's face. Velasquez also had another reason to smile. Entering June, he had been the hottest jockey on the circuit, having won 36 percent of his races. Although rivals, Cauthen and Velasquez were professionally friendly; each respected the other and more than once complimented one another.

When Cauthen and Velasquez reached the track on their extraordinary horses in full view of the crowd, a large roar erupted from the stands. Electricity was in the air, and Affirmed and Alydar illuminated Belmont like nothing before them. In Veitch's Civil War historical reference, it was Lee meeting Grant, only in the horse world, Alydar wasn't about to surrender, as Veitch had promised.

The cheers followed Affirmed and Alydar all the way to the end of the grandstand on their gallop to the starting gate. The serene scene of five beautiful thoroughbreds limbering their limbs ended. Alydar, as he often did, balked at being led to the gate. Judge Advocate was even more indignant and had to be helped into his position. As soon as he was in place, the gates immediately sprang open to eliminate any more delays. The Belmont was too big a race for that.

With no speed horses in the race to set the pace, Cauthen directed Affirmed to the middle of the track and into an opening lead. Horse and rider remained that way until the first turn, when Cauthen started to control the pace by pulling Affirmed back ever so slightly. As Veitch had instructed, Velasquez kept Alydar close behind in third place. Cauthen maintained the leader's pace until they reached the backstretch, when who else but Velasquez brought up Alydar to join him. The Kid recognized the move and accelerated Affirmed enough to maintain the lead on the rail.

The pace quickened. Over the next several furlongs, Alydar kept after Affirmed by matching his speed in what was developing into a furious early duel before they even reached the far turn. Veitch's strategy looked good at this point in that Alydar would be Affirmed's shadow. The two champions still had a long way to go in their one-upmanship before the vital stretch drive that would require every bit of stamina the horses possessed. Was Alydar's challenge too early?

The two distinct styles of Alydar and Affirmed would come into play. Alydar, the bigger horse, was powerful in finishing a race. He was never a front-runner. Instead, he excelled in coming from behind at the top of the stretch before fully exerting himself as a strong closer.

Affirmed was very much the opposite and was a bit faster than Alydar. He was comfortable staying close to the leader or just in front, setting the pace if he had to, but didn't exert himself unless he was challenged. Affirmed, too, was a strong stretch runner and really opened up if a horse began passing him. More often than not, he wouldn't let that happen.

Cauthen and Velasquez were relentless as they headed for the stretch amid the noise of the crowd. No one was seated as the horses matched each other stride for stride. Heads bobbed up-down, up-down, as on a merry-go-round. Velasquez kept Alydar so close to Affirmed's right that Cauthen would have difficulty extending a right-handed whip. Alydar collared Affirmed and poked his nose in front for a brief moment. Would Affirmed feel the pressure and yield to his antagonist for the first time?

It was a classic duel all right, in full view of everyone. Driving, driving, driving for every inch. It was like Jake LaMotta and Sugar Ray Robinson in Madison Square Garden, two warriors flailing away with both fists against each other, punch after punch, with no one falling to the canvas. It was a back-and-forth until one horse relented.

Track announcer Chic Anderson aroused the crowd when he bellowed, "Alydar and Affirmed are side by side with a mile to go."

Once Alydar nudged in front at the midpoint of the stretch, only he couldn't sustain the lead. Both came thundering down the stretch almost as one. Affirmed and Alydar showed no signs of yielding. Stride for stride, nose to nose. It would continue this way in front of a widely vociferous gathering until the end of an exhausting journey. With the finish line fifty yards away, the crowd was one collective chorus: cheering for Affirmed. Yelling for Alydar.

In one Herculean effort, Affirmed lunged forward from a

final urging from Cauthen and made history by a head. It was the most beautiful head in racing in what was the greatest stretch run in turfdom's annals. Cauthen the ultimate maestro. It was Leonard Bernstein at the Philharmonic, Cauthen's left hand the baton. It was a photo finish, but Cauthen knew after he crossed the finish line that he had won, raising his stick like a magic wand high with his left hand to signal the victory to everyone.

The crescendo of noise bellowed ever upward and wafted into the air above the track before reaching the Long Island countryside. Affirmed had created it. Cauthen had encouraged him. Horse and man, a man of only eighteen years on a twelve-hundred-pound thoroughbred who'd endured only two defeats in a taxing two-year stretch. No horse ever worked harder for it in what was indeed a race of two champions.

A beaming Cauthen headed to the winner's circle aboard Affirmed to the chants of "Stevie, Stevie, Stevie." The bodacious Triple Crown was his; he was a young David in the land of the Goliaths. Velasquez passed him on Alydar and said, "Great race, Steve." Cauthen's smile widened. "Thank you," answered the youngest jockey even to win the Triple Crown. What more could anyone want out of a horse and rider?

When Cauthen reached the winner's circle, a large number of well-wishes were already there waiting for him. And why not? He'd just ridden the greatest Belmont in the track's history. It was the closest stretch run and the closest margin of victory in the history of the challenging Belmont. After the hugs and the customary handshakes, which took some time, Cauthen embraced the Belmont Trophy. Barrera spoke first over the trackside microphone, and he spoke for all of racing.

"This Belmont was the greatest injection racing ever had," he proudly announced. "I am very proud that one of my horses participated in a race that has done the sport so much good. Racing has done so much good for me and my family, and I feel good about making a contribution in return. The Belmont was a race that thrilled millions all over the country."

Cauthen was rushed to a hurried press conference in the jockeys' quarters, where he had to prepare to ride in the ninth race, one he would eventually win. But the Belmont was the only one that mattered. Did it ever. Cauthen rode a flawless race. The choreography between man and horse was almost human.

"I can't believe it" were the first words he uttered. "This was a tremendous race. It meant so much to me to win like that. I wanted to go as slow as I could, and if Alydar passed me, I would try to stay in front but not too far. Alydar came to me early and tried to run me into the ground, but he didn't make it. I wanted to keep my horse a little bit in front as long as I could without pressing him.

"The last sixteenth of a mile, my horse was really tired. Alydar was a head in front of me. I felt he needed something. I had to get as much out of him as I could. I had never hit him left-handed in my life, but I switched to my left and he seemed to respond to it. They only time I'd seen him hit left-handed was in a race he got beat in the Great American ridden by Angel Cordero, when Alydar beat him. But I had to switch my stick. He responded good and dug in again."

Cauthen gave an unbelievable ride, one for the ages. He had to be perfect and was despite the pressure applied by Velasquez and Alydar alongside him. He never flinched from the ordeal, an eighteen-year-old in the death valley of Belmont's torturous stretch, duking it out with the veteran Velasquez.

"You have to know your horse," continued Cauthen. "You have to know what he can do and what he can't do. You have to judge the pace. You have to ride your own race and stick to the game plan. Affirmed likes to run ahead and he did it at the finish. My horse likes company. He likes to run with other horses, but he can't stand another horse to have a nose in front of him.

"It was the longest race I've ever ridden." Cauthen finished gulping down a soft drink. "Now please excuse me, I have to get ready to ride another race."

Barrera was still around. He didn't have a horse to saddle in the ninth race. As he always, the affable Cuban had time for the media.

"When Affirmed put his head in front at the start of the race, I was confident because I know no horse can pass him," disclosed Barrera. "Alydar was the only horse we had to worry about, and if he had broken out in front, which I didn't think likely, my instructions to Cauthen was to go with Alydar from here to China.

"I told Steve not to let him get an inch away. I knew we had to beat him, and he had to beat us in order to win the race. Everything worked out perfectly. It was the greatest race I ever saw in my life."

Veitch remained gracious in yet another heartbreaking loss. He was buoyant and witty as ever. Once again he reverted to his Civil War lore. He must have loved history in college.

"It was a helluva race," exclaimed Veitch, anticipating what was going to be asked. "I just couldn't appreciate the race from an artistic standpoint. I was too closely involved. It was like Pickett's Charge. You look at the picture and you say, 'That's fantastic.' But if you were at Pickett's Charge, you'd say, 'That's not the way it was.' When some SOB was sticking a bayonet in your gut, you weren't thinking how pretty he was."

As always, Veitch was supportive of Velasquez. He wanted to absolve the jockey of any blame if any of the media were going in that direction after Alydar's third straight defeat to Affirmed in the biggest races of 1978.

"Jorge Velasquez is the best jockey in America," claimed Veitch, something he had said before. "Maybe if Jorge hadn't been riding, we'd have been beaten by three lengths. I was just hoping we had the better horse today. The difference was three inches, that's all I can tell you. It was very much as I had expected. Jorge knew we couldn't let Affirmed get too far ahead and he didn't."

In the jockeys' quarters, Velasquez was greeted with respect by some of the other riders. He is an excellent jockey and they all knew it. He rode as masterfully as Cauthen.

"Great race, Jorge."

"Jorge, that was one of the best I've ever seen."

The words were comforting, but they couldn't mask Velasquez's feelings.

"I'm disappointed in this race," he revealed. "I believe that maybe by the three-sixteenth we got a head in front. They proved they are the greatest. You see how far they beat the rest every time they run.

"Today was kind of difficult for my horse because Affirmed was trying to slow down the pace and I had to go and chase him. I'd rather see someone else chase him and come up at the end and surprise him."

Louis and Patrice Wolfson accepted more congratulations in the Directors Lounge. They were a popular couple again. Winning does that. Despite the success, Wolfson wasn't thirsting for publicity and wasn't much for press conferences.

"I'll let Laz handle that," he said, shrugging his shoulders. "It was the greatest race I've seen in all my years in racing. I just couldn't believe it. It really meant a lot to us."

Patrice's bubbly smile radiated in the stodgy room. She was gracious and proud but almost speechless.

"Phenomenal, just phenomenal," she kept repeating.

It was all that indeed. Racing history has seldom seen two three-year-olds like Affirmed and Alydar in the same year, and with the Belmont they enhanced their legacy. Not only will Affirmed be remembered for winning the Triple Crown, but Alydar, too, even as a trivia question, being the only horse to finish second in all three races. After months of hype and anxiety, it all came down to the final thrust by Affirmed, who paid $3.20 while Alydar returned $2.20 with no show betting.

Never but never has there been another thoroughbred rivalry to compare with theirs. In Affirmed's seven conquests of Alydar, one by a nose, two by a neck, one by a head, and one by a half-length, over two years, which encompassed more than nine miles of racing, Affirmed's total margin over Alydar was about twenty-five feet. It never got any closer than that over in a century of racing.

Ed Comerford of *Newsday* was distinctly impressed. He wrote, "One of these days an inventive racing secretary is going to write a race goal around the world, 25,000 miles on the equator. Affirmed will win it. But Alydar will be at his throat all the way and it will take a photo to separate them at the finish."

Joe Hirsch of the *Daily Racing Form* was just as effusive: "The most remarkable chapter in the Triple Crown has been written in one of the greatest races ever run."

Ray Kerrison, the knowledgeable turf writer of the *New York Post*, had the best summation regarding the Triple Crown: "A horse may luck into winning the Derby or the Preakness but not the Belmont. Luck never wins a Belmont. Heart wins a Belmont."

That was every inch Affirmed.

Art Buchwald in his nationally syndicated column got caught up in the Triple Crown magnetism.

"Affirmed, Alydar stand head and withers above Howard Cosell and Muhammad Ali," proclaimed Buchwald, the cigar-chomping humorist.

Veteran horsemen who viewed the race up close spoke in awe of the pulsating Belmont. Woody Stephens, the dean of trainers, gushed, "Been around fifty years, and Affirmed and Alydar in the Belmont, probably the best horse race that's ever been run. Whatever it is that these two horses have cannot be bought or manufactured. It's the greatest act horse racing has ever had."

Charlie Rose, one of Alydar's handlers, felt the same way. He appeared sad and forlorn and spoke with tears in his eyes as he looked at Alydar cooling down. "He tried so hard, gave it everything he had. I guess you finally have to admit that Affirmed is a little-better horse. But it was the greatest race I've ever seen.

"Damn!" Rose yelled, shaking his head. "Why did these two horses have to come along in the same year? In almost any other year they'd be Triple Crown winners."

Rose stood looking as a groom walked Alydar by him. Rose just clapped his hands.

"Hey, you," shouted Rose at Alydar, who stopped for a moment, then turned away toward the stable. "You saw two courageous horses today. I thought we had him beaten in the end. The Derby and the Preakness were tough to take, but this was the toughest one of all. I thought we had him."

Back at his barn, Veitch was mellow and managed to smile. He said that he had talked with the Markeys. Naturally, they didn't say much, only two minutes' worth.

"They were disappointed, of course, but they thought their horse had acquitted himself very nobly, very bravely," relayed Veitch. "He did the best he could and he never gave an inch all the way."

Leaning on a railing, Veitch talked philosophically in the closing sunset. "You live in hopes, you die in despair. That's why I'm not much for carrying on disappointment. I'm just looking forward to tomorrow."

How many tomorrows were left for the Markeys? The disappointments were embedded in two solitary figures. Both in their eighties, though no one knew Lucille's real age, they had become increasingly frail from age and illness and weren't at any of the Triple Crown races. Somehow they mustered enough strength to watch Alydar on television. The dedicated owners had fought a long campaign to restore the glory of Calumet. Now, bundled together, they had clung to the hope that the Belmont would give them one jewel in the legs of a gallant

Alydar. With their deteriorating health, combined with financial problems, this was their last hurrah for their falling empire.

It was a magical season, one made for Hollywood. An owner who sought redemption after prison; an innocent teenage jockey; a wily immigrant trainer; and a horse who wouldn't quit.

"Affirmed was the catalyst to the return of my father, and that's what has meant the most to me," his son Steve said.

For Affirmed, he was destiny's child. He didn't have to win another race. *Sports Illustrated* heralded it as "The Race of a Lifetime." Indeed it was.

ELEVEN

The Final Turn

It is never enough in racing, especially so for a horse like Affirmed. He was the most celebrated thoroughbred in America after arduously capturing the Triple Crown with Alydar breathing down his neck. He did so in a dream Hollywood movie in a pulsating duel with the Calumet challenger, which was ordained as the greatest two-horse race in the history of racing. But racing fans wanted more. Affirmed and Alydar's pugnacious rivalry was unmatched in the sport.

But how much more is more? Would the two combatants face each other again in the six months remaining in the 1978 campaign? How much did Wolfson want out of his prized champion? On the business side he had an answer. He established stud fees of $400,000 and didn't lack for investors, who were standing in line at Affirmed's hallowed stable. The market was there and Wolfson had retained fifteen of the thirty-six shares that were sold.

But the betting public was only concerned with Affirmed on the track. It was left to Wolfson and Barrera to strategize on what races they would send their conqueror out on during the last half of the year. Wolfson and Barrera talked often about Affirmed's future while he was enjoying a two-month rest from racing. After all, Affirmed deserved as much after what he had accomplished. He had the perfect jockey in Cauthen, and like Bonnie and Clyde they ran over anyone in their path. Affirmed's return would begin in Saratoga on August 8 with the Jim Dandy Stakes, followed by the Travers Stakes on August 19 at the same track. Those two races were a certainty. Affirmed's performance would determine if there would be any more.

Saratoga is one of the nation's oldest tracks and has been standing since the Civil War. It is a historical treasure for New York State, and for one month in summer the bucolic town with its Victorian houses and flower plantings awakes from its slumber with millionaires, tourists, and the railbirds. A two-and-a-half-hour drive from New York, or a three-and-a-half-hour trip by train up the scenic Hudson Valley, it has kept its old-world charm because its residents resist change for the fear of destroying this special place. It was just that for the Wolfsons, who owned a house in the tranquil countryside.

By 1963, Saratoga had been a vacation spot for fifty years. Vacationers imbibed its naturally carbonated mineral waters and inhaled its piney air. Its spas were medicinal for arthritis sufferers. The sleepy village had remained unchanged since the presidency of Ulysses S. Grant, and by the turn of the century, Saratoga was a showcase where the egos of the American tycoons were shamelessly exhibited.

Affirmed was training punctually the week before the race and appeared to like the track in his daily gallops under Barrera's watchful eyes. Affirmed's celebrity had excited racing fans everywhere. He was mentioned in the same sentence as other Triple Crown champions such as Secretariat, Citation, Whirlaway, and Seattle Slew, the elite among all the eleven thoroughbreds that wore the crown. He was every bit a Madison Avenue darling, handsome, well-defined, and amazingly intelligent. Yet, there were no endorsements or marketed products such as T-shirts, caps, on other sundry items bearing his image. The Wolfsons preferred it that way.

"Nothing has been sold," announced Patrice Wolfson, whose father, Hirsch Jacobs, had more winners than any other trainer in racing. "There are no endorsements. Hopefully, there won't be any. He won't be promoting anything but horse racing itself."

With Affirmed, her husband was the only owner to have bred a Florida-foaled Triple Crown champion. His Harbor View Farm in Ocala was resourceful with over three hundred hopefuls, while some fifty others were competing at Belmont and on the West Coast at Santa Anita and Hollywood Park. He even refused to ship Affirmed to California for the Swaps Stakes on July 2 despite an attractive $300,000 purse.

"We're not going to run this horse just for the money," emphasized Wolfson. "I never count my money anymore. As long as I have enough money to do just about anything I want to do, it doesn't mean that much. We won't be syndicated until next year because we want to race him as a four-year-old. That means his value will probably go down a little, but that doesn't bother us in the least. All it amounts to is money. The pleasure he's going to give us and the racing public is worth the risk. We might get as much as five million dollars more by syndicating him now. But five million dollars isn't going to make that much difference in the way we live."

The erudite Wolfson was known on Wall Street as "the father of the modern conglomerate." He is a distinguished man of letters with a decorous and noble appearance. He was still involved in the business world as a consultant to a number of large corporations. But racing had his devoted love. However, beyond the pastoral world of the sport of kings, a determined Wolfson continued a tenacious fight, costing him millions, to overturn his criminal conviction, which resulted, he claimed, from "people in higher places who united to frame me." It had been over eight years since that one stained year of his life, and he wouldn't let go.

"Do you think I'm foolish enough to sue if I've got any skeletons in my closet?" posed Wolfson. "Thousands of people have sold unregistered stocks, and all they got was a slap on the wrist for a technical violation of the Security and Exchange Commission rules. Mine was the only case that was treated as a criminal offense. Why? Because I made the mistake of saying Wall Street had more crooks, proportionally, than any other place, and because I said the insiders manipulate the market the way they want."

Leslie Gould, a prominent SEC attorney, represented Wolfson in his defense and perhaps, as several of Wolfson's family members believe, lost the case with his closing argument. Gould, in his remarks to the jury, characterized Wolfson as someone "who was soaring high like an eagle in the sky."

Michael Armstrong presented the government's rebuttal.

With Gould's description of Wolfson fresh in the jurors' minds Armstrong cleverly said in his opening remarks, "Mr. Gould is right. Louis Wolfson was there soaring above the law." It impressed the jury.

The catchy name Jim Dandy came from the nondescript horse that upset the Triple Crown winner Gallant Fox in his Travers Stakes at Saratoga in the summer of 1930. The prodigious eight-length upset produced by Jim Dandy, a 100–1 shot, was compared to the 1919 defeat of Man o' War by, appropriately enough, a horse named Upset. On paper, Jim Dandy had no business being in Saratoga that August afternoon. He'd finished last in a prep race eight days before only to face Gallant Man and Whichone. The Fox was listed at 8–5 while Whichone attracted odds of 12–1.

The race appeared nonconsequential to the prestigious *New York Times*. Its coverage of two sentences, practically like a classified ad, was at the bottom of one of its sports pages: "Three horses are named, in addition to Gallant Fox and Whichone, but two of them (Caruso and Jim Dandy) are doubtful starters and none is given the slightest chance among handicappers to run second, not to speak of winning. Seldom has been a race which so patently lay between horses."

Affirmed was expecting to meet Alydar in either one or both races at Saratoga. Wolfson looked at the Jim Dandy as somewhat of a prep race for Affirmed. In Alydar's last win, he'd developed some soreness in his legs, and Veitch decided to skip the Jim Dandy and pointed to the Travers, a more prestigious race with a bigger purse, two weeks later. By race day, Wolfson looked at the Jim Dandy as more of a "tightener."

"He's not as tight as we would want him," observed the owner. "He needs this race."

And so did Cauthen. For the first time in his young career, he was mired in a slump. In the last two months, he'd produced only two wins, which was very un-Cauthen-like. If Alydar was waiting down the road, Cauthen needed this one as much as Affirmed.

Despite the absence of Alydar, a Tuesday-record crowd of 21,544 gathered to see Affirmed in his first outing since annexing the fabled Triple Crown. As many as possible jammed the paddock area to get a glimpse of Affirmed, who now had the adulation of a movie star.

Five other horses were waiting for Affirmed. Only one, Sensitive Prince, had an outside chance of making it a race. While Affirmed attracted most of the money, Sensitive Prince accounted for some action as the second choice. He was considered as a hunch bet because of his trainer, Allen Jerkens, who had a reputation as a superb conditioner and had upset such champion horses as Kelso and Secretariat.

Barrera definitely approached the Jim Dandy as a prep race for the bigger Travers Stakes. Affirmed hadn't raced in two months, not since the thrilling Belmont on June 10. Admittedly, Barrera's only concern was Sensitive Prince, who was in prime shape and had won six consecutive races. An Affirmed victory would boost his earnings for the year over $800,000 and put him within easy reach of Secretariat's single-year mark of $864,404. Yet, Barrera expected it to be a tough race.

While Affirmed was assigned 128 pounds, the heaviest of his career, Sensitive Prince would carry 119 for the nine-furlong race. With a nine-pound weight advantage, could Jerkens devise a way to surprise Affirmed? Nothing is certain in horse racing except its uncertainty, which accounts for upsets. The other questions in the air around the track that afternoon were if Affirmed was ready after a two-month layoff and would Cauthen break his slump?

Sensitive Prince provided the first answer. He broke clearly from the starting gate and took the lead. Did Jerkens want to break out fast and stay there for the entire race? Apparently so. Affirmed didn't offer any challenge as Sensitive Prince took advantage and widened his lead. It had all the appearance of a wire-to-wire front run. Affirmed looked sluggish, nothing like the Triple Crown champion he was. Around the turn, Sensitive Prince opened a seven-length advantage, and jockey Jacinto Vasquez never used his whip once.

Affirmed backers were getting more nervous with every increased length of Sensitive Prince's advantage. At the top of the stretch, at Cauthen's urging, Affirmed began to rally and trimmed Sensitive Prince's edge to four lengths. Only one-eighth of a mile was left. "He's not gonna get him," yelled a reporter in the press box. Trepidation was on the faces of both Louis and Patrice Wolfson.

Track announcer Chic Anderson picked up the action: "Affirmed is driving. Sensitive Prince is hanging on gamely. Affirmed is coming like a shot now. Can he catch him? We'll find out!"

Cauthen needed more from Affirmed. But could he get it? The Kid went to the whip and Affirmed began to respond. He pricked his ears and started driving and thundered past the front-running Sensitive Prince to snatch a half-length victory. Once again, Affirmed had demonstrated his great competitive quality. He would not let a horse he could see beat him. He would not be denied. Affirmed's stretch run was what champions are made of, and his thrilling finish was much to the relief of Cauthen.

"He was hesitating a bit because of the muddy track," claimed the smiling youngster, who got a much needed win. "I had to let him settle."

Barrera was exceptionally pleased. He called it one of Affirmed's greatest races in overcoming a number of handicaps.

"Affirmed showed a lot of guts in winning that race," proclaimed Barrera. "He just does what he has to. There is only one other horse on the racetrack that has as much guts as Affirmed, and that's Alydar, who keeps coming on and coming on."

For a moment it appeared that Affirmed wouldn't make it when Sensitive Prince opened up a nine-length had in the backstretch. Cauthen was instructed by Barrera to stay close to Sensitive Prince and not allow him to grab a big lead at any time.

"Affirmed was treading a little gingerly on the track and was not really grabbing hold early in the race," revealed Cauthen, who'd snapped his slump if only for a day.

"I guess Cauthen knows the horse better than I do," quipped Barrera.

In Patrice Wolfson's eyes, the win was big. "Unbelievable," she exclaimed. "I've never seen anything like it in my entire life."

Jerkens was every inch the gentleman he was portrayed to be.

"We have no excuses," he remarked. "We just got beat by a great horse. Cauthen's been in a little slump, and the youngster that he is, there would have been a natural tendency for him to be nervous. But he kept his cool at all times. He never rides a horse the way he doesn't want to ride him. To my way of thinking it is the mark of a great rider."

The afterglow of the Jim Dandy reflected the excitement of the Belmont for an entire week in Saratoga leading to the much awaited Travers. Veitch announced that Alydar was sound following his latest win at Monmouth Park, and that he would indeed go after Affirmed, conjuring up memories of the thrilling Belmont contest between the pair. In the final challenge for the Triple Crown two months earlier, Alydar, running furiously, had closed the gap in chasing Affirmed, improving in his relentlessness from 1½ lengths behind in the Derby to only a neck in the Preakness, and only a nose in the Belmont. Racing buffs never forget moments like that, and the townsfolk in Saratoga braced for what would be a record invasion of people into their idyllic hamlet, which has stood almost motionless in a time capsule except for one month each summer for the last 114 years.

Early one morning, Sylvester Veitch, John's father, was at the stable where his son was readying Alydar for a workout. He was affectionately called Syl and was well liked by the racing fraternity. He'd been around horses all his life and was comfortable in his world. "Horse training is a terrible disease," he reflected. "If it gets into your blood, what do you do?" Which explains why he liked being at a stable every day.

Syl did what was expected of him. For almost a century, a Veitch family member had been training at Saratoga. It began with his father, who handed it down to him, and Syl in turn passed it on to John. Syl saddled enough winners to get him into the Hall of Fame. The nostalgia surrounding Saratoga was refreshing, and old-timers such as Syl were one reason why.

The sport in the summer rapture enjoyed the present and savored the past. Over the years the greats of racing had been here. Saratoga was where Man o' War suffered his only loss. All the outstanding jockeys, from Earl Sande to Eddie Arcaro, and now Steve Cauthen, were astride the spectacular thoroughbreds of the pinnacle stables such as Calumet, Vanderbilt, Whitney, and Greentree.

The old guard who knew Saratoga best were rooting for Veitch and Alydar. Elliot Burch, a classy trainer who won the 1969 Travers with Arts and Letters, stopped by Calumet's barn to extend his good wishes to the thirty-two-year-old Veitch after exchanging pleasantries with his father.

"It's time for this guy to win," announced Burch. "He's done such a great job and he has tried so hard. He deserves it."

Veitch resumed his training chores when Burch left, continuing in the footsteps of his father and grandfather doing the same thing at the same place, years and years ago. Veitch was philosophical about it:

"Training is basically the same today as it was back then. The only thing that modernization has done is make trainers be less concerned with perfection. Today, the trainers aren't as good as they used to be. They don't have to be. They have too many people to help, the assistants, jockey agents.

"My father taught me a long time ago that if you can't accept defeat as well as victory, then you have no business in the game. There are more defeats than victories, you know."

In the seven days before Saturday, enough bickering was going on between the adversaries to portend a bitterly fought afternoon. The two-year odyssey between Affirmed and Alydar had apparently taxed the tolerance of both Veitch and Barrera. By the week's end, their tempers were frayed and remained so right into race day. Three days before, Veitch had expressed his disappointment that Sensitive Prince would not start in the Travers. That was the start of it, and nothing like it had ever appeared between the two before.

Barrera was a bit sad. Two days before the race, he had to replace Cauthen, who was noticeably limping, with Laffit Pincay. He described Cauthen and Affirmed as "a beautiful team." Still, he was confident with Pincay.

"Pincay rode Affirmed in the Juvenile and the Santa Anita Derby on the West Coast," said Barrera. "He knows the horse, and I expect him to ride a prefect race Saturday. Pincay will be able to work at one hundred and ten percent, whereas Stevie wasn't able to do that. That's why we made the switch. But no matter how well Pincay does in the Travers, Stevie will ride Affirmed next time. Laffit has a lot of plane connections to make. He's got to go to San Diego, to Los Angeles, to Chicago, to New York, to Saratoga. It's not easy to get to Saratoga."

Veitch didn't see any advantage in the switch of jockeys.

"Affirmed is Affirmed," he emphasized. "That's about all you can say. He'll be tough to beat no matter who rides him. I don't think the strategy will change any, because Pincay has ridden him so well before. The only change I hope for is for Alydar's nose to be in front of the wire this time. If that happens, it certainly won't be Pincay's fault."

Veitch appeared more upset about Sensitive Prince's absence than Cauthen's.

"I was certain that Sensitive Prince would go in the Travers after he had run so well against Affirmed in the Jim Dandy," sighed Veitch. "When Allen Jerkens decided not to enter Sensitive Prince, it came as quite a surprise. I figured that Sensitive Prince would run with Affirmed from the start, and that might allow Alydar to lay up close to both of them and then make his big run through the stretch. Without Sensitive Prince to help, we'll have to come up with another plan. About the only thing I can think of is to force Pincay into a tactical error, to catch him asleep somewhere along the line."

A testy Barrera was upset at Veitch's reference to forcing Pincay into a tactical error. What was Veitch planning? It made Barrera wonder what a horse such as Shake Shake Shake with Angel Cordero was doing in the Travers, the oldest continuously run stakes race in the country, and one of Saratoga's featured events. Barrera shook his head while perusing the horse's past performance, doing so with a suspicious eye that gave meaning to "a tactical error."

"For a young man who is supposed to be a good trainer, Veitch certainly says some stupid things," remarked Barrera. "Won't this ever end? He always says he has a new way to beat Affirmed. What new way? Seven out of nine and four in a row to Affirmed doesn't show me any new way. The record is seven wins for Affirmed and two for Alydar. If this was boxing, he wouldn't get any more shots at the title."

Barrera had always been a fight buff, and in the context of a heavyweight fight, this was round ten. The *Albany Times-Union* looked at it that way with its day-of-the-race headline, "Affirmed, Alydar: It's Round 10." Affirmed had won seven rounds and Alydar two, and Calumet needed a knockout, a big win, one bigger than Affirmed had inflicted in the nine meetings. Like Ali and Frazier, Affirmed had stung like a bee and overcome Alydar's furious late-stretch thunder. At the Travers, both combatants were ready, not just ready but primed.

The scorecard in boxing lexicon, which Barrera, a big boxing fan, liked to use, read:

Round 1: The Youthful
Even though he hadn't yet raced, Alydar was a surprising 9–5 favorite. Affirmed was at 3–1 and won by a neck. Alydar encountered difficulty in finding running room and lost by five lengths.

Round 2: The Great American
Once again, Alydar emerged as the favorite, a strong one at 4–5. He demonstrated why in swimmingly running past Affirmed to win by 3½ lengths. Affirmed was shipped to the West Coast after the loss.

Round 3: The Hopeful
Alydar and Affirmed were the class of the Saratoga race, Alydar at 1–1 and Affirmed at 2–1. That's how they were matched. Affirmed had the lead at the turn, and when Alydar made his stretch run, Affirmed withstood the challenge to win by half a length.

Round 4: The Belmont Futurity
For the first time, Affirmed emerged as the favorite at 6–5. It was the most exciting race yet between the two. Affirmed won by a nose in a grueling stretch run. A disappointed Veitch replaced Eddie Maple with Velasquez.

Round 5: The Champagne

On a muddy track, Alydar blew by the favorite Affirmed for a length-and-a-quarter victory. Affirmed was occupied trying to get past Darby Creek Road when Alydar flew by him.

Round 6: The Laurel Futurity

It looked like another win for Alydar, the 2–5 favorite, when he got his head in front of Affirmed. However, he couldn't hold it, and Affirmed fought him off and crossed the finish line ahead by a neck. Affirmed was given the rest of the year off to rest in California, while Alydar remained on the East Coast to begin their three-year-old challenge.

Round 7: The Kentucky Derby

The homebred Alydar was made the 6–5 favorite at Churchill Downs, but ran a poor race. He didn't appear into it and, despite Velasquez's urging, finished a 1¼ lengths behind Affirmed.

Round 8: The Preakness

In a thriller, Affirmed withstood a furious charge by Alydar to win by a neck. It was only the third time in their duels that the favorite won.

Round 9: The Belmont

In what many consider the greatest Belmont of them all, Alydar and Affirmed were entwined in perhaps the most memorable stretch run in the Belmont's history. It went down to the wire with Affirmed winning by a nose after Alydar had been a nose in front at the sixteenth pole.

Here they were again at Saratoga. On Friday, Alydar had his final workout for the next day's joust. Sipping a Coke under a tree, Veitch expressed his satisfaction and confidence after Alydar's week of workouts:

"Alydar is going to beat him. It's a question of how much Alydar has improved in relation to how much Affirmed has or who is at the top of his game. We've been playing this game all along. Saturday is the same old thing, that's all."

Barrera pointed out that the horse in front has a big advantage in match races, which was what Affirmed and Alydar had been running. He felt better after Affirmed rallied from ten lengths behind to catch Sensitive Prince ten days earlier.

"He needed that kind of race," revealed Barrera. "My horse was ready. He's lost weight from the Belmont, but he's got it all back now. These are the two most consistent horses you've ever seen. It brings back to racing what we need. It gets fans to believe."

On Saturday, the Saratoga track swarmed with a mass of people such as never experienced before in the old town. It even caught track officials by surprise when a record of 50,359, more than the town's population, maneuvered their way into the ornate venue. As many as possible crowded the paddock an hour before race time to capture a glimpse of Affirmed and Alydar, the darlings of the three-year-olds, and they could not care less about the other two horses, Shake Shake Shake, and Nasty and Bold.

New York governor Hugh Carey arrived by helicopter in ample time for the first race. His chopper landed on the John Hay Whitney training track. He was accompanied by family members and well-known musical conductor Morton Downey. The governor was cheerful and had apparently done his research on racing. As he sat down for lunch in the clubhouse, he said he felt lucky because a horse named Carey had won the Travers in 1887.

Both Affirmed and Alydar looked fit and seemed to acknowledge one another. Affirmed, looking calm, appeared first before the idolaters to a ripple of applause. It disappeared moments later when Shake Shake Shake and Nasty and Bold came out. Only Alydar was left. When he entered with several bandaged ankles, he, too, like Affirmed, heard applause. And like his rival, he also looked ready. A majority who were there thought so. They made Alydar a surprising favorite 1–2, while Affirmed was listed at 9–5. There never was much separating the two in all the times they fought.

The opening odds were a reflection of the uncertainties festering over the race. Yes, it was Affirmed and Alydar, but this time Cauthen wouldn't be riding him. A day after he won the Jim Dandy, he got hurt in a spill for the second time in his short career. Skeptics wondered if Affirmed would be uncomfortable without Cauthen. It was like Gene Autry without Champion. Yet Pincay had been on Affirmed twice before and won both times. The first time was in 1977 at Hollywood Park.

The second time, Cauthen's agent, Lenny Goodman, had taken him west to fulfill commitments in California. Two days before Cauthen was scheduled to ride Affirmed in the Santa Anita Derby, his horse bumped into another rounding the turn for home. He was disqualified for five days for the incident. Goodman and Cauthen appealed, but they were rejected, and Pincay took Steve's place on Affirmed for the Santa Anita Derby.

Barrera wasn't fazed now by the switch: "Pincay rode Affirmed in the Juvenile and the Santa Anita Derby and knows the horse well. But no matter how well Pincay does, Stevie will ride Affirmed the next time."

By post time, Affirmed assumed the favorite role at 3–5, while Alydar, as in his other races, was right behind at even money. It spoke volumes about the race's being visualized as still another two-horse fracas for supremacy. When the gates opened, Cordero jumped Shake Shake Shake out quickly on the rail but didn't extend to a decisive lead, which Veitch was looking for in the ten-furlong race. It enabled Affirmed to hang close. Although Velasquez held Alydar back in last place, he wasn't that far behind. Pincay had the speedy Affirmed positioned to grab the lead, but Shake Shake Shake held him off and continued to challenge him, much to Veitch's delight.

However, Shake Shake Shake couldn't sustain the pace and began to swerve, pushing Affirmed farther away from the inside. With Pincay holding steady and not breaking stride, he got Affirmed in front a half mile from the finish line. Velasquez then made his move. He saw a lane opening along the rail and led his champion there. The sudden move annoyed Pincay, who pulled to his left in a dangerous tactic that abruptly cut off Alydar, who was only a head behind.

When Affirmed veered in, it stunned Velasquez, who almost lost his mount in quickly yanking on the reins to pull Alydar's head back. He fortunately kept control and avoided a collision, but Alydar pulled up abruptly. He hit the rail, breaking his stride, and fell six lengths behind. But the great horse didn't quit. Velasquez righted Alydar and had him running with speed around the turn into the stretch. Alydar was coming and the crowd began to roar at his patented tactic of barreling home. He came within a length of Affirmed but couldn't get any closer and finished 1½ lengths behind.

Affirmed had beaten his tormentor for the eighth time in ten trials. But did he? A moment after Affirmed crossed the finish line, the stewards flashed the inquiry light. It didn't take them long to view the film and decide that Pincay had interfered with Alydar, causing him to bang into the rail. The foul made Alydar the winner as Affirmed was dropped to second by disqualification. In some regards, it was a shallow victory. But Veitch and Velasquez would take it regardless of the circumstances. A win is a win.

Barrera wasn't so sure and said, "I have to see the film before I can make a judgment. Everything happened so quickly. From what I saw of the fast-action film, Affirmed's number had to come down, but I want to see it in slow motion."

Pincay defended his action: "I didn't think there was enough room for him to get through. He was going through a blind spot."

Not everyone was happy with the result. It was not the race the record crowd had waited with anticipation to view. Boos echoing from the stands demonstrated their displeasure, and Veitch didn't remain long in the winner's circle accepting the customary congratulations. He was every bit concerned about Alydar. When he reached the horse in the barn, it was evident why. Alydar had cuts on both his front legs. Veitch grimaced. He was angry and let everyone around him know it.

"Pincay should get ten days on bread and water," he vented. "I think he knew he blew the race and panicked. There is no place on a racetrack for any rider who does that. No, I'm not happy winning this way. It's hollow as hell. Do you realize that one of the best horses to come along in years was almost killed out there in front of the biggest crowd in Saratoga history? Jorge told me that he was within an inch of being dropped, going down. He said he was lucky Alydar didn't fall.

"It was bad riding on Pincay's part. You might be able to do that in California, but it doesn't go here. It looked to me that Pincay went to sleep on his horse when he took the lead, left a little opening there on the rail, and the horse that Cordero was on was tiring and drifted from the rail. Jorge very shrewdly dropped in on the rail, had the rail, and was moving up on the inside of Shake Shake Shake very easily. Pincay realized it, dropped back down, and shut off my horse. It was a blatant foul."

Alydar's win didn't provide any satisfaction for Veitch at all. "I don't consider that we won the race," he confessed.

Velasquez felt equally as bad: "I didn't want to win in that way. I'm very upset right now."

Barrera was sitting in a box waiting for the ninth race when he was apprised of Veitch's remarks. His temper flared. He was convinced that Cordero and Velasquez, who were close friends, had conspired to manipulate Affirmed's defeat.

"Alydar had no business to be in there on the rail if he didn't know Cordero was going to open the inside for him," pointed out Barrera. "My horse was head and head with Cordero's horse, and all of a sudden the other horse took my horse out and delivered the rail to Alydar. I don't plan to run anymore against Alydar."

Veitch, intently observing Alydar being cooled down by the barn, was informed of Barrera's remarks. Veitch wasn't pleased at what he heard, especially about not facing Alydar again. His anger remained.

"That's chicken," snapped Veitch. "If Alydar is okay, he'll be in the Marlboro Cup. Who the hell is Barrera to say that? Velasquez couldn't go on the inside? Does he own the track?"

At that moment Velasquez came by with a bottle of champagne but never opened it. He wasn't in a mood to celebrate. Still numb from the near fall that could have caused a serious injury, he was worried about his horse. He began talking to him in his stall. Velasquez was as close to Alydar as Cauthen was to Affirmed. A bond forms between a jockey and a horse that's priceless. Almost human.

"We're going to get him next time," Velasquez promised. "It's a shame we couldn't have done it our way. You were going to beat him. This way is the worst way for the thing between you and Affirmed."

Affirmed's owners wouldn't comment on the race. They reserved their opinions until watching the film with Barrera.

"I'm glad that both horses came out of the race okay," related Louis Wolfson. "That's the most important thing."

It certainly was, because Alydar could have gotten seriously injured and perhaps been finished in his career. Don Veitch, John's cousin, made a pertinent observation, saying it was lucky for Alydar that Saratoga still had old-fashioned rails, rather than the newer plastic ones.

"Instead of bouncing off the rail as he did, he'd have gone right through a plastic rail and doubtless gone down and been seriously hurt," deduced Veitch. "We were in the best position we had ever been in our races against Affirmed, but who could tell what would have happened from then on. Affirmed is a great horse."

A sullen Cauthen, who watched the race in the Wolfsons' box, absolved Pincay of any blame. If not for his injury, Steve would have been aboard Affirmed and none of the controversy would ever have evolved.

"I think it's unfair to put blame on Pincay," he offered. "He rode him good. It happens every day. People said I wouldn't win after I lost my allowance bug, but they were wrong, too."

No one knew it then, but it would be the last time Affirmed and Alydar would ever duel.

Affirmed had been flawless until the Travers mishap. Before that race he had fashioned a smooth line of eight straight victories that went from Santa Anita to Hollywood Park across the country to Churchill Downs, Pimlico, Belmont, and now at Saratoga.

For several days after the Travers most observers conjectured that Alydar would have beaten Affirmed with his furious stretch run if not for his near collision. He courageously stormed back with his trademark stretch rumble and almost caught his nemesis. Despite Barrera's assertion that he didn't want any part of Alydar anymore, it was only wishful thinking. Barrera had already charted plans for the Belmont fall session, and the next two races circled on his calendar were the Marlboro Cup on September 16 and the Jockey Club Gold Cup on October 14. Veitch had the same agenda for Alydar. Their simmering feud wasn't on either one's calendar, but it was there nevertheless.

Racing fans were giddy about the continued rivalry between Affirmed and Alydar, which had been proclaimed as the greatest in racing history just on their three encounters in the quest for the Triple Crown. It was all that and more for the railbirds. In the weeks leading to the Marlboro, the Barrera-Veitch rivalry, which had been on the edge of a breakout, abated. A solemn Veitch suffered a paramount setback, one that no trainer, even Barrera, would ever want to happen to someone else. Alydar had broken a bone in his left front foot. There would be no Marlboro for Alydar, and no more racing either. He was done for the year, and it was a sad day for racegoers everywhere.

Instead, the Marlboro's focus turned to a battle between Affirmed and Seattle Slew. It was the first time in history that two Triple Crown winners faced each other. Comparisons were made between the two, but it was much too early to be definitive. The experts preferred to pass judgment after Affirmed's final season. Yes, Alydar would be missed. But what better a scenario than two Triple Crown champions snorting at one another? For fantasy fans, it had the atmosphere of the Derby, one with a heartwarming feel. Had Alydar been healthy, it would have felt even bigger.

"This race was set up for Alydar," said Mickey Taylor, one of Seattle Slew's owners. "It's too bad."

With Alydar in it, the 1⅛-mile race would probably have gotten off with Sensitive Prince and Seattle Slew, both speed horses, charging to the front with Affirmed close behind while everyone waited for Alydar to make his burst at the stretch. Veitch picked Affirmed to win the race.

"Affirmed by far," he remarked unhesitatingly. "He's trained very well. And without Alydar in the race, I give Affirmed an easier chance to beat the rest."

Slew, who captured audiences in 1977, was returning in 1978 from a viral infection in January that had threatened his life. Dr. Jim Hill, one of Slew's owners, had prayed back than that his horse would make a miraculous recovery from a blood infection. Days later, Slew showed some positive signs.

"I've just seen the results of some blood tests, and I know Slew isn't going to die," exclaimed Hill. "I can't say now if he'll run again. It's going to take a long time for him to even get back on the racetrack. The last few days have been hell for everybody, but I hope the worst is finally over."

By May, Slew had recuperated well enough to run again. But how much did he have in him? Did the infection take too much out of him? He hadn't won a big race since the Belmont during his Triple Crown year. He showed no ill effects in winning a few allowances in May and August as he was being brought along slowly. He looked impressive in a win at Saratoga, but created concern with a loss to Dr. Patches under Cordero in a tune-up race at the Meadowlands in September.

The win earned Cordero the mount on Slew. His regular jockey, Jean Cruguet, was taken off Slew after he criticized the horse's training regimen and further remarked that Slew was "a short horse' and would not be able to seriously challenge Affirmed in the Marlboro. Trainer Doug Peterson was enraged when he read Cruguet's remarks. So was Taylor. They didn't hesitate in pulling Cruguet off Seattle Slew.

"When Jean said what he said, it proved to us that he didn't have any confidence in Slew," charged Taylor. "We didn't want a jockey on our horse who didn't believe in him. It was as simple as that. Angel has ridden for our stable before, and he's ridden against Slew and watched his race. He's got confidence in him and so do we."

Barrera looked upon that development with a jaundiced eye

after what had happened in the Travers a month earlier. This time Barrera had Cauthen back for the nine-furlong race. Slew carried the top weight of 128, while Affirmed was assigned 124 pounds, much to Barrera's liking. Could the top three-year-old overtake an older champion? Was Slew fit enough for a competitive one-two battle with Affirmed? Taylor seemed to think so.

"Slew is right where we want him to be," he ventured. "He'll run his race. There is one thing you have to remember about Slew. He loves Belmont Park. It's his racetrack. He has never lost at Belmont."

Barrera infused Cauthen with his thinking. When Sensitive Prince was scratched because of an inflamed jaw, Barrera was concerned about the pace. The only speed left in a five-horse field belonged to Slew. If he could get away, he'd be hard to beat. When he was out in front, it was difficult to run him down.

"Don't break too fast," Barrera instructed Cauthen. "Stay one length away at most off that horse. He's the only one you have to beat."

Slew did take the early lead with a long way to go. Affirmed was second, two lengths behind, and remained that way for most of the race. Rounding the clubhouse turn, Slew swung wide, which provided a lane for Affirmed to go through. The crowd yelled for Cauthen to make his move. It never transpired. Instead, Seattle Slew put on a burst of speed that carried him to a three-length victory. He did so with a record time for the last five-eighths in eclipsing Secretariat's world record by two-fifths of a second. Seattle Slew was indeed back, and Cordero gained more prominence after the horrible Travers incident.

"I knew when we were able to go to the lead that we could win it," claimed Cordero. "Slew is such a nice horse, and I was able to relax him on the backstretch. There isn't a horse in the world that could have beaten him today."

Cauthen had run the race that Barrera wanted, but Slew was too much horse. Cauthen alluded to that as Slew commanded the entire race.

"Affirmed ran a good race, but he just couldn't cut into Slew's head," he pointed out. "I thought at the top of the stretch that I might get to him, but Cordero just let him out a little bit and we couldn't pick up any ground. I don't know if it would be the same if they ran again or not."

A revived Slew filled the vacuum created by Alydar's unfortunate absence. Slew had been the poster boy during his Triple Crown season not only for what he had done but how it all came about, and racing fans reached out and welcomed him back following his serious illness.

Slew's was one of those feel-good stories that occur in racing at times. He was a paltry $17,500 purchase in 1975 by Mickey and Karen Taylor, two newcomers to racing from White Swan, Washington. Slew wasn't exactly impressive as a yearling as he stood at the Keeneland sales with a clubfoot. However, he did have some good bloodlines as the great-grandson of Bold Ruler. Slew demonstrated his potential as a two-year-old, winning all six races he was entered in.

The public liked him so much that they made Slew a 1–2 favorite in the Kentucky Derby despite the critics' disdain in saying he had never beaten anyone. Despite getting off to a bad start, Slew recovered and won the Derby by three lengths. Two weeks later, Slew got off to a trouble-free start and won again. The Belmont was waiting, and Slew responded with a three-length triumph to win the 1977 Triple Crown.

Taylor was a logger who got into racing with a $100 bet on a long shot at Santa Anita while his financée, a stewardess at the time, was on a flight. The Triple Crown was the end of the fairy tale for the Taylors, who had beaten racing's Gatsbys at their own game.

Affirmed would get a chance for redemption against Seattle Slew in the Jockey Club Gold Cup a month down the road. However, this time he had to be aware of another dangerous adversary, a horse named Exceller. It would appear that Slew would open as the favorite off his glowing performance in the Marlboro on the same Belmont course. But track logic doesn't always produce a positive result. As Mark Twain once remarked, "It were not the best that we should all think alike; it is difference of opinion that makes horse races."

The three principals produced a marquee billing for the Gold Cup. Affirmed was the best three-year-old, Slew was the best four-year-old, and Exceller was the best five-year-old. Then, too, it was the first time the three million-dollar winners had got together, in what was construed as the definitive race of the year with three of racing's top jockeys, Cauthen, Cordero, and Shoemaker in the chase for the $321,000 prize.

Slew was established as the favorite, Affirmed was second, and Exceller was third in the wagering. Not much was known about Exceller, who had run most of his twenty-eight races in Europe. He was an American-bred horse who was purchased by Texas millionaire H. L. Hunt for only $25,000 in the 1974 yearling auction at Keeneland. He was immediately shipped to

France and raced in England and Canada before trainer Charlie Whittingham got him in California. He performed well there, winning all three races he competed in, and Whittingham took him East for the remainder of the 1978 season.

"I'm gonna win it," predicted Whittingham one night the week of the Gold Cup after dinner at the "21" Club. "Exceller's a lot better horse than people think, and he is real good right now."

Barrera had other ideas. Along with Affirmed, he entered another horse, Life's Hope, so as to push Slew. Barrera didn't want Slew to get off so fast by himself and dictate the pace. He told Cauthen that with Life's Hope pressing Slew, he should remain about a length behind him. Cauthen, who was still mired in a slump, agreed.

Slew did get away fast, and Life's Hope and Affirmed rushed to meet him. It was the plan Barrera had looked for until the horses reached the first turn. Cauthen was having difficulty controlling Affirmed, and Barrera didn't know why. A few moments later he found out. Through his binoculars, he detected that Cauthen's saddle was slipping, a severe mishap for a jockey. It became dangerous for Cauthen as his saddle kept moving forward. He wisely pulled up Affirmed when he reached the far turn to prevent any damage to himself or the horse.

The three-horse duel had suddenly became a one-horse race as Exceller was an unbelievable last, twenty-two lengths away! Slew's bettors started withdrawing to the windows to cash their bets. It wasn't unusual. But Shoemaker wasn't finished. He urged on Exceller, who began to respond. He was moving swiftly on the rail and gaining on Slew with every stride. But did he have enough to catch the leader a half mile from the finish? Exceller kept driving and caught Slew. They battled back and both, crossing the line in a photo finish, which Exceller won by a nose. It was a heroic effort by the stranger, and for the first time in his remarkable career, Affirmed finished out of the money.

"I was so far back I couldn't really tell what was going on up front," admitted Shoemaker. "But I didn't need to know too much anyway. With Exceller, the winner gets done in one long move. I didn't move on him until the three-quarters pole. When I did, he really took off."

The loss left Karen Taylor in tears. "I cried and cried and cried," she sobbed. "Not because he had lost but because he tried to win so hard."

"Your horse ran a great race and deserved to win," offered Mickey Taylor.

"Well, thank you," countered Hunt. "I really didn't think he'd get there. When he was so far back on the backstretch, I thought we'd be lucky to get third money."

"You really have a great horse. He just never did give up. Came back and caught us at the end. You have to be very proud of him the way he ran today."

"We are. We're very satisfied with his race."

No one could recall another such dramatic run by Exceller. It left the crowd breathless.

"He is one heckuva racehorse," averred Whittingham. "The best thing that probably happened to him is that he raced in Europe as a two-year-old. This meant that Exceller didn't have to be rushed for speed as would have been the case had he raced in this country. The two-year-old races in Europe are longer and less frequent, so the pressure isn't as intense as it is in the U.S."

There was no explanation why Affirmed's saddle slipped. It had never happened to Cauthen before. Perhaps Barrera didn't tighten the saddle enough? Or was there foul play? It certainly caught Cauthen by surprise.

"The saddle was up around Affirmed's withers and I couldn't get any balance," he explained. "I thought I was going to get pitched off. The damned thing was nearly up on his neck."

Barrera's son, Larry, offered a remote possibility, alluding to a muddy track: "Maybe it was the water splashing from the horses on the other side of him, it may have stretched the elastic. There was nothing that could be done. Every time Steve pulled back, the saddle went forward. It was halfway off the number. Steve rode a good race. On the far turn, Steve thought, 'What's the use of going on?' He gave up on him and didn't ride him the rest of the way."

Affirmed's neck wasn't the issue now. Far from it. What was instead was Cauthen's. His slump had reached epidemic proportions, which created serious concern for Barrera and Wolfson. No one had an answer. Maybe a month's respite from riding would benefit Cauthen. A slumping fighter takes time off. So does a baseball player in a batting slump. Wouldn't it make sense for a jockey who couldn't find a winner's circle?

But Cauthen kept riding, and he kept losing on all the other mounts Goodman got for him. It was mind-boggling. How could he fall from grace so quickly? He, too, was looking for answers as the racing world wondered.

"I try to be pretty much myself," Cauthen said. "I try to get the best out of my ability. This game is an up-and-down game. I've known this since the beginning. And when things are not going right, it's not necessarily your own fault.

"I've gone to people I respect and trust, my dad, Lenny, and some trainers, and I've asked them what I'm doing wrong. And the answer usually is, 'Steve you're riding as good as ever. You just do the best you can.'"

It just wasn't enough.

Following the Gold Cup, Wolfson and Barrera decided that Affirmed wouldn't run the rest of the year, but instead wait for his four-year-old campaign. Barrera would leisurely train him in California, then go all out in preparation for Affirmed's first race on January 7 in the Malibu Stakes at Santa Anita, a track both Barrera and Affirmed were familiar with, and besides, Barrera always liked California. When Cauthen joined them, he told Barrera that he'd decided to move to California and ride there all year.

"I'm very enthusiastic about this meeting," exclaimed Cauthen. "I'd like to see Affirmed have a great season. I've been telling people all along that he's going to be a better horse as a four-year-old. Affirmed really deserved the Horse of the Year award. I don't have to defend him, but he deserved it. He went through one of the toughest Triple Crowns of all time, and he was tired when he got beat by Seattle Slew in the Marlboro. Slew had reached his peak at that time, don't forget.

"There is a terrific difference between a three-year-old and a mature four-year-old. It's like asking a ten-year-old kid to run against a twenty-year-old man. Affirmed is still growing and developing. You haven't seen anything yet. Riding him is like floating. Other horses float, too, but they don't cover as much ground as Affirmed. The sensation is hard to describe but it's like floating and knowing you can get the job done anytime you ask him. Just take over at any time.

"I like California and I like the people here. New York was a tough town. For someone who comes from the country and togetherness, New York is a cold place to walk into. Some of this is good, but I get claustrophobia there."

On the evening of the Malibu, Barrera had another concern aside from Cauthen. Heavy rain during the day left the possibility of an off-track on Sunday. Barrera never liked to send his horses to the post in conditions like that.

"I will check the track on Sunday afternoon, and if I think it's in good shape, Affirmed will run," reported Barrera. "I am keeping my fingers crossed the track will be fast because Affirmed is ready for a race."

Affirmed had four horses waiting to challenge him after a record 1978 campaign in which he earned $901,541 and won Horse of the Year honors. He was a true champion in his first two years, producing 16 victories and three second-place finishes in twenty lifetime races. The only time he finished out of the money was in his last race, the Jockey Club Gold Cup over a sloppy track at Belmont Park three months earlier. In recent weeks, Barrera had worked hard to get him ready for the Malibu.

"He put on more than one hundred pounds since his last race, and it's all muscle," disclosed Barrera. "He needed the work, and when he came off the track, he never acted tired. In fact, he's always on the muscle, wants to do more. He's muscled up and more mature-looking. It's hard for me to say if he's going to be a better horse in 1979. I'm hopeful but honestly I'd be happy if he's as good as he was last year."

Barrera never expected what would happen when the race got under way. Cauthen broke Affirmed in front and had him on the rail throughout the race, but unfortunately with little racing room at any part of the seven-furlong race. Radar Ahead saw to that. He kept Affirmed locked in before he tired as Little Reb took over while Affirmed finished a shocking third, over two lengths behind. Barrera was left to wonder if Cauthen had had a bad race as his slump continued.

Affirmed's loss in the Malibu attracted a larger field for the San Fernando. Seven horses, three more than the Malibu, entered to challenge him. Were other trainers taking aim at Affirmed? Still, the crowd didn't quit on him and made Affirmed a solid 1–2 favorite at top weight of 126 for the San Fernando. Cauthen had remarked that Affirmed would be fine and a much tighter horse this time. It was indeed a critical race not only for Affirmed but for Cauthen as well.

As he did in the Malibu, Little Reb took off fast and jumped in front with Radar Ahead next, followed by Affirmed. Radar Ahead stayed with Little Reb until the top of the stretch, when he turned it on and assumed the lead. Affirmed, who had fallen to fifth, advanced to third but went wide on the far turn. Cauthen didn't want any part of the close quarters he'd encountered in the Malibu. Cauthen had room this time and urged Affirmed faster with a snap of the whip. He overtook Little Reb for place, but finished 2¾ lengths behind Radar Ahead.

It was the second successive disappointing loss for the three-year-old champion, and questions abounded about his tribulations. Was it him or the jockey? It grew even worse for Cauthen, who was wallowing in a rough winter in California. He had now gone 110 times without a victory and was incurring the wrath of the fans, who began booing him even before the races commenced. What a difference a year made. But that's the way it is in horse racing. Never is the old cliché "What have you done for me lately?" more prominent than in racing. Cauthen began thinking of going back to New York.

As disappointed as Barrera was after the Malibu, his remorse deepened after Affirmed finished second in the San Fernando Stakes two weeks later. It was clearly a poor start for his star thoroughbred's final campaign. The media were wondering just what was wrong with Affirmed. Several days before the $200,000 Charles Strub Stakes, Barrera, never losing confidence in Affirmed, offered some encouraging words while at the same time replacing Cauthen with Pincay in an attempt to stem the losing streak.

"There's not a thing wrong with Affirmed," assured Barrera. "He needed the first race, the Malibu, and he may have dropped a little too far out of it in the San Fernando. He has trained sensationally for the Strub. Last week, he did a five-furlong breeze in fifty-seven seconds. If there was anything wrong with him, he couldn't have done that."

Barrera even looked past the Strub, exuding confidence about his champion: "After the Strub, his next start will probably be the Santa Anita Handicap. I plan to keep him here on the West Coast through the spring and early summer for the Californian and the Hollywood Gold Cup and then return to New York. It might be time to try him on the grass. If he were to show something, it would mean many more options. I am not crazy about grass racing, but this is a great horse and I think he can do anything asked of him."

Barrera was ebullient when discussing the upcoming annual Eclipse Award Dinner. A wagonful of trophies was already cataloged for the Harbor View Farm contingent. Affirmed was responsible for practically all of them: the Horse of the Year trophy; the trophy as the best three-year-old; Louis Wolfson as Owner of the Year; Louis Wolfson as Breeder of the Year; Laz Barrera as Trainer of the Year; and Steve Cauthen as Jockey of the Year. It was quite a war chest.

An emotional Barrera was looking forward to the evening in San Francisco, and he made certain that members of his family would be there to share his joy.

"My daughter is coming from Mexico City," said Barrera. "My oldest son is coming from New York. There will be brothers and sisters-in-law, nieces and nephews. I want them all there because it will be a special evening."

Barrera shook his head and bit his lip. He was filled with emotion but still preferred to talk. After all, he loved his profession and was *numero uno*, as the Latinos would yell.

"I never in my life believed it could all have happened in one year," weighed in the fifty-four-year-old Cuban conditioner. "It's given me a sense of pride I can't describe. I just hope the same thing happens to somebody else so that another trainer can know the feeling. If all the other good things hadn't happened with J. O. Tobin and It's In The Air, and if Affirmed had just won the Triple Crown, that would have been more than enough. There never was a Triple Crown like it, and you have to wonder if there will be another with two horses matched as closely as Affirmed and Alydar."

The largest crowd of the Santa Anita meet, 50,220, assembled on a sunny Sunday afternoon to see if Affirmed, with his new jockey, Laffit Pincay, could end the slump, which had elongated to five straight defeats. The horse and rider were no stranger to each other. Pincay had appeared with Affirmed three straight times in the winner's oval. However, the last time they were together, Affirmed was disqualified for interfering with Alydar in Saratoga's Travers Stakes. Ironically, that was the beginning of Affirmed's winless stretch.

Barrera was confident that the Affirmed-Pincay union would be advantageous and result in triumph. He didn't even protest when Affirmed was assigned the maximum weight of 126 pounds after five straight losses. What added to his confidence was that Affirmed had drawn the No. 10 post position.

"That's good," he acknowledged. "Nobody will bother him out there. Going a mile and one-quarter, there's a long run to the first turn, and we'll have plenty of time to get good position."

Affirmed had some familiar rivals, notably Radar Ahead and Little Reb, on the track with him. However, this time Little Reb didn't break out on top. Quilligan Quail, a 57–1 entry, led the early going. Affirmed, running easily, wasn't far behind in the third position. At the five-furlong pole, without any urging from Pincay, Affirmed began to run with a purpose. He was defiant in running away from the field in amazing fashion to a prodigious ten-length triumph. Pincay handled him perfectly.

"The only thing Laz told me before the race was to use my best judgment," disclosed Pincay. "The colt broke right on top so I just waited to see how things went past the grandstand the first time. I could tell he was full of run, so I was only concerned with keeping him clear and out of trouble.

"At the five-length pole, he breezed to the leader, and I just waited until the stretch to ask him to run. I hit him right-handed but he didn't seem to notice. He has a tendency to loaf when he gets in front so I hit him three or four times more just to keep his mind on business. I didn't want to take any chances."

Cauthen and his agent, the incorrigible Lenny Goodman, realized Steve had no chance of being on board Affirmed again. Pincay was in perfect harmony with Affirmed with the ostentatious display in the Strub. Cauthen made up his mind to leave for New York, but Goodman urged him to remain in California, and he did so for a week without any progress. Despite all the speculations regarding Cauthen, Goodman was hoping Steve would rebound and eliminate them.

One speculation was that Cauthen had lost his nerve because of two bad spills in 1977 and 1978. Another was that Cauthen had become complacent after his overnight, wealthy success. A third was that Goodman wasn't getting him the best horse in any given race. A final far-reaching one was that young Steve had discovered girls and was out late too much.

"Wrong, wrong, wrong," protested the cigar-chomping Goodman. "All these things are stupid. Arcaro went zero for one hundred once. Sure he goes out with girls, but he's not running around. He wouldn't know how because he doesn't drink anything stronger than orange juice. His weight is fine and his attitude is beautiful.

"Stevie went zero for twenty-two once in 1977," continued the smooth-talking agent, "and they all started saying that he'd had it. He won six the next day before the ink was even dry. You know something? It may sound crazy, but I think the Kid is riding better now than he ever rode."

Goodman was a proud agent. He was desperately trying to reestablish Cauthen since trainers were looking past him. But going 105 days without a winner was like Joe DiMaggio going hitless for two months. What indeed was going wrong with Cauthen, the first jockey whose horses earned $6 million in a single year, who brought home 487 winners in 2,075 outings? In New York, where he was worshipped, he won 433 of them, obliterating the previous record of 299.

It was unfathomable that the hottest apprentice jockey since Bill Shoemaker in 1949, and Cauthen was hotter, in less than a year lost more consecutive races than any other jockey in history. Cauthen was emotionally devastated and was beginning to look toward England and an offer from British horse owner Robert Sangster. Although slumps are usually confined to the world of sports, they do occur in other fields. Companies and large corporations experience them. Actors and actresses have them, as do authors. Even Ernest Hemingway was affected. He overcame one slump with *The Old Man and the Sea* and won a Pulitzer Prize for it.

Yet athletic slumps are more publicized, more so in baseball than any other sport, simply because of their seemingly unending categories of statistics. Once the unwelcome albatross of a slump appears, it unquestionably becomes prolonged by pressure. One classic example was Brooklyn Dodgers star Gil Hodges, going 0 for 21 in the seven-game series against the Yankees. Dodgers fans were praying and lighting candles in church on his behalf.

"All I needed was a horse who could run fast enough," lamented Cauthen. "I was just getting a lot of crappy mounts. Nobody wins with slow horses. It's impossible. I just needed the right mount. I was supposed to do some good once, then why not again?"

Several factors possibly contributed to Cauthen's dilemma. Goodman didn't arrive in California until the racing season began. Most agents are on the grounds well before then lining up mounts for their clients. Besides, the leading trainers in Southern California work closely with the local agents, who are available all year long. It's a distinct advantage.

Another factor was that Barrera's stable was also undergoing a slump. In the first thirty-six days of the meet, Barrera had saddled only eleven winners. Trainers understandably shy away from a jockey who isn't going good, which is compounded when a stable is also down. If Cauthen wasn't getting the good mounts he was expecting, this was doubly why.

Frank Kilroe, Santa Anita's vice president of racing, cited another reason. Kilroe was highly regarded in racing circles. He had years of experience in New York both as a handicapper and a racing secretary. He pointed out the difference in racing styles between the West and the East:

"The tracks out here are harder and faster, and that means your racing tactics have to be a little different. In the East, the softer tracks tend to slow the fast horses down a little bit and give the come-from-behinders a chance to come back.

"Out here on the faster tracks, you have to be more aggressive at the start. The jockeying for position in the first furlong is a critical factor because the leaders aren't coming back to you later in the race."

When a story broke in a Los Angeles newspaper that Cauthen was on the verge of signing a lucrative contract for Sangster, Barrera was enraged.

"I knew nothing about this," he fumed. "Last year we were very close. He lived with my son Larry. This year he has his own apartment. Larry still goes to dinner with him almost every night, but he said nothing of this."

Cauthen confirmed it at a press conference several days later. The contract specified a salary, reportedly a million dollars a year along with incentives.

"I'm not running away," confessed Cauthen. "A man sometimes gets an offer to go to a better job. I think I got a better offer."

The surprising events stirred memories of a lyric from one of George M. Cohan's songs, and a popular one indeed:

> *Yankee Doodle went to London*
> *Just to ride the ponies . . .*

Maybe Cauthen was more comfortable in New York, or perhaps the grind was getting too much for his liking, although Cauthen said that he hadn't lost his desire to ride. On the contrary, he wanted to continue, but he found keeping his weight down to ride a burden. The jockeys' world is complex. They love the glamour of the track and the financial rewards for winning. But they have to pay a heavy physical price to remain fit every day of the year.

No athlete suffers more for his sport than a jockey, with the constant pressure to win. He must tax his body to keep his weight almost inhumanly low to secure mounts to earn enough money to exist, hoping for that one big payday, such as a Derby, that will give him that one glorious day in the sun. The food abstinence was insane, as being two or three pounds overweight meant the death sentence.

The scale looks down upon a jockey like an executioner. The defining weight was 114 pounds, and many jockeys dreaded being weighed. It was a hellish encounter. Some would regurgitate to arrive at the prescribed weight, and the lighter the better. How much can the human body endure every day? Six hundred calories a day was the standard. Steam rooms were the Shangri-la. Diarrhea was an ally. Laxatives, too. It didn't bode well for a jockey's personality. It was a helluva tariff to pay to achieve fame.

Steve Cauthen didn't want that anymore. He had the fame and the glory and the money, and he was still a kid.

TWELVE

Laffit Pincay: Affirmed's New Jockey

Cauthen had been unsuccessful with Affirmed, losing four successive races on both coasts: two in New York and the other two in California. As personally disturbing as it was because of his closeness with Cauthen, Barrera had to make a change. He reached out to Laffit Pincay, who had won two of the three times he was on Affirmed, with the only loss being a disqualification in the Travers at Saratoga in August.

Under Pincay, Affirmed resumed winning, as Cauthen left for New York and a new start. In the $312,800 Santa Anita Handicap, Affirmed was a tight 13–10 favorite over Tiller, who was listed at 17–10. It didn't matter to Pincay. In the early moments of the mile-and-a-quarter outing, he turned Affirmed loose after Painted Wagon set the pace. Without any urging, Affirmed assumed command in the backstretch without any trouble. He moved swiftly and increased his 1½-length lead at the quarter pole to a healthy 4 at the eight pole and won effortlessly by 4½ lengths, beating two old rivals, Tiller and Exceller. The win inflated Affirmed's earnings to $1,609,318, fourth on the all-time list.

"This is easily the best horse I have ever ridden," praised Pincay, who won the Santa Anita Handicap for the fifth time.

At thirty-two, Pincay had been riding for twelve years in America. Born in Panama, he came to the United States in 1966 and four years later won the prestigious George Woolf Memorial Jockey Award. The coveted award is given to the jockey whose career and personal conduct exemplify the best among those participating in the sport. He had been successful in California in winning such major stakes as the Del Mar Derby, San Bernardino Handicap, Hollywood Gold Cup, and the Bing Crosby Handicap among others.

Pincay had other trophies on his shelf. He won the Eclipse Award in 1971, 1973, 1974, 1979, and 1985. He also was the United States Champion Jockey by earnings for five successive years, 1970–74. He was every inch a champion jockey, and now he had a champion horse for the rest of the year. Pincay's career couldn't have been more fulfilling. Any jockey would relish half of what the popular Panamanian had accomplished, whose defining strength was his willpower in controlling his weight, the daily nemesis of jockeys.

Trainer D. Wayne Lukas witnessed an exemplary instance of it on a California–New York flight. Incredibly, Pincay ate only a single peanut on the lengthy cross-county flight. And he did so systematically. Pincay ate one-half of a solitary peanut at takeoff, and the other half on landing. Lukas marveled at Pincay's control, which was beyond belief. Ever since 1969, Pincay had been battling a weight problem. He ate diet pills like jelly beans, only the pills left him nervous and sleepless. The daily water pills he took caused him cramps. For a brief time he stopped taking pills, but returned to them when his weight began to climb.

"You think it's great that you lost some, and then later on you start feeling cramps in your legs, then your back, and dizziness," confessed Pincay. "Little by little it starts getting into your system and you start feeling the weakness and the cramps. I was tired all the time.

"Even when I was going good, I had a very empty feeling. I used to get up in the morning and think, 'Oh, man, you got to do it again, the pills, the hot box, and there's nothing you can do about it. Do I have to do this the rest of my life?' It was a terrible feeling, day after day.

"Yet, I was making so much money. I had a beautiful family and I was not enjoying it. I don't know why I was so intense about winning. I was trying so hard, sometimes I was too active on a horse and he would lose his balance and foul other horses and I was getting suspensions.

"Pushing too hard, trying too hard, was what I was doing. I would lose my temper very easily. Get in fights all the time with other jockeys. In 1973 I started to get very depressed. I wasn't satisfied with anything. I'd win four races in a day and think about the one that got away. I'd get mad thinking I should have won five today. It was always the win that got away. I don't know why. It wasn't the money. It was the pressure. Just too much pressure."

In that year, 1973, Pincay became the first jockey to win $4 million in purses in a single year. The following year he topped that with $4.251 million. But he was paying a price for all that he was doing. In 1975, he broke his collarbone twice in five months, the first time in March and the next in July. Was it all worth it? The excruciating infirmities, coupled with the death of his best friend and fellow jockey Alvaro Pineda, along with the rigid diet, were enough to make Pincay seriously think about quitting. He was at a breaking point.

"What am I doing here?" Pincay asked himself. "Alvaro had been working very, very hard. He gets killed trying so hard. It was like I was putting myself in his position. Why do I have to suffer like this? To get killed like he did? I questioned whether what I was doing was right. I didn't know if it was worth it. What's important? What means something to me?"

Since that time Pincay had been at peace with himself. His consuming obsession with winning had mellowed to some degree, but his intensity remained.

"There's no pressure now," he admitted. "I hope to ride until I'm forty. I just do my job, come home, and eat my dinner. There's nothing to worry about anymore. If I get into a bad streak, or something goes wrong, I know how to handle it better."

Pincay's demeanor wasn't lost on his former agent Vince DeGregory. "Laffit is riding better than ever," observed De-Gregory. "I still think he's the greatest rider in the world and will always think that."

Pincay's California challenge shifted to Hollywood Park and the $272,400 Californian on May 20 in a mile-and-sixteenth run. Affirmed's 130-pound impost didn't deter his backers, who made him a 3–1 favorite in the field of eight, among them Little Reb and Sensitive Prince. At the outset, they were a trio, with Affirmed in the middle, flanked on either side by the two familiar challengers. They remained locked that way for a half mile, then Sensitive Prince dropped back, followed by Little Reb a few seconds later.

Pincay took over. Did he ever. He opened a two-length lead at the eighth pole, then extended it in the final furlong for another facile five-length triumph. It was a special victory for Barrera, who was hugging Affirmed in the winner's circle for the first time since he had recently undergone open-heart surgery. If Barrera needed a jolting get-well lift, Affirmed gave it to him.

"He's a great horse, no doubt about it," praised Pincay. "Laz told me to lay about second, but after he broke so good, I went to the front with him. I didn't want to take any chances. He was really starting to play around in the stretch. He seemed like he was looking for someone to go with him again. That's why I kept getting after him so much."

Affirmed with Pincay appeared unbeatable. They had one more challenge in California in the Hollywood Gold Cup on June 24 before heading East to close out Affirmed's career. The prize money was enriched from $350,000 to $500,000 in a direct attempt to bring Alydar and Affirmed together again. However, Lucille Markey recommended that her prize thoroughbred remain in the East.

"I wanted Affirmed to relax," disclosed Barrera in the weeks before the Cup. "He puts so much into his workouts that he needs to taper off. I've been working him a mile and he'll lose his speed completely, so I shortened up. This was a very good workout, not too slow, not too fast."

Some two weeks after the purse was announced, handicapper Eual Wyatt began assigning the weights for the Gold Cup.

Barrera wasn't idly standing by. He was shrewdly playing the old con game when talk of Affirmed's carrying 132 pounds became lively.

"I don't want him to carry so much weight that he gets hurt," warned Barrera. "From now on, I'm going to be very careful running him with weight. He don't have to prove anything no more. He established his value. More important to me is that he will be a good stallion."

When the weights were officially announced, Barrera got his number. Affirmed would carry 132 pounds. D. Wayne Lukas was displeased.

"It was an out-and-out gift," charged the veteran trainer. "He should have had at least one thirty-five."

Wyatt defended his judgment. "I think it's a fair weight. We'll see on Sunday."

Still, seven other trainers wanted to challenge Affirmed's dominance in California. Despite toting the heaviest impost of his career, Affirmed was the bettors' pick at 3–10. The crowd of 48,884 would get its money's worth. From the start, Affirmed and Sirlad went at each other along with Text, another challenger. They were within a length of each other all the way until the stretch, Affirmed on the rail, Sirlad next to him, and Text on the outside. No one yielded an inch, and it had all the drama of a classic Affirmed-Alydar duel.

It brought the crowd to its feet screaming. The three began to turn it on for one last drive. Pincay thumped Affirmed three times. Darrel McHargue was swatting Sirlad, and Bill Shoemaker was doing the same on Text. With about a furlong left, Text yielded. The duel between Affirmed and Sirlad continued. They were neck and neck inside the sixteenth pole. Could

Sirlad pull the upset? Affirmed sensed the danger. He began to pull away by a neck, then a half-length, finally disposing of his rival by three-quarters of a length in an exhilarating finish that thrilled the crowd.

The emotion carried to the winner's circle. The fans cheered Barrera along the way. He was numbed by the spectacle he had witnessed just minutes ago as he joined Patrice Wolfson, who was wiping her face from the tension the race had created.

"What a race. What a race," he excitedly remarked. "A great horse, isn't he? A great horse."

When Pincay appeared with Affirmed, Barrera yelled, "Thank you."

Pincay broke out a smile. "Congratulations, Lazaro," he piped up.

"If you had to pick the five greatest horses in all history, Affirmed would have to be right there," added Pincay. "When we were all right there at the head of the stretch, I knew I was going to have to ask for a lot from him, but I had confidence that he would go on. He always does. Sirlad was the one to beat, and the pace wasn't that fast. The only way they'll beat my horse is with more weight."

Louis Wolfson didn't get to see the race. He was at his Bal Harbour home scratched by the flu. But his wife Patrice's cheeks were flushed with victory.

"Laz has done just the most phenomenal job," she gushed. "The record speaks for itself. Never has there been a Triple Crown winner who came back and raced the way Affirmed has as a four-year-old."

Barrera, too, was moved by the win, saying, "The money record means a lot to me because Affirmed did it in so much shorter time than Kelso and because I know it will last for a very long time. This is a day that the people who were here will always remember. You can't take the Santa Anita Handicap, the Laurel Futurity, or the Belmont Stakes away from Affirmed, but this day was just as beautiful, a great day for Affirmed and the people who came to see him. When he is retired in December, racing will lose its best friend."

Just then, the voice of the track announcer bellowed through the loudspeaker, "Ladies and gentlemen, the richest racehorse in thoroughbred history, Affirmed!"

Sirlad's jockey, Darrel McHargue, was awed by Affirmed's performance. He bestowed the ultimate compliment, which also served as warning to others.

"There is no way any horse is going to beat Affirmed," he predicted. "I think he'll go down as one of the greatest that ever raced. My horse ran real big, but look what happened to him when it counted."

After triumphantly conquering California with four consecutive victories, Affirmed, Pincay, and Barrera headed to New York. Affirmed's farewell appearance would come in the fall. "Affirmed will go to Saratoga for the summer for a rest and run in New York in the fall," disclosed Barrera, who'd already docketed him for the Woodward Stakes on September 22 and the Jockey Gold Cup on October 6 at Belmont, a track that was to Affirmed's liking. The only pitiable part was that Cauthen wouldn't see him for the last time. He was in Europe racing for owner Robert Sangster, who had made him an attractive offer to ride without worrying about maintaining a 115-pound weight standard.

With the winner's share of $275,000 from the Hollywood

Gold Cup, Affirmed jumped past Kelso as the richest horse in turf history. Barrera was ecstatic, saying, "Affirmed showed what kind of horse he was. He showed all his courage and he gave them a historic race. And I'll tell you something else. With that kind of race, if I didn't have my heart surgery, I would have been buried. I knew that I was taking my chances that I would drop dead at the racetrack any moment.

"Between the afternoon of March fifth and the morning of March seventh, they worked on me for seven hours. My wife and my sons and daughter were in the hospital waiting. The doctor told me beforehand of the chances of stroke and heart attack during the surgery. I told him not to tell them, that they had enough to worry about."

It had been a strenuous year for the fifty-four-year-old horse lover, whose hair was producing more strands of white. A number of factors contributed to Barrera's travails regarding Affirmed, not the least of which was the removal of Cauthen, with whom he had a father-son relationship, in favor of Pincay. Affirmed had opened his four-year-old campaign with shocking losses in two races with Cauthen in the Malibu and the San Fernando, which left Barrera distraught.

"There was a point where Affirmed lost four straight races and I had to do something," agonized Barrera. "Affirmed was in tip-top shape and was training tremendously. But Cauthen was riding him easy, and obviously I can't change the trainer."

Since the change, the doughty Affirmed and the determined Pincay had harmonized for four consecutive victories. They were as compatible as mustard on a hot dog at any racetrack. But New York was another challenge awaiting them, and Barrera had to be wary about the reception he would receive there, the races he was considering, and the weights his horse would be saddled with. He had two months to decide, and Affirmed welcomed the rest after a hectic California season.

Affirmed returned to competition on August 29 in an allowance race at Belmont that offered no wagering. Barrera scheduled this prep race before sending Affirmed into the Marlboro Handicap at the Long Island track. With two other horses to test him over a mile, Affirmed performed excitingly. He was never pushed and led from wire to wire in an impressive six-length victory in the near record time of 1:34. He showed himself ready for the $300,000 Marlboro Cup.

"This race today did Affirmed a lot of good," remarked Pincay. "He was going along easily and he didn't seem to get tired."

Affirmed's torrid return came only three days after Spectacular Bid set a track record at Delaware Park in his first outing since being upset in the Belmont Stakes. His appearance in the Marlboro would make a fascinating duel with Affirmed. Buddy Delp, Bid's trainer, was excited about the matchup.

"I'm really looking forward to the Marlboro," he confessed. "We're going for Horse of the Year, and you don't win big ones like that by staying in the barn. My horse couldn't be better now. He's done everything we've asked. I'm not sure he's ready for Affirmed, but he's ready for today.

"I'm like Laz. He thinks he has a great horse and I think I have a great horse. Now we have to see which one is right."

Racing officials were apparently impressed with Affirmed's exhibition race. When Racing Secretary Leonard Hale published the assigned weights for the Marlboro, it made Barrera flinch. Hale gave Affirmed the heaviest impost yet, a glaring 133 pounds, nine more than Spectacular Bid. An irate Barrera immediately reacted with the warning that he might not enter Affirmed in the Marlboro at that weight, opting instead for the Woodward Stakes two weeks later.

"I would have been willing to give Spectacular Bid seven pounds, but nine is too much," argued Barrera. "I don't think it's right either to give General Assembly thirteen pounds when he just got through setting a track record in winning the Travers at Saratoga.

"In last year's Marlboro Cup, Seattle Slew, an outstanding horse, carried 128 pounds to Affirmed's 124. I think Affirmed would be taking the worst of it and I'm opposed to running."

Wolfson was quick to support Barrera's decision and bellowed, "I've always followed my trainer's recommendations. If after further thought Laz continues to recommend to me that we pass the Marlboro, Affirmed will not run."

Barrera withheld Affirmed. Spectacular Bid did run and Shoemaker conducted a masterful ride. While the field of eleven was still maneuvering for position in the backstretch, Shoemaker quickly sent Bid to the front. He never got caught. Riding him easily, Shoemaker only tapped him once, at the sixteenth pole, just to keep him interested, and Bid stormed across the finish line well in front of everybody else. As the handicappers would say, he wasn't even tested. They were already analyzing an Affirmed-Bid challenge in the Woodward.

However, it wasn't to be. Bid developed a fever a week before the race and the much anticipated duel was postponed.

Sirlad, who'd finished second behind Affirmed in the Hollywood Gold Cup, was looked upon as Affirmed's chief rival following an impressive win in the Sunset Handicap. Another who drew attention with his speed was Coastal. The weather on race day wasn't promising. It had already begun to rain Saturday morning some eight hours before the Belmont race as Barrera stood under the shedrow by Affirmed's stall. Barrera never liked muddy tracks. Yet, he had the capacity to get the most out of his horses, making the adjustment from the firmer fast tracks of the West to the deeper, slower ones of the East. He was in a philosophical mood.

"The only difference between Laz Barrera who trains horses at Santa Anita and Hollywood Park, and the Laz Barrera who trains horses at Saratoga and Belmont, is in the license plates on the cars," he mentioned. "In California my license reads *Laz*. In New York, it's *Barrera*. But I'm the trainer in both places.

"Today is September twenty-two, the last day of summer. In the East that can mean when you wake up in the tomorrow, there will be snow on the ground. The bees know that summer is ending. That's why they are so mean right now. They sting for no reason at all. At this time of year the bees will get down inside your shirt and crawl up the legs of your pants and sting the hell out of you. But the bees also get slower now. You can swat them a lot easier than you could two weeks ago. Watch!"

Was the colorful conditioner with his philosophy making reference to a muddy track that could conceivably slow his horse down? Yet, he had proven that he could make adjustments from California to New York. He had been criticized for skipping the Marlboro. And with his temperament, he didn't forget those things.

"Experts are just like bees at this time of the year," he began. "They get slow and dumb. Two weeks ago these experts said that Barrera ducked the Marlboro Handicap because he was afraid Affirmed could not beat Spectacular Bid. But I was up-front in giving my reasons for not running in the Marlboro. I thought the weights for that race were way out of line. A lot of people said I was a lousy sport for not running in the Marlboro, that I owed it to the game.

"What I owe to the game is for the public to see Affirmed at his very best in the best race. A trainer's job is to do the best thing for his horse. I think I have, and I know that if Affirmed loses the Woodward today, I'll look like a fool. The field is rough and the racetrack is going to be sloppy. But Affirmed is ready. I'll let him speak for me."

Affirmed had difficulty getting adjusted to the muddy track in the early segment of the race. He hadn't made anything of a move. With a quarter of a mile remaining, he was pinched along the rail. Pincay eased his grip on the reins, and in an instant Affirmed electrified the thousands who had come to see him with a burst of speed that shot him through a gap and into the lead. In the stretch for home, Pincay lightly tapped Affirmed twice for a 1¼-length victory with consummate ease over Coastal.

Pincay said he felt in control the entire way despite a slow start and even being in close quarters on the rail. He never showed any signs of panic.

"I wasn't ready to make my move yet," he explained. "I just waited for the three-eighths pole and he went from there. I was concerned about the track condition because of his layoff, and he dropped back early because of the mud."

The race went according to what Barrera had outlined, bees or no bees. He was a magnificent trainer, a virtuoso in every sense.

"I wasn't worried when Affirmed dropped back to fourth," divulged Barrera. "I told Laffit not to fight with the others for the lead. Affirmed proved what a great horse he is. I'm not afraid to face Spectacular Bid because the Jockey Gold Cup will answer all those questions about who is the best."

The Jockey Gold Cup was exactly two weeks away in what would be Affirmed's final race. Under Pincay, he had won six consecutive races and wasn't seriously threatened in any of them. He was every bit a champion. The $375,000 Gold Cup was all that was left, and much of the talk before the race centered on Affirmed's syndication.

Kentucky breeder Brownell Combs, who would manage Affirmed's stud fees, knew Affirmed's value. The previous January, Combs had syndicated Affirmed for $14.4 million, thirty-six shares at $400,000 each. He collected buyers for twenty-one shares. Wolfson retained the remaining fifteen shares, while Combs's Spendthrift Farm accumulated four free breeding services a year to manage the syndicate's care of Affirmed.

"The value of this horse keeps going up all the time," revealed Combs. "There have been offers of $650,000 to buy a share, but no one has been willing to sell. I suppose that if a person really wanted to sell a share in his horse now, he could get one million dollars. If you were syndicating now, if he wins today, you'd be looking at a twenty-five-million-to-thirty-million-dollar horse."

The race finally matched the four-year-old Affirmed and the best three-year-old, Spectacular Bid, along with the 1979 Belmont Stakes winner, Coastal, who was looked upon as a spoiler. The winner would undoubtedly determine the Horse of the Year. The jockey would play a significant role: Pincay with his strong hands, and Shoemaker with the smoothest hands on the circuit. The heavy wagering was on Affirmed at 3–5 and Spectacular Bid at 7–5. Coastal followed at 8–1. Affirmed opened the twelve-furlong race in front from the No. 3 post, trailed by Spectacular Bid. Pincay had Affirmed moving briskly at the clubhouse turn.

In the backstretch, the duel that everyone was expecting began to form. Bid was running freely from his earlier fourth spot and was only a half-length behind Affirmed. However, at the mile marker, Bid lost several strides, and Coastal moved along the rail to challenge Affirmed and actually drew even with him. As they headed into the stretch, Affirmed relished Coastal's challenge and began pulling away from him. He disposed of Coastal, but what about Spectacular Bid?

Affirmed wasn't home free yet. Shoemaker got Bid moving with speed again in full stride and was only a half-length behind at the eighth pole. It prompted Pincay to revert to his stick. Affirmed responded instantly. He stretched out and surged to the finish line to a wildly screaming crowd. Affirmed completed his charge over the last hundred yards to win by three-quarters of a length. Four times Bid challenged Affirmed, and four times the great champion rebuffed him. Affirmed had in perfect rhythm achieved his seventh straight triumph to close a brilliant career as the first horse to win $2 million.

The win was extrasweet for Barrera. When he pulled Affirmed out of the Marlboro for what he considered an unfair weight disadvantage, he was heavily criticized, even though he explained, "I gotta do what's best for my horse." Any horsemen should accept that. But they didn't. The talk around Belmont by knowledgeable people accused Barrera of being "chicken." A bit of machismo is part of the Latin male personality. Being called a chicken is the ultimate insult.

"How come nobody asked me why now that I didn't run Affirmed in the Marlboro?" he asked his son Larry. Barrera's pride surfaced by his sarcastically answering his critics without reprimanding them. But down deep Barrera was hurt and angry but kept his composure and didn't say anything. Subtly he only remarked, "I'll let Affirmed do my talking for me," and the wonder horse did.

"Once my horse went to the lead, I knew the party was over," rhapsodized the happy Barrera. "Spectacular Bid is a helluva horse, no doubt about it. He's been used to winning by fifteen or twenty lengths, but when you hook up with Affirmed, it's different. Spectacular Bid is a great horse but Affirmed is a little better.

"Affirmed is a superhorse, the best in America or in Europe. I don't want anyone calling me prejudiced, but I think Affirmed is the best horse I ever saw."

No horse had ever withstood the excruciating pressure in the Derby, Preakness, and Belmont as Affirmed did from the relentless challenge of Alydar. Affirmed was racing's golden boy, a keen, intelligent horse almost human in his composure. If Affirmed had his way, he'd wear dark celebrity glasses, polo shirts, and sip Moët champagne. He was that kind of guy.

Barrera wanted a final look at his horse. He wanted to whisper good-night. When he reached the barn, the sky had darkened. He looked up at Affirmed and shook his head, a bit teary-eyed.

"Look at him," sighed Barrera. "It looks like he didn't even run. He knows he's a champion. No horse can look like that and not be a champion."

Steve Cauthen was right. Affirmed was indeed better as a four-year-old. The Kid knew his horse. But he wasn't with him at the end. The Kid without his horse. That was the only sad moment.

EPILOGUE

In the crucible of sports that has spanned centuries, Affirmed has etched his name, with other celebrated icons of the 1970s, with such luminaries as Babe Ruth, Red Grange, Johnny Unitas, Bill Tilden, Arnold Palmer, Gordie Howe, and Bill Russell, with a nod to Man o' War. Affirmed didn't do it alone and had a challenger and a champion in Alydar, who pushed him to the limits. Racing had never seen a more intense rivalry than Affirmed and Alydar in 1978 in the taxing journey of the Triple Crown. To this day, racing has never seen another Triple Crown champion, let alone a greater rivalry than that of the two chestnut thoroughbreds.

The story behind Affirmed was every bit an Ernest Hemingway novel. Affirmed was foaled and raised in Florida. Louis Wolfson, the crestfallen owner, was a kingmaker, a brilliant financier who established the art of the corporate takeover, which continues today; Steve Cauthen was a teenage jockey who won the Kentucky Derby five days after his eighteenth birthday; and Lazaro Barrera was a shrewd trainer who emigrated from Castro's Cuba to Mexico and arrived in California almost penniless. The story had all the essentials of a movie directed by John Ford.

Affirmed and Alydar were indelibly ensconced as the most intense rivalry in racing's colorful history. There were other rivalries in the past, but none with the background of Affirmed's storybook characters. Citation's battle with Noor in 1950 conjured memories, as did Kelso and Gun Bow in 1964. Track historians can scour the archives but won't find any rivalry the equal of Affirmed and Alydar. Talent and courage were their earmarks. Both were homebred chestnuts nurtured by owners who disdained going to market at Keeneland or Saratoga to buy a horse. Both thoroughbreds ironically inherited bloodlines from Native Dancer.

The spring of 1978 left an immutable memory of racing like no other. It started with a cheering crowd at the Derby that escalated to a roar at the Preakness and reached a crescendo at the Belmont, where Affirmed and Alydar ran side by side the entire distance of the stretch as one. Even the most stoic expert would accept it as the epiphany of the Triple Crown with the greatest mile-and-a-half stretch duel ever extracted. It captured a nation with anticipation and more thrills imaginable with every stride of the two superlative thoroughbreds.

The beauty the two horses presented was transferred to the jockeys who rode them. Both were professionally savant, Cauthen a mere youth at eighteen and Jorge Velasquez a cagey veteran of thirty-one. The beauty here was that each respected the other. They would compliment one another after a race and remain friendly in the confines of the jockeys' quarters, offering help if one needed it. On the tracks for a rigorous two minutes or so, they were like a Hemingway description of a bullfight in Spain. Cauthen and Velasquez, like matadors demonstrating their craft, rode flawlessly on their mounts and would have received an "Olé!" from Hemingway himself.

In 1998, the jockeys enjoyed a twenty-year reunion at Turfway Park in Florence, Kentucky.

"I still get butterflies," claimed Velasquez. "I know I got beat, but I feel like I'm going through the same thing again."

Cauthen pointed to the Belmont finish, which will forever be embedded in racing lore.

"It knew it was the greatest way you could win a Triple Crown, with a great finish," emphasized Cauthen. "That's my lasting memory that we pulled it off.

"People ask me, do you think you would have won the Triple Crown if you rode Alydar? No, I'd have finished worse than second. Alydar was more difficult to ride. He didn't switch leads. Affirmed was easier because he had speed. You could put him where you wanted him."

Ten years later at the Kentucky Derby in 2008, they were still recalling the dramatic Belmont stretch duel that provided Affirmed with the cherished Triple Crown.

"I was getting a little nervous and was starting to sense that we might be in trouble," admitted Cauthen. "I didn't want to make a mistake and be the reason we didn't win the Triple Crown. I really respected Alydar. He was always putting the pressure on and he never gave up. He kept coming back. I had to ask Affirmed for everything that day. His desire, his heart, is what got him home that day."

It was all that and more. Velasquez had given Alydar a masterful ride.

"I believe I pulled a head in front of Affirmed," recalled Velasquez. "I thought I was a winner. I was trying to ride Steve a little close, making sure I didn't get my number taken down or something like that. I just didn't want him to be able to hit his horse right-handed. I said to myself, 'Well, I got him this time.' Then I saw the little head coming again and I said, 'Oh my God, here we go again!'"

The inspired move that Cauthen made in switching his stick from his right hand to his left was ultimately the margin of victory.

Racing gave Wolfson back his self-respect and admiration in energizing Harbor View Farm into a champion stable. It reached its pinnacle in 1978 when Affirmed won the Triple Crown.

The Wolfson name is evident all over the city of Jacksonville. As chairman of the Wolfson Family Foundation, Wolfson directed much of the foundation's gifts to Jacksonville's medical, educational, research, and charitable entities. They included Wolfson Children's Hospital, and the Wolfson Student Center at Baptist Medical Center Downtown.

He was a man for the ages.

Yet, 1978 was a bittersweet for Gene and Lucille Markey. In Alydar, they had a worthy challenger, the only one who could duel Affirmed, especially in the melodramatic races of the Triple Crown. Alydar, too, was a champion, and he generated a notoriety to Calumet that had been absent for so many years.

Hiring young John Veitch as head trainer two years earlier turned out to be the miracle that brought Calumet out of the backstretch and ultimately out of debt. It provided a great deal of comfort to both Markeys in the fading years of their lives. The Admiral died in 1980 and Lucille in 1982. Yet Alydar continued to add to Calumet's coffers with his $300,000 breeding fees.

Unfortunately, under J. T. Lundy, Calumet once again spiraled into debt. Lundy, who was married to Lucille's granddaughter, was given control of Calumet. One of the first moves he made was to release Veitch and replace him with Frank Whiteley, who in turn appointed his son, David, as trainer. It was an awkward situation since Veitch and David were good friends. Lundy wanted no part of Veitch and had been instructed by the Markeys not to allow him on the property.

By 1991, Calumet had incurred over $100 million in debts after being grossly mismanaged by Lundy. One of his severe mistakes was his mismanagement of Alydar. Some years he bred Alydar over ninety times, more than twice the average for a stallion. In 1990, Alydar mysteriously broke a leg in his stall and had to be destroyed, much to Veitch's chagrin.

"I was offended, yes," remarked Veitch. "They had a great stallion, and instead of breeding him to a select group of high-quality mares, they were jeopardizing his life by breeding him so much. I guess nobody realized how badly they needed the cash. Everything was a house of cards based on Alydar, and when he died, it all collapsed."

Alydar's insurance was worth $36 million. However, it wasn't enough to save Calumet, which declared bankruptcy and was purchased by Henryk de Kwiatkowski in 1992. Alydar left a legacy in siring 1987 Kentucky Derby winner Alysheba and 1991 Derby victor Strike The Gold. In 2000, Lundy was convicted of fraud and bribery, casting a further pall on the proud Calumet farm, which had been a model for the industry.

Time has claimed the lives of the leading characters in the historic year. Besides the Markeys, Laz Barrera has died, and so has Wolfson, who succumbed in 2007 at the age of ninety-five, sadly without successfully cleansing his name. Jimmy the Greek died in 1996, in Las Vegas naturally, without ever collecting on his $100,000 bet on the Triple Crown. After the Belmont in 1978, the police raided a Miami bookie's joint and sent the unfortunate bookmaker to jail for a long time.

Horse racing is rife with hard-luck stories, albeit none other of the magnitude of the Greek's misfortune. Yet, for every bad-luck story, there is also a palmy one. Louie Petho, a horseplayer from Port Huron, Michigan, was attending his first Derby in 1978 while visiting his brother-in-law, Carl Working, in Louisville. Petho, with a $100 winning ticket on Affirmed in his pocket, got lucky and got close to Arcaro at the paddock just before the jockeys were to mount their horses. Petho found himself standing next to Arcaro and Howard Cosell as Banana Nose was wishing Cauthen luck and has the photo to prove it.

Suddenly, from out of nowhere, Petho heard someone shouting, "Howie, Howie." He looked around and discovered his brother-in-law standing on a trash can with a beer held high in his hand, yelling. Some ten seconds later the cover gave way, dumping Working into the can.

Surprisingly, Petho never got around to cashing the winning ticket. "I want to keep it as a souvenir," explained Petho years later, and he has the $560 ticket framed in his office to remind him of what a lucky day it was at the 1978 Derby.

Ten years after Alydar's death, Affirmed died in 2001. Cauthen had a lasting memory of Affirmed. He visited the horse often and savored every moment, knowing that Affirmed knew him.

"We had a connection, no doubt," remarked Cauthen. "I believe he knew me because he was such an intelligent horse. I think he knew exactly who I was, and he knew exactly what I was asking him to do. My connection with him was on his back. That's when he knew me, when I was on his back."

Veitch remained in racing as chief steward of the Kentucky Horse Racing Commission; Cauthen has a horse farm poetically named Dreamfield in Verona, Kentucky; and Velasquez became a jockeys' agent. They were such a vibrant part of the most exciting year in racing's history.

ACKNOWLEDGMENTS

The amount of research needed to produce a book of this magnitude wouldn't remotely have been possible without the help of so many others. I'm so grateful for the enormous contribution I was accorded by Phyllis Rogers at Kentucky's Keeneland Library and by Allan Carter at the National Museum of Racing. Phyllis never went out for lunch in the days I was there, and Allan came into his office from a morning on the tennis court to provide his time on his day off. Racing needs more of such dedicated individuals, who were unselfish in rendering insight to an author of twenty-four books who had never before written any on horse racing. Every author should have such a punctilious editor as Rob Kirkpatrick at St. Martin's Press, who got the horses on the track, and also Margaret Smith, who kept it all flowing. And Steve Boldt, an eagle-eye copyeditor if there ever was one. Thank you, also, to Kenneth J. Silver, who expertly coordinated the book's production. Finally, I was fulfilled brainstorming with Joe Rinaldi, on the marketing to get *Affirmed* off and running. And for Joan Higgins in getting the word out for *Affirmed*.

I must confess, in the kingdom of the horse I was energized by some wonderful people, especially the likes of Steve Cauthen, Hank Goldberg, Tom Werblin, and Dusty Mormando. Special acknowledgment to Marcia Wolfson, who supported the project from day one. I would like to thank a number of others for their parts: Ron Glass and Kristen Stewart of the Palm Beach County Library; Miriam Meier of the Saratoga Springs Public Library; Brien Bouyea at the National Museum of Racing; Richard Hancock and Becky Robinson of the Florida Thoroughbred Breeders and Owners Association; Rob Giltner of the Kentucky Derby / Churchill Downs; Ashley Herriman, Adam Coglianese, and Erin McLaughlin of the New York Racing Association; Denise Larzo; Kim Tribley of Impressions in Saratoga; Mandy Minger; Sarah Feldman and Melissa Ullmann of the *Daily Racing Form;* Erin Spaulding; Bob McNair; Ruben Sanjur; Blair Dimitro; Herb Levy; Tara Westerfield; Michael Palermo; Nick Mormando; Brant James; Ruben Mercado; Bill Straus; Katey Barrett; Candace Chew; Mallory Brinkhorst; Mitch and Melanie Mansour; Rocco Muriale; Monsignor Luciano; Marian Ciaccia; Ron Peterson; Theresa Stephens; Ernie Salvatore; Chuck Landon; and Randy Burnside.

I would be remiss if I didn't acknowledge my agent, Marianne Strong, in a special way. She approached me with the project fully realizing I had never written a tome about racing. It definitely was a challenge, and much like Affirmed, I had the desire and the courage to undertake countless hours of travel and the research it required. I would like to think that I rewarded Marianne's faith in me, and I feel I did. Also Roseanne Wells, every inch an editor, at Strong Literary.

Finally, I would like to express a special thank you to Amy Blalock, who crossed every *t* and dotted every *i* of a wordy manuscript.

The single most memorable experience of my journey into the equine world was meeting Steve Cauthen at Keeneland. He was every bit a champion, as he was in 1978, and I include him among the many star athletes that I have had the opportunity to interview over the years. I was so absorbed in my journey that I came away feeling that I was indeed at the Triple Crown races in 1978 myself.

Thanks for the memories.

THE HORSE AFFIRMED: FACT SHEET

1. Affirmed was the first $2 million money earner in the history of thoroughbred racing.
2. His record: 29 starts, 22 wins, 5 seconds, and 1 third, finishing out of the money only one time.
3. He was a champion at two, three, and four years of age.
4. Affirmed was named Horse of the Year in 1977, 1978, and 1979.
5. Affirmed won the Triple Crown in 1978, and no horse has done so since.
6. As a three-year-old in 1978, Affirmed won eight consecutive races, including the Triple Crown in head-to-head meetings with Alydar.
7. The Affirmed-Alydar rivalry is regarded as the greatest in the history of thoroughbred racing here and abroad.

8. Affirmed and Alydar met ten times. Affirmed won seven times, with one of the losses as a result of a controversial disqualification.

9. Affirmed concluded his great career by winning his last seven races, culminating with a scintillating victory in the Jockey Club Gold Cup over Spectacular Bid and Belmont winner Coastal.

10. Affirmed was retired following the Gold Cup. His lifetime earnings totaled $2,393,818, which made him the world's leading money winner of all time.

APPENDIX I

Affirmed Stats

Record: 29: 22-5-1
Earnings: $2,393,818

Affirmed Major Racing Wins

1977 – Hollywood Juvenile Championship Stakes
1977 – Futurity Stakes
1977 – Hopeful Stakes
1978 – Santa Anita Derby
1978 – Kentucky Derby
1978 – Preakness Stakes
1978 – Belmont Stakes
1979 – Hollywood Gold Cup
1979 – Santa Anita Handicap
1979 – Woodward Stakes
1979 – Jockey Club Gold Cup

Racing Awards

1977 – Champion 2-Year-Old Colt
1978 – 11th U.S. Triple Crown Champion

1978 – Champion 3-Year-Old Male Horse

1978, 1979 – American Horse of the Year

—— Honors ——

1980 – United States Racing Hall of Fame

#12 – Top 100 U.S. Racehorses of the 20th Century

Affirmed Handicap at Hollywood Park Racetrack

Affirmed Street in Napa, California

APPENDIX II

—— *Bloodlines: 1975 Chestnut Colt* ——

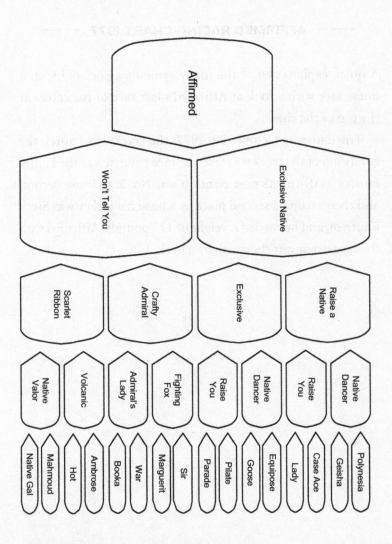

Affirmed

Won't Tell You

Exclusive Native

Scarlet Ribbon

Crafty Admiral

Exclusive

Raise a Native

Native Valor

Volcanic

Admiral's Lady

Fighting Fox

Raise You

Native Dancer

Raise You

Native Dancer

Native Gal

Mahmoud

Hot

Ambrose

Booka

War

Marguerit

Sir

Parade

Pilate

Goose

Equipose

Lady

Case Ace

Geisha

Polynesia

APPENDIX III

────── **AFFIRMED RACING CHART 1977** ──────

A quick explanation of the many symbols associated with a horse race with a look at Affirmed's last race of his career at the top of the chart:

The date was October 29, 1977; the track was Laurel; the condition of the track was fast; the race entered was the Laurel Futurity; Affirmed's post position was No. 3; he broke second and then assumed second place by a head his jockey was Steve Cauthen, and he carried a weight of 122 pounds. Affirmed won the race driving at the finish by a neck.

Date	Track	Condition	Distance	Furlongs	Race	Post	Start	1/4	Finish	Jockey	Weight	Comment
29Oct77	Laurel	Fast	$1\frac{1}{16}$ M	:48^4	Laurel Futurity	3	2	2^{hd}	1^{nk}	Cauthen	122	Long hard drive
15Oct77	Belmont	Muddy	1 M	:24^2	Champagne	5	3	3^2	2$^{1\!/\!4}$	Cauthen	122	2nd best
10Sep77	Belmont	Good	7 F	23^3	Futurity	2	2	2$^{1\!/\!2}$	1no	Cauthen	122	Strong drive
27Aug77	Saratoga	Fast	$6\frac{1}{2}$ F	:22^4	Hopeful	4	1	3^2	1$^{1\!/\!2}$	Cauthen	122	Good handling
17Aug77	Saratoga	Fast	6 F	:21^4	Sanford	3	2	3$^{5\!/\!2}$	1$^{2\,3\!/\!4}$	Cauthen	124	Driving very wide
23Jly77	Hollywood	Fast	6 F	:21^3	Juvenile Champ (Div 1)	6	3	1^{hd}	1^7	Pincay	122	Easily
6Jly77	Belmont	Fast	$5\frac{1}{2}$ F	:22^2	Great American	1	1	1^1	2$^{3\,1\!/\!2}$	Cordero	122	No match
15Jun77	Belmont	Fast	$5\frac{1}{2}$ F	:22^2	©Youthful	1	1	2$^{1\!/\!2}$	1^{nk}	Cordero	119	Driving
24May77	Belmont	Fast	$5\frac{1}{2}$ F	:23	Maiden Special Weight	10	1	1$^{1\!/\!2}$	1$^{4\,1\!/\!2}$	Gonzalez	117	Ridden out

© 2000 by Daily Racing Form, Inc.

——— AFFIRMED RACING CHART 1978 ———

A quick explanation of the many symbols associated with a horse race with a look at Affirmed's last race of his career at the top of the chart:

The date was October 14, 1978; the track was Belmont Park; the condition of the track was sloppy; the race entered was the Jockey Club Gold Cup; Affirmed's post position was No. 2; he broke second and then assumed second place by a head; his jockey was Steve Cauther, and he carried a weight of 121 pounds. Affirmed was fifth at the finish by 18¾ lengths because the saddle slipped.

Date	Track	Condition	Distance	Furlongs	Race	Post	Start	1/4	Finish	Jockey	Weight	Comment
14 Oct 78	Belmont	Sloppy	1½ M	:45^1	JC Gold Cup	2	2	2^{hd}	5^{18¾}	Cauthen	121	Saddle slipped
16 Sep 78	Belmont	Fast	1⅛ M	:47	Marlboro Cup	1	2	2^{2½}	2^3	Cauthen	124	No excuse
*19 Aug 78	Saratoga	Fast	1¼	:48	Travers	3	2	2^{hd}	1^{1¾}	Pincay	126	Came over
10Jun78	Belmont	Fast	1½ M	:50	Belmont	3	1	1^1	1^{hd}	Cauthen	126	Driving
20May78	Pimlico	Fast	1³⁄₁₆ M	:47^3	Preakness	6	2	1^1	1^{nk}	Cauthen	126	Brisk handling
6May78	Churchill Downs	Fast	1¼ M	:45^3	Kentucky Derby	2	2	3^{5½}	1^{1½}	Cauthen	126	Fully extended
16Apr78	Hollywood	Fast	1⅛ M	:45	Hollywood Derby	2	1	1^{hd}	1^2	Cauthen	122	Driving
2Apr78	Santa Anita	Fast	1⅛ M	:45^4	Santa Anita Derby	7	2	1^{1½}	1^1	Pincay	120	Handily
18Mar78	Santa Anita	Fast	1¹⁄₁₆ M	:24^1	San Felipe	4	2	2^{hd}	1^2	Cauthen	126	Driving
8Mar78	Santa Anita	Fast	6½ F	:21^3	Allowance	4	1	4^{3½}	1^5	Cauthen	124	Easily

*Disqualified and placed second.

© 2000 by Daily Racing Form, Inc.

——— AFFIRMED RACING CHART 1979 ———

A quick explanation of the many symbols associated with a horse race with a look at Affirmed's last race of his career at the top of the chart:

The date was October 6, 1979; the track was Belmont Park; the condition of the track was fast; the race entered was the Jockey Club Gold Cup; Affirmed's post position was No. 3; he broke second and then assumed a 1½ length lead; his jockey was Laffit Pincay, Jr., and he carried a weight of 126 pounds. Affirmed won the race driving at the finish by 1¾ lengths.

Date	Track	Condition	Distance	Furlongs	Race	Post	Start	1/4	Finish	Jockey	Weight	Comment
6Oct79	Belmont	Fast	$1\frac{1}{2}$ M	:49	JC Gold Cup	3	2	$1\frac{1}{2}$	$1\frac{3}{4}$	Pincay	126	Driving
22Sept79	Belmont	Sloppy	$1\frac{1}{2}$ M	$:47^3$	Woodward	3	2	2^4	$1^{2}\frac{1}{2}$	Pincay	126	Ridden out
*29Aug79	Belmont	Sloppy	1 M	$:22^2$	Allowance	3	1	1^1	1^6	Pincay	122	Ridden out

Date	Track	Condition	Distance	Furlongs	Race	Post	Start	1/4	Finish	Jockey	Weight	Comment
24Jun79	Hollywood	Fast	$1\frac{1}{4}$ M	$:45^3$	Hollywood Gold Cup	1	2	1^{hd}	$1\frac{3}{4}$	Pincay	132	Driving
20May79	Hollywood	Fast	$1\frac{1}{16}$ M	$:22^2$	Californian	2	1	1^1	1^5	Pincay	130	Driving
4Mar79	Santa Anita	Fast	$1\frac{1}{4}$ M	$:46^2$	Santa Anita	3	2	2^1	$1^{4}\frac{1}{2}$	Pincay	128	Speed to spare
4Feb79	Santa Anita	Good	$1\frac{1}{4}$ M	:47	Charles H Strub	8	2	3^1	1^{10}	Pincay	126	Handily
20Jan79	Santa Anita	Good	$1\frac{1}{8}$ M	$:45^3$	San Fernando	4	3	$4^{9}\frac{1}{2}$	$2^{2}\frac{3}{4}$	Cauthen	126	Drifted out
7Jan79	Santa Anita	Fast	7 F	$:22^2$	Malibu	2	1	3^2	$3^{2}\frac{1}{4}$	Cauthen	126	Hemmed in to stir

*No wagering. Exhibition race run between 7th and 8th races

APPENDIX IV

Race Histories

Kentucky Derby

EIGHTH RACE
Churchill
MAY 6, 1978

1 ¼ MILES. (1.59 2/5) 104th running THE KENTUCKY DERBY. $125,000 Added 3-year-olds. By subscription of $100 which covers nomination for both The Kentucky Derby and Derby Trial. All nomination fees to Derby Winner. $4,00 to pass the entry box Thursday, May 4, $3,500 additional to start, $125,000 added, of which $30,000 to second, $15,000 to third, $7,500 to fourth, $100,000 guaranteed to winner (to be divided equally in the event of a dead heat.) Weight 126 lbs. Starters to be named through the entry box Thursday, May 4, at time of closing. The maximum number of starters for The Kentucky Derby will be limited to twenty. In the event more than twenty entries pass through the entry box at the usual time of closing, the twenty starters will be determined at that time with preference given to those that have accumulated the highest lifetime earnings. For those that entered and are eliminated under this condition, the nomination fee and the fee to pass through the entry box, will be refunded. The owner of the winner to receive a gold trophy. Closed with 319 nominations.
Value of race $239,400, value to winner $186,900, second $30,000, third $15,000, fourth $7,500. Mutuel pool $4,425,828.

Name of Horse	Assigned Weight	Post Position	¼ Stretch	½ Stretch	¾ Stretch	1 Stretch	Stretch	Finish	Jockey	Odds $1
Affirmed	126	2	2^{head}	$3^{2\frac{1}{2}}$	$3^{1\frac{1}{2}}$	2^{3}	1^{2}	$1^{1\frac{1}{2}}$	Cauthen S	1.80
Alydar	126	10	9^{head}	9^{5}	8^{head}	4^{head}	3^{3}	$2^{1\frac{1}{4}}$	Velasquez J	1.20
Believe It	126	9	4 ½	4 ½	5^{3}	1^{head}	2^{2}	$3^{4\frac{1}{4}}$	Maple E	7.40
Darby Creek Road	126	7	7 ½	7^{2}	7^{2}	5 ½	4^{2}	$4^{2\frac{1}{4}}$	Brumfield D	33.00
Esops Foibles	126	3	$5^{1\frac{1}{2}}$	5^{4}	4^{1}	6^{3}	5^{3}	$5^{5\frac{1}{4}}$	McCarron C J	49.70
Sensitive Prince	126	11	$3^{2\frac{1}{2}}$	$1^{1\frac{1}{2}}$	1^{2}	$3^{1\frac{1}{2}}$	6^{3}	6 ½	Solomone M	4.50
Dr. Valeri	126	8	11	11	10^{4}	10^{5}	$7^{1\frac{1}{2}}$	$7^{3\frac{1}{4}}$	Riera R Jr	96.10
Hoist the Silver	126	5	8^{2}	8 ½	9^{5}	7^{3}	8^{5}	8^{7}	Depass R	123.70
Chief of Dixieland	126	6	6^{3}	6^{2}	6 ½	9^{1}	9^{1}	9^{1}	Rini A	121.70
Raymond Earl	126	1	1^{2}	2^{4}	2^{2}	8^{1}	10^{2}	10^{2}	Baird R L	117.10
Special Honor	126	4	10^{3}	10 ½	11	11	11	11	Nicolo P	177.10

OFF AT 5:41 EDT. Start good for all but SPECIAL HONOR, Won driving. Time, :22 3/5, :45 3/5, 1:10 4/5, 1:35 4/5, 2:01 1/5 Track fast.

$2 Mutuel Prices:

	Payoff		
2-AFFIRMED	**$5.60**	**$2.80**	**$2.60**
10-ALYDAR	----	**$2.60**	**$2.40**
9-BELIEVE IT	----	----	**$2.80**

Ch. c, by Exclusive Native—Won't Tell You, by Crafty Admiral. Trainer Barrera Lazaro S. Bred by Harbor View Farm (Fla).

AFFIRMED away alertly but held in reserve for six furlongs, moved up boldly along outside thereafter to take command on second turn, relinquished the lead momentarily a quarter mile out but responded to a rousing ride to regain command in upper stretch and was fully extended to holy ALYDAR safe. The latter, under snug restraint early, commenced to advance from the outside after six furlongs, continued wide into the stretch, swerved in to bump with BELIEVE IT in closing sixteenth and finished strongly when straightened. BELIEVE IT reserved off the early pace, moved up with a bold rush while bearing out on second turn to gain command momentarily a quarter mile away, continued wide while lacking a further response and was bumped by ALYDAR in the closing stages. DARBY CREEK ROAD lacked speed and hung after making a rally on the final bend. ESOPS FOIBLES faltered after making a mild bid on the second turn. SENSITIVE PRINCE sent to the fore on rounding the first turn, continued to make a swift pace while along the inside to final bend where he gave way suddenly. dr. valeri was without speed. CHIEF OF DIXIELAND was bumped about before going a quarter mile. RAYMOND EARL showed brief early speed and tired badly. SPECIAL HONOR reared at the start.

Owners— 1, Harbor View Farm; 2, Calumet Farm; 3, Hickory Tree Stable; 4, Phillips J W; 5, Frankel J; 6, Top the Marc Stable; 7, Renzi V & R; 8, Dasso-Golob-Levinson-Solomon; 9, Dixie Jake Inc; 10, Lehmann R N; 11, Gaston Linda T & Haynes A D.

Trainers— 1, Barrera Lazaro S; 2, Veitch John M; 3, Stephens Woodford C; 4, Rondinello Thomas L; 5, Rettele Loren; 6, Jerkens H Allen; 7, Perez Aurelio M; 8, Fischer Richard J; 9, Morreale Jake; 10, Adams W E Smiley; 11, McCann Edward T.

(*Reprinted with permission from the* Daily Racing Form.)

Preakness Stakes

EIGHTH RACE

Pimlico

MAY 20, 1978

1 3/16 MILES. (1.54) 103rd Running PREAKNESS. $150,000 Added. 3-year-old by subscription of $100 each, this fee to accompany the nomination. $1,000 to pass the entry box, starters to pay $1,000 additional. All eligibility, entrance and starting fees to the winner, with $150,00 added, of which $30,000 to second, $15,000 to third and $7,500 to fourth. Weight 126 lbs. Starters to be named through the entry box Thursday, Mat 18, two days before the race by the usual time of closing. A replica of the Woodlawn Vase will be presented to the winning owner to remain his or her personal property. Closed Wednesday, February 15, 1978 with 247 nominations.

Value of race $188,700, value to winner $136,200, second $30,000, third $15,000, fourth $7,500. Mutuel pool $1,335,965, Minus place pool $17,998.60, Minus show pool $17,914.65. Exacta Pool $262,946.

Name of Horse	Assigned Weight	Post Position	St.	¼ Stretch	½ Stretch	¾ Stretch	Stretch	Finish	Jockey	Odds $1
Affirmed	126	6	1	2^1	1^1	1^1	1½	1^{neck}	Cauthen S	.50
Alydar	126	3	2	6^2	6^4	4^{1½}	2^{1½}	2^{7½}	Velasquez J	1.80
Believe It	126	2	5	3^1	3^2	3^{head}	3^{3½}	3^{2½}	Maple E	6.70
Noon Time Spender	126	1	7	5^{2½}	4½	2^1	4^3	4^8	Hinojosa H	80.80
Indigo Star	126	7	3	4½	5^1	6^{2½}	5^6	5^6	Fitzgerald R	89.80
Dax S.	126	5	4	7	7	7	6^1	6^4	Kurtz J	93.30
Track Reward	126	4	6	1^{head}	2^1	5^2	7	7	Gonzalez B	88.70

OFF AT 5:41 EDT. Start good, Won driving. Time, :23 3/5, :47 3/5, 1:11 4/5, 1:36 1/5, 1:54 2/5 Track fast.

$2 Mutuel Prices:

	Payoff		
6-AFFIRMED	$3.00	$2.10	$2.10
2-ALYDAR	----	$2.10	$2.10
2-BELIEVE IT	----	----	$2.10

$2 EXACTA 6—3 PAID $4.00.

Ch. c, by Exclusive Native—Won't Tell You, by Crafty Admiral. Trainer Barrera Lazaro S. Bred by Harbor View Farm (Fla).

AFFIRMED, taken under light restraint after breaking alertly, quickly joined TRACK REWARD from the outside, gained the advantage leaving the first turn, made the pace under clever rating, responded gamely to rousing when challenged by ALYDAR in the upper stretch and turned back that rival under brisk handling. ALYDAR, under restraint and allowed to settle early, advanced willingly outside of horses in backstretch, engaged AFFIRMED well out from the rail approaching the stretch to nearly reach even terms then couldn't get to that rival when set down in a steady drive. BELIEVE IT saved ground under a snug gold while maintaining a good striking position, came around TRACK REWARD when that rival began to retire on the final turn then quickly regained the rail and couldn't stay with the top pair when the real test came. NOON TIME SPENDER, saving ground while not far back, eased outside of horses in backstretch and steadily gained ground, loomed boldly on the final turn and weakened in the drive. INDIGO STAR had good early speed and gave way readily on the final turn. DAX S. showed little. TRACK REWARD was quickly sent up to join for the lead soon after the start, saved ground while prompting the pace into the last bend and gave way readily.

Owners— 1, Harbor View Farm; 2, Calumet Farm; 3, Hickory Trees Stable; 4, Miami Lakes Ranch; 5, Procopio R F; 6, Scherr N; 7, Aisquith Stable.

Trainers— 1, Barrera Lazaro S; 2, Veitch John M; 3, Stephens Woodford C; 4, Arocodia Antonio; 5, Leatherbury King T; 6, Gross Mel W; 7, Barrera Albert S.

(Reprinted with permission from the Daily Racing Form.)

Belmont Stakes

EIGHTH RACE
Belmont
JUNE 10, 1978

1 ½ MILES. (2.24) 110th running THE BELMONT. $150,000 Added. 3-year-olds. By subscription of $100 each to accompany the nominations; $500 to pass the entry box; $1,000 to start. A supplementary nomination may be made of $2,500 on Wednesday, June 7 plus an additional $10,000 to start, with $150,000 added, of which 60% to the winner, 22% to second, 12% to third and 6% to fourth. Colts and Geldings, weights, 126 lbs. Fillies, 121 ___. Starters to be named at the closing time of entries. Thursday, June 8. The winning owner will be presented with ___ August Belmont Memorial Cup to be retained for one year, as well as a trophy for permanent possession and trophies will be presented to the winning trainer and jockey. (Closed Wednesday, February 15, 1978 with 268 nominations.)

Value of race $184,300, value to winner $110,580, second $40,546, third $22,116, fourth $11,058.

Name of Horse	Assigned Weight	Post Position	¼ Stretch	½ Stretch	1 Stretch	1 ¼ Stretch	Stretch	Finish	Jockey	Odds $1
Affirmed	126	3	1¹	1¹	1^½	1^{head}	1^{head}	1^{head}	Cauthen S	.60
Alydar	126	2	3^{1½}	2¹	2⁵	2⁸	2¹²	2¹³	Velasquez J	1.10
Darby Creek Road	126	1	5	5	5	3^{1½}	3⁴	3^{7½}	Cordero A Jr	9.90
Judge Advocate	126	4	2^{1½}	3^{2½}	4³	5	4^{head}	4^{1¼}	Fell J	30.10
Noon Time Spender	126	5	4¹	4³	3^½	4^{head}	5	5	Hernandez R	38.40

Mutuel pool $1,186,662, TB pool $1,389,646.

OFF AT 5:43, EDT. Start good, Won driving. Time, :25, :50, 1:14, 1:37 2/5 , 2:01 3/5, 2:25 4/5, Track fast.

$2 Mutuel Prices:

		Payoff	
3 – (C) – AFFIRMED	$3.20	$2.10	----
2 – (B) – ALYDAR	----	$2.20	---
1 – (A) – DARBY CREEK ROAD	----	----	---

(No Show Wagering)

Ch. c, by Exclusive Native—Won't Tell You, by Crafty Admiral. Trainer Barrera Lazaro S. Bred by Harbor View Farm (Fla).

AFFIRMED went right to the front and was rated along on the lead while remaining well out from the rail. He responded readily when challenged by ALYDAR soon after entering the backstretch, held a narrow advantage into the stretch while continuing to save ground and was under left-handed urging to prevail in a determined effort. ALYDAR, away in good order, saved ground to the first turn. He came out to go after AFFIRMED with ___ furlongs remaining, raced with that rival to the stretch, reached almost even terms with AFFIRMED near the three-sixteenths pole but wasn't good enough in a stiff drive. DARBY CREEK ROAD, unhurried while being outrun early, moved around horses while rallying on the far turn but lacked a further response. JUDGE ADVOCATE broke through before the start and was finished at the far turn. NOON TIME SPENDER raced within striking distance for a mile and gave way.

Owners— 1, Harbor View Farm; 2, Calumet Farm; 3, Phillips J W; 4 Phipps ___; 5, Miami Lakes Ranch.

Trainers— 1, Barrera Lazaro S; 2, Veitch John M; 3, Rondinello Thomas L; 4, Russell John W; 5, Arcodia Antonio.

BIBLIOGRAPHY

Louis Wolfson: *Life*, 1953; *Saturday Evening Post*, July 24, 1954; *Sports Illustrated*, September 27, 1961; *Time*, May 29, 1978; *Backstretch*, November/December 2000; *Post Time USA*, February 2008.

Steve Cauthen: *Newsweek*, February 14, 1977; *New York Times Magazine*, February 20, 1977; *Sports Illustrated*, March 7, and December 26, 1977; *The Kid* by Pete Axthem (Viking Press, 1979).

Derby Lore: *10 Best Kentucky Derbies* (Bloodhorse Publications, 2005).

Derby and Calumet: *Sports Illustrated*, March 17, 1978, September 2, 1991; *Wild Ride* by Ann Auerbach (Henry Holt, 1994).

Road to the Derby: *Los Angeles Times,* January 8, 1978; *Sports Illustrated,* March 6, April 10, and May 3, 10, 1978; *New York Times,* May 8, 1978; *Daily Racing Form,* May 9, 1978.

The Derby: *Lexington Herald,* April 26, 27, 29, 30, and May 2, 6, 7, 8, 1978; *Kentucky Sports World,* June 1978; National Public Radio, July 2, 2009.

The Preakness: *Lexington Herald,* May 22, and June 6, 9, 11, 13, 1978; *New York Times,* May 21, 1978; *Blood Horse,* May 28, 1978; *Sports Illustrated,* May 29, 1978.

The Belmont: *New York Times,* May 21, and June 2, 8, 9, 1978; *Lexington Herald,* May 26, and June 6, 9, 11, 13, 1978; *Los Angeles Times,* June 4, 1978; *Daily Racing Form,* June 9, 10, 13, 1978; *Louisville Courier Journal,* June 11, 1978; *Miami Herald,* June 12, 1978; *Sports Illustrated,* June 12, 1978; *Jimmy the Greek by Himself* (Playboy Press, 1975).

Final Turn: *Daily Racing Form,* January 7, and August 29, 1978, March 3, 4, 5, 1979, October 6, 1979, September 4, 1979; *Sports Illustrated,* July 2, and October 29, 1979; *New York Times,* August 28, 30, 1979, September 22, 1979, October 6, 1979; *American Racing Manual,* 1979; *Blood Horse,* June 20, 2001; *USA Today,* May 5, 2008.

Interviews: Marcia Wolfson; Karla Wolfson; Steve Cauthen; Hank Goldberg; Melvin James; Dusty Mormando; Sal Marchiano; Lou Petho.

INDEX